Congressional Ethics

Congressional Ethics

History, Facts, and Controversy

CONGRESSIONAL QUARTERLY INC.
WASHINGTON, D.C.

Photos: 11, 17, 101—Library of Congress; 22, 34, 43, 45, 48, 82, 91, 96, 118, 120, 133, 139—R. Michael Jenkins; 29, 38, 42, 52, 62, 64, 67, 74, 87, 88, 95, 96—AP/Wide World Photos; 32, 38, 48, 94, 95, 113—Steve Karafyllakis; 40—Paul Conklin; 40, 69, 177—Sue Klemens; 52—Office of Tom Evans; 52—Office of Dan Quayle; 69—Stan Barouh; 80—Congressional Quarterly; 91—Marty LaVor; 94—Ken Heinen

Copyright © 1992
Congressional Quarterly
1414 22nd Street, N.W.
Washington, D.C. 20037

Printed in the United States of America

Library of Congress Cataloging-in-Publication Data

Congressional ethics : history, facts, and controversy.
    p. cm.
    Includes bibliographical references and index.
    ISBN 0-87187-624-8
    1. Political corruption--United States--History.   2. Political ethics--United States--History.   3. United States. Congress--Ethics--History.   I. Congressional Quarterly Inc.
JK2249.C64   1992
328.73'0766--dc20   92-254
                          CIP

Editor: John L. Moore
Contributors: Chuck Alston, Mary Cohn, John R. Cranford, Thomas Galvin, Stephen Gettinger, Hoyt Gimlin, Martha V. Gottron, Janet Hook, Nancy Kervin, Phil Kuntz, Patricia Ann O'Connor
Production Editor: Jenny K. Philipson
Indexer: Max Franke
Book Design: Kaelin Chappell

CONTENTS

Preface   vii

Introduction   1

Chapter 1   Disciplining Congress:
An Unpopular Chore   5

Chapter 2   Expulsion:
The Ultimate Sanction   15

Grounds for Expulsion   15
Twentieth-Century Senate Cases   18
House Leadership Resignations   19

Chapter 3   Censure/Reprimand:
A Public Scolding   25

Censure by the Senate   26
Censure by the House   36
Reprimand in the House   41
Senate Reprimand of Cranston   44

Chapter 4   Other Forms of Discipline:
Loss of Chair or Right to Vote   47

Loss of Chairmanship   47
Suspension in the House   49
Suspension in the Senate   50

Chapter 5   Influence Buying:
Lobbying Gone Wrong   51

Lobby Disclosure: "More Loophole
Than Law"   52
Lobbying Investigations   55
Individuals Prosecuted   59

Chapter 6   Money: Root of Most
Congressional Evils   61

"Abscam," 1980   63
Wedtech, 1988   68
Criminal Prosecutions, 1941-80   70
1980s and 1990s: Bumper Crop of Cases   73

Chapter 7   Danger Zones:
Sex and Alcohol   85

Cases in the 1970s   85
Cases in the 1980s   89
Cases in the 1990s   93

Chapter 8   Staff and Perks:
"The Last Plantation"   97

Questionable Hiring Practices   98
Aides' Misuse of Power   102
Legislative Work vs. Politics   104
Aides and Ethics   107

Chapter 9   Hill Immunity: Shielding
Legislators   109

Chapter 10   The "Keating Five":
A Special Case   117

Decision: End of an Ordeal   118
Testimony: Complex and Rancorous   122
Closing Views: Bennett and Committee   138
Compromise: No Floor Vote   139

Chapter 11   The Cleanup Begins:
Three Decades of Reform   145

Codes of Conduct   145

Code, Pay Relationship   149
Honoraria   151
1989 Revision: Pay Hiked, Loopholes
    Closed   154
"Contrition Acts"   159

Appendix   **163**

Senate Cases Involving Qualifications for
    Membership   165
House Cases Involving Qualifications for
    Membership   166
Cases of Expulsion in the House   167

Cases of Expulsion in the Senate   168
Censure Proceedings in the Senate   169
Censure Proceedings in the House   170
Reprimand Proceedings in the House   172
Party Abbreviations   173
Senate Rule XXXV   174
Senate Rule XXXVII   175
House Rule XLIII   178
Ethics Committee Chairs, 1966-92   179

Selected Readings   **181**
Index   **183**

Preface

Congress celebrated its recent bicentennial with appropriate speeches and ceremonies honoring the institution and the thousands of men and women who served there since 1789. Understandably, the speakers glossed over or skipped entirely the darker side of congressional history—the crimes and other misdeeds committed by a relative handful of senators and representatives.

But in its workaday world of lawmaking, Congress cannot look the other way when one of its members is caught acting illegally or immorally. It must face up to the fact and punish or clear the alleged wrongdoer.

Congress carries out this constitutional obligation with a variety of disciplinary tools, including one spelled out in the Constitution—expulsion if two-thirds of the chamber concur that it is warranted.

In recent years the House and Senate ethics committees have been busier than ever investigating complaints against members and recommending whatever action is necessary. Usually the parent body goes along with the committee's recommendation.

The 1980s and early 1990s in particular produced a bumper crop of ethics cases, including one that resulted in the first expulsion for corruption in either house of Congress. The same period has seen three senators formally disciplined for misconduct involving personal or campaign funds, and six representatives censured or reprimanded for sexual or financial offenses. Numerous others were admonished by the ethics committees, defeated for reelection, or escaped punishment by resigning.

Congress's already low standing in public opinion polls was further degraded by other scandals, such as surreptitious pay raises and wholesale check kiting at the House's own bank. Small wonder that Congress moved in 1989-91 to improve its image by passing tougher ethics codes and doing away with the acceptance of honoraria—a popular means for interest groups to circumvent restrictions on gifts to lawmakers.

How This Book Is Organized

Congressional Ethics covers all aspects of the congressional disciplinary process, from the basic methods of punishment to the specific cases that triggered the various investigations and the resulting committee or floor action.

The Introduction provides an overview of Congress's efforts to police itself in the context of an apparent decline of ethical standards throughout American society, marked by a proliferation of scandals in religion, the financial world, politics, and government.

Chapter 1 examines the early history of ethics in Congress, including the constitutional underpinnings of the disciplinary process and Supreme Court decisions regarding qualifications for office.

The most severe punishment available to Congress—expulsion—is discussed in Chapter 2, along with cases where members facing near-certain removal decided instead to resign voluntarily.

Chapter 3 offers a rundown on censure or reprimand—the leading alternative to expulsion in the most serious cases of misconduct by members of Congress.

When senators or representatives are indicted or convicted in the courts, a question remains as to whether they should continue to chair committees or to vote on legislation. Chapter 4 looks at Senate and House procedures for dealing with this question.

Chapter 5 reviews the relationship between lobbyists and Congress—a delicate one that has gone wrong in some instances, resulting in major scandals.

Chapter 6 deals with bribery and other money-related abuses that have sent some members to jail.

Chapter 7 enumerates the sex scandals that have ruined some congressional careers and tainted others. Alcohol is often a factor.

The perquisites that go with being a member of Congress, including the services of a large staff, often invite abuse. Instances where this has happened are discussed in Chapter 8.

Congressional immunity from arrest or prosecution is the subject of Chapter 9.

Chapter 10 examines the Senate's Keating Five investigation, which raised far-reaching questions about the thin line between proper and improper legislative actions.

Chapter 11 outlines Congress's recent efforts to clean up its act with stiffer ethics codes.

The Appendix provides tables listing the members subjected to disciplinary action since the beginning of Congress, excerpts from Senate and House rules on ethical conduct, and a list of political party abbreviations used throughout the book.

The material in this book was updated, expanded, and revised from *Congressional Quarterly's Guide to Congress,* fourth edition.

Introduction

The United States Congress polices itself. It is empowered by the Constitution to keep its members in line, and by and large it succeeds in doing so.

While Mark Twain could joke that "there is no distinctly native American criminal class except Congress," the vast majority of senators and representatives have not been lawbreakers or even home wreckers.

But some of them have broken laws or marriages, and their illegal acts and embarrassing antics have posed some of the most difficult decisions their peers have ever had to face. In a handful of extreme cases Congress has resorted to its ultimate punishment: booting out the offender—an action formally known as expulsion.

More commonly the discipline administered has been a good old-fashioned tongue lashing, euphemised as a *censure* or *reprimand*. There is little or no difference between the terms, except that in the House the member being censured is required to stand before his colleagues as the Speaker reads the censure resolution. (The masculine *his* is sufficient here. As of early 1992, no female member had been censured.) Neither the House nor the Senate imposes the indignity of a formal dressing-down in reprimand cases. The Senate issued its first reprimand in 1991 against Alan Cranston, D-Calif., one of the so-called Keating Five senators accused of improperly helping a troubled California savings and loan in exchange for campaign contributions.

The Senate shies away from both expulsion and censure. No senator has been expelled since 1862 or censured since 1967. The two senators most recently disciplined before Cranston were "denounced" instead of censured, although, here again, there is no clear dictionary difference in the meanings of the two words.

Nor, apparently, does calling a censure by another name make it any more palatable to the senators handing out the punishment. William L. Armstrong of Colorado, who participated in the unanimous denouncement of his Republican colleague, Minnesota's Dave Durenberger, in 1990, put it this way: "When this is all over and after we have voted to denounce him, we will still want him to be our friend. We will still want to go down to the dining room and have lunch with him."

Senators and representatives have even less enthusiasm for another aspect of the disciplinary process. They generally shun service on the ethics committees, which must deal with *all* the behavior problems of the colleagues, not just those that reach the Senate or House floor and thus require every member to take a stand. The two relatively unpopular panels are the Senate Ethics Committee and the House Standards of Official Conduct Committee.

Julian C. Dixon, D-Calif., who stepped down as chairman in 1991 after leading the House ethics committee through a mine field of cases in the 1980s, reflected at one point: "Members always think you're not being fair to them, and the public thinks you're bending over backwards for the member. It's a no-win situation."

The Sleaze Factor

The ethics chairmen's job has not been made easier by the proliferation of ethics cases in both chambers. The larger House, particularly, handled a massive docket of difficult cases in the 1980s and early 1990s, including for the first time three that resulted in censure/reprimand of members for sexual misbehavior.

The increase of cases paralleled a rise in morals problems throughout American society, with a barrage of scandals in religious evangelism, the White House, Wall Street investment houses, banking, and other areas once considered solid bedrocks of the nation's value structure.

Time magazine devoted fourteen pages to the decline in its May 25, 1987, cover story headlined, "What Ever Happened to Ethics: Assaulted by sleaze, scandals and hypocrisy, America searches for its moral values." The story surveyed the indices of turpitude: more than one hundred Reagan administration officials indicted, resigned under a cloud, or suspected of questionable activities; laws violated and Congress lied to in the Iran-contra affair; Gary Hart out of the 1988 presidential race amid questions of adultery; Wall Street high rollers guilty of insider trading; televangelist

Jim Bakker defrocked over a tryst with a church secretary; business leaders convicted in assorted white-collar scams; and so on and on.

The worst was yet to come. The year 1991 proved to be a motherlode of scandals: the sensational trial and acquittal of William Kennedy Smith on charges that he raped a woman outside the family Palm Beach compound while his mother and uncle, Sen. Edward M. Kennedy, D-Mass., were inside; Anita F. Hill's lurid allegations of gross sexual speech by her former boss, Supreme Court nominee Clarence Thomas; televangelist Jimmy Swaggart caught again with a different prostitute; former defense secretary Clark F. Clifford's stumbling attempts to explain his ties to the collapsed, disreputable Bank of Commerce and Credit International (BCCI), which comedians quickly dubbed the "Bank of Crooks and Criminals"; and the revelations of wholesale check bouncing and unpaid restaurant tabs by scores of House members.

"Scandal fever has taken over," said political scientist Larry J. Sabato. "It used to be that you'd get one good scandal every few years. Now it is scandal du jour."

In her 1991 book, *Scandal: The Crisis of Mistrust in American Politics,* Suzanne Garment observed that unprecedented numbers of public scandals erupted in the fifteen years after the botched Watergate coverup drove Richard Nixon from the presidency in 1974. Garment counted "more than 400 relatively senior federal officials and candidates for federal office who have been publicly accused in the national press of personal wrongdoing" during those fifteen years.

In the century between Watergate and 1875, when the Whiskey Ring breakup convicted 110 officials for conspiring to skim federal alcohol taxes, the government of course grew enormously. But since Watergate the scandal rate soared without a corresponding growth in government. Garment noted that "the incidence of scandal has risen

Former senator Gary Hart was prompted to withdraw from the 1988 presidential race when his relationship with model Donna Rice was exposed. After major newspapers disclosed that Hart and Rice had spent a night together in his Washington townhouse, a tabloid published color photos of the pair on a yacht called *Monkey Business*. This 1992 *Newsday* cartoon refers to a new sex scandal involving presidential candidate Bill Clinton.

exponentially in recent years even though the number of federal employees has remained relatively stable over the same period of time."

The proliferation, she said, "reflects not so much an increase in corruption at the federal level as it does our growing capacity and taste for political scandal production."

That would help to explain the rash of arrests, indictments, complaints, and exposés that brought the congressional cases before the House and Senate ethics committees for investigation. Just having such committees, which are fairly new in their current form, was thought by some to have generated business for them. When there was no mechanism for handling complaints, there was less incentive to file them.

Heightened awareness of the moral climate, akin to the "green" concern for the physical environment, was another possible factor in the reduced tolerance of questionable or unethical behavior.

Misdeeds winked at in years past were no longer acceptable. Although Watergate was an executive branch scandal, it sparked reforms in the legislative branch as well. New laws were passed requiring the first mandatory disclosures of congressional campaign contributions and putting teeth into ethics codes that urged public officials to lay their financial cards on the table.

As recently as 1976, House members shouted down a move to throw out a colleague, California Republican Andrew J. Hinshaw, who had been convicted of bribery. Four years later the climate had changed so much that representatives could overcome their distaste for the job and expel a member of the Democratic majority, Michael J. "Ozzie" Myers of Pennsylvania, who had been snared in the FBI's bribery sting operation, Abscam. It was the first expulsion for corruption in either house.

By 1989 House members brought sufficient

pressure in a less clear-cut case to bring about the first midterm resignation of a Speaker, Democrat Jim Wright of Texas. Wright was accused of financial misconduct, including the use of a rigged book deal to skirt income limitations.

Over in the Senate, the Keating Five hearings came at a soul-searching time in the evolution of congressional ethics. The issues were complex, with many gray areas, and they raised questions that went far beyond the immediate one of the senators' guilt or innocence. Is it enough for senators to steer clear of anything illegal? Or should they be held to a higher standard, as the special counsel argued, avoiding even the *appearance* of impropriety?

The legacy of the scandal-ridden late twentieth century was certain to fuel the debate well into the next one.

CHAPTER 1

Disciplining Congress:

An Unpopular Chore

One reason that members of Congress have not always met the highest ethical standards is that the Constitution put up so few barriers to who could be a senator or representative. Having revolted against autocracy and aristocracy, the Founders created an egalitarian legislature for the new democracy. Clearly they expected members to be wise, educated, and virtuous, but none of these qualities were required.

The Constitutional Convention of 1787 set up only three qualifications for membership in the House of Representatives. The representative had to be at least twenty-five years old, have been a U.S. citizen for at least seven years, and, when elected, be an inhabitant of the state from which the person was elected.

Senate membership was only slightly more restricted. A senator had to be at least thirty, a citizen for nine years, and a resident of the state represented.

The result was a not-so-exclusive club that almost anyone could enter if he or she obtained enough votes or, in the case of the Senate before 1913, was selected by the state legislature. And as Congress grew along with the country, the chances increased that some of the hundreds of persons selected as lawmakers would be less than upstanding.

In laying down Congress's authority to seat, unseat, and punish its own members, the Constitutional Convention drew inspiration from its favorite concept: checks and balances. The Constitution put bounds on that power and the judicial branch has been called upon from time to time to interpret the extent of those limits.

The exclusive power of Congress to determine its members' qualifications has come into conflict, over the years, with the voters' right to decide who shall represent them. When Congress rules on controversies such as disputed elections, the uncertain citizenship of a member elect, or other questions of competence, senators or representatives from all parts of the country are, in effect, deciding whether the residents of a state may or may not be represented in Washington by the person selected by those residents.

Although Congress has often had to determine the winner in contested elections, the voters' clear choice has been rejected, for lack of the requisite qualifications, in fewer than twenty cases since 1789.

Congress also has infrequently used its constitutional power to expel or punish members for

Constitutional Standards
for Members of Congress

- A senator must be at least thirty years old and have been a citizen of the United States not less than nine years. (Article I, Section 3, clause 3)
- A representative must be at least twenty-five years old and have been a citizen not less than seven years. (Article I, Section 2, clause 2)
- Every member of Congress must be, when elected, an inhabitant of the state that he or she is to represent. (Article I, Section 2, clause 2, and Section 3, clause 3)
- No one may be a member of Congress who holds any other "Office under the United States." (Article I, Section 6, clause 2)
- No person may be a senator or a representative who, having previously taken an oath as a member of Congress to support the Constitution, has engaged in rebellion against the United States or given aid or comfort to its enemies, unless Congress has removed such disability by a two-thirds vote of both houses. (Fourteenth Amendment, Section 3)

disorderly or improper conduct. As of early 1992, ten senators, twenty-two representatives, and one territorial delegate had been formally censured by their colleagues for misconduct. There have been fifteen expulsions in the Senate and four in the House. (One of the fifteen Senate expulsions was posthumously revoked.)

The authority of Congress to judge qualifications and punish members rests on two clauses in Article I of the Constitution. The first is clause 1 of Section 5, which reads in part: "Each House shall be the Judge of the Elections, Returns and Qualifications of its own members. . . ." This clause would appear to give each house carte blanche in the validation of elections and the seating of mem-

bers-elect. However, the election of members is regulated elsewhere in Article I and in the Seventeenth Amendment, which provides for direct election of senators. In addition, the Constitution specifically lists the qualifications required for membership in Congress.

The second clause on seating, unseating, and punishment of members is clause 2 of Article I, Section 5, reading: "Each House may determine the Rules of its Proceedings, punish its Members for disorderly Behavior, and, with the Concurrence of two thirds, expel a Member." The original draft of this clause did not include the words "with the concurrence of two thirds." When the clause was considered in the Constitutional Convention, August 10, 1787, James Madison of Virginia said that the right of expulsion was "too important to be exercised by a bare majority of a quorum, and in emergencies might be dangerously abused." He proposed requiring a two-thirds vote for expulsion.

Gouverneur Morris of Pennsylvania opposed Madison's proposal. He said: "This power may be safely trusted to a majority. To require more may produce abuses on the side of the minority. A few men from fractious motives may keep in a member who ought to be expelled." But Edmund Randolph and George Mason of Virginia and Daniel Carroll of Maryland spoke in support of Madison's proposal, and it was adopted by a vote of ten states in favor, one (Pennsylvania) divided, and none opposed.

Litigation on the seating and disciplining of members of Congress reached the Supreme Court in the latter part of the nineteenth century in suits focused mainly on legalistic questions such as the power of Congress to subpoena witnesses when considering the qualifications of members. These suits afforded the Court an opportunity to indicate bases upon which to judge the qualifications of members and to suggest the scope of punishment that may be imposed on members. In cases argued during the twentieth century, the Court has ruled more directly on the nature of the power of Congress to exclude members-elect and to punish or expel sitting members.

Effect of Crédit Mobilier Scandal

The Supreme Court, in its 1880-81 term, handed down a decision that upheld the right of Congress to punish its members. Although the case, *Kilbourn v. Thompson* (103 U.S. 168), directly involved only private persons under investigation by the House, it occurred at a time when the Crédit Mobilier scandal had aroused suspicions of financial misdeeds by several members of the House, including Speaker James G. Blaine, R-Maine.

The number of congressional investigations had soared during Ulysses S. Grant's eight years as president (1869-77). According to Joseph Harris, author of *Congressional Control of Administration,* Congress undertook thirty-seven maladministration inquiries during Grant's tenure, including the Crédit Mobilier of America probe. Two committees in the House and one in the Senate investigated charges that the company's construction of the last 667 miles of the Union Pacific Railroad, completed in 1869, had been marked by wholesale corruption.

The charges first appeared when the New York *Sun* of September 4, 1872, reported that Rep. Oakes Ames, R-Mass., a principal stockholder in both the Union Pacific and Crédit Mobilier, had used Crédit Mobilier stock to bribe Vice President Schuyler Colfax, Sen. Henry Wilson, R-Mass., House Speaker Blaine, Sen. James W. Patterson, R-N.H., Rep. James Brooks, D-N.Y., and Rep. James A. Garfield, R-Ohio. The reported bribes represented an attempt to head off a congressional investigation of railroad transportation rates.

Ownership of the railroad and the construction company were the same. The Union Pacific promoters bought Crédit Mobilier and awarded it inflated contracts made possible by government subsidies to help link the two coasts by rail. The company name derived from a Paris-based bank that made loans backed by movable property rather than real estate.

Blaine proposed the first inquiry, and the House on December 2, 1872, appointed a select committee headed by Rep. Luke P. Poland, R-Vt., "to investigate and ascertain whether any member of this House was bribed by Oakes Ames, or any other person or corporation, in any manner touching his legislative duty." A month later, January 6, 1873, the House appointed another select committee, headed by Rep. Jeremiah M. Wilson, R-Ind., to investigate the financial arrangement between the Union Pacific and the Crédit Mobilier.

As the House investigations proceeded simultaneously, the Poland committee discovered evidence implicating members of the Senate. Upon receiving the information, the Senate on February 4, 1873, established a select committee of its own to look into the alleged bribery. The committee was headed by Sen. Lot M. Morrill, R-Maine.

The Poland committee filed a report February 18, 1873, clearing Blaine but recommending that Ames and Brooks be expelled from the House. The committee said Ames had been "guilty of selling to members of Congress shares of stock in the Crédit Mobilier of America, for prices much below the true value of such stock, with intent thereby to influence the votes and decisions of such members in matters to be brought before Congress for action." Brooks had purchased stock in his son-in-law's name but for his own benefit, the committee added. The House ultimately censured the two representatives but did not expel them.

The Wilson committee issued its report March 3, saying that Crédit Mobilier had been making exorbitant profits, and that some persons connected with it were holding bonds illegally. The committee recommended court action.

The Senate's committee had meanwhile come out with its report on March 1, saying that Patterson had bought Crédit Mobilier stock from

Rules Governing Members' Conduct: Constitution, Hill Rules, and Criminal Laws

Concern for the ethical conduct of members of Congress is reflected in the Constitution, federal statutes, and Senate and House rules. Some key provisions affecting members' conduct follow:

Constitutional Provision

"Each House may determine the Rules of its Proceedings, punish its Members for disorderly Behavior, and, with the Concurrence of two thirds, expel a Member." (Article I, Section 5, clause 2)

"...They shall in all Cases, except Treason, Felony and Breach of the Peace, be privileged from Arrest during their Attendance at the Session of their respective Houses, and in going to and returning from the same; and for any Speech or Debate in either House, they shall not be questioned in any other Place." (Article I, Section 6, clause 1)

"No Senator or Representative shall, during the Time for which he was elected, be appointed to any civil Office under the Authority of the United States, which shall have been created, or the Emoluments whereof shall have been encreased during such time; and no Person holding any Office under the United States, shall be a Member of either House during his Continuance in Office." (Article I, Section 6, clause 2)

"No Title of Nobility shall be granted by the United States; And no Person holding any Office of Profit or Trust under them, shall, without the Consent of the Congress, accept of any present, Emolument, Office, or Title, of any kind whatever, from any King, Prince, or foreign State." (Article I, Section 9, clause 8)

"The Senators and Representatives before mentioned ... shall be bound by Oath or Affirmation, to support this Constitution...." (Article VI, clause 3)

Criminal Statutes

A series of laws in Title 18 of the U.S. Code make it a federal crime for members of Congress to engage in certain actions. Prohibited acts, excluding those relating to campaign spending, include:

- Soliciting or receiving a bribe for the performance of any official act, for the violation of an official duty, or for participating in or permitting any fraud against the United States. The penalty is a $20,000 fine or three times the monetary equivalent of the thing of value, whichever is greater, or imprisonment for not more than fifteen years, or both, plus possible disqualification from holding office. (18 USC 201c)
- Soliciting or receiving anything of value for himself or because of any official act performed or to be performed by him. The

Ames at below-market prices. The committee recommended Patterson's expulsion, but his retirement upon the expiration of his term on March 3 precluded Senate action to expel him.

Colfax, whose involvement was not satisfactorily explained, had fallen from favor with the regular Republicans before the scandal broke and was not renominated in June 1872 for a second term on the Grant ticket. Henry Wilson, who replaced Colfax

as vice president, and Garfield, elected president in 1880, never explained away their connection with the affair.

The Crédit Mobilier affair moved the Court to go beyond its ruling on private citizen Kilbourn and discuss the power to punish members of Congress. Speaking in the context of calls for punishment of members accused of unethical financial involvement in the business under investigation, it said:

penalty is a $10,000 fine or imprisonment for not more than two years, or both. (18 USC 201g)

- Soliciting or receiving any compensation for services in relation to any proceeding, contract, claim, or controversy in which the United States is a party or has a direct and substantial interest, before any department, agency, court martial, officer, or civil or military commission. The penalty is a $10,000 fine and imprisonment for not more than two years, or both, plus disqualification from holding office. (18 USC 203a)

- Practicing in the Court of Claims. The penalty is a $10,000 fine and imprisonment for not more than two years, or both, plus disqualification from holding office. (18 USC 204)

- Receiving, as a political contribution or otherwise, anything of value for promising use of or using influence to obtain for any person an appointive office or place under the United States. The penalty is a $1,000 fine, or imprisonment for not more than one year, or both. (18 USC 211)

- The campaign laws prohibit buying a vote, promising employment, soliciting political contributions from federal employees, and threatening the job of a federal employee who fails to give a campaign contribution. (18 USC 597-606)

Chamber Rules

Prior to the adoption of formal codes of conduct beginning in 1958, the chief ethical curbs on members' activities related to voting. *(Provisions of 1958 code, p. 146)*

In 1801, when he was vice president and presiding over the Senate, Thomas Jefferson wrote in *Jefferson's Manual:*

Where the private interests of a Member are concerned in a bill or question he is to withdraw. And where such an interest has appeared, his voice has been disallowed. . . . In a case so contrary, not only to the laws of decency, but to the fundamental principle of the social compact, which denies to any man to be a judge in his own cause, it is for the honor of the House that this rule of immemorial observance should be strictly adhered to.

Jefferson's rule gave rise to Rule 8 of the House, which requires each member present to vote "unless he has a direct personal or pecuniary interest in the event of such question." In most cases this decision has been left to the member. Under an 1874 ruling a representative may vote for his or her private interests if the measure is not for the member's exclusive benefit, but for that of a group.

Under Rule 12 senators may be excused from voting, provided they give their reasons for abstaining, and senators have been excused in the past because of such a direct interest in the outcome.

- "The Constitution expressly empowers each House to punish its own members for disorderly behavior. We see no reason to doubt that this punishment may in a proper case be imprisonment."
- "Each House is by the Constitution made the judge of the election and qualifications of its members. In deciding on these it has an undoubted right to examine witnesses and inspect papers, subject to the usual rights of witnesses in such cases; and it may be that a witness would be subject to like punishment at the hands of the body engaged in trying a contested election, for refusing to testify, that he would if the case were pending before a court of judicature."

In a later case, *In re Chapman* (166 U.S. 66),

decided in 1897, the Court reaffirmed the right of Congress to compel testimony on matters within its jurisdiction. It also defined the circumstances under which either chamber might expel one of its members: "The right to expel extends to all cases where the offense is such as in the judgment of the Senate is inconsistent with the trust and duty of a member."

Automatic Expulsion

In 1906 the Supreme Court expanded upon its *Chapman* ruling while interpreting a law Congress had approved on June 11, 1864. The act provided that any senator or representative found guilty of illegally receiving compensation for services provided in connection with a claim, contract, or other proceeding before a government agency "shall ... be rendered forever thereafter incapable of holding any office ... under the government of the United States." Sen. Joseph R. Burton, R-Kan., had been convicted under this law. In fighting to keep his seat, Burton's lawyers contended that the 1864 law violated the constitutional right of the Senate to decide on expulsion of its members.

In the Court's decision May 21, 1906, Justice John M. Harlan said that "The final judgment of conviction did not operate, *ipso facto,* to vacate the seat of the convicted senator nor compel the Senate to expel him or to regard him as expelled by force alone of the judgment" *(Burton v. United States,* 202 U.S. 344). On the following day, the Senate asked its Committee on Privileges and Elections to recommend what action, if any, should be taken. Burton resigned on June 4, 1906, before the committee reported.

Primary Election Misconduct

Misconduct by a member-elect provided the next major case for the Supreme Court to rule on congressional power to judge members' qualifica-tions. This case came from the Federal Corrupt Practices Act of June 25, 1910, as amended August 19, 1911. The two laws limited the amount of money that a candidate for Congress could spend on a campaign.

Sen. Truman H. Newberry, R-Mich., and sixteen others were found guilty of conspiring to violate the corrupt practices legislation in the Democratic senatorial primary election of August 27, 1918, in Michigan. Newberry's opponent had been auto manufacturer Henry Ford.

Acting on Newberry's appeal, *Newberry v. United States* (256 U.S. 232), the Court ruled May 2, 1921, that Congress did not have power to control in any way a state's party primaries or conventions for designating candidates for the Senate or House.

Twenty years after *Newberry,* the Supreme Court reversed itself on the right of Congress to legislate on primary elections. In a decision May 26, 1941, *United States v. Classic* (313 U.S. 299), the Court said that the power to regulate national elections, which the Constitution assigned to Congress, "includes the authority to regulate primary elections when, as in this case, they are a step in the exercise by the people of their choice of representatives in Congress."

Denial of Representation

The constitutional clause on the qualifications of members-elect has raised more questions of interpretation than has the authority to punish members. One of the most serious issues is whether exclusion of a member-elect deprives a state unwarrantedly, even for a short time, of its constitutionally guaranteed representation in Congress.

The Supreme Court in 1969 said a state may send to Congress anyone it chooses, if that person meets the qualifications in the Constitution and is legally elected. In 1969 the Court reversed the

House of Representatives' exclusion of Adam Clayton Powell, Jr., because Powell met the basic constitutional requirements. *(Powell case, below)*

Earlier, in 1929, the Court had ruled that Republican William S. Vare of Pennsylvania had not been legally elected to a Senate seat in 1926 because of corruption in the election campaign. The issue of whether this deprived the state of its right to representation was before the justices only peripherally, but they decided the matter anyway.

The Court, in *Barry et al. v. United States ex rel. Cunningham* (279 U.S. 597), said the Senate, which barred Vare from a seat by voiding the election, had acted legally within its authority "to exclude persons asserting membership who either had not been elected or, what amounts to the same thing, had been elected by resort to fraud, bribery, corruption, or other sinister methods having the effect of vitiating the election."

The Court then went on to the key issue of representation. The justices said the Article V equal representation language prohibited a state from being deprived of its equal suffrage in the Senate. The Court said this was "a limitation upon the power of amendment" and did not apply in the Vare situation.

"The temporary deprivation of equal representation" from not seating a person while an election controversy is resolved, the Court said, "is the necessary consequence of the exercise of a constitutional power, and no more deprives the state of its 'equal suffrage' in the constitutional sense than would a vote of the Senate vacating the seat of a sitting member or a vote of expulsion."

The Vare case was significant for one other question answered by the Supreme Court: whether Congress, in judging election cases, violated the principle of separation of powers by exercising a judicial function. The Court said that the Constitution, by authorizing Congress to be the judge of its members' qualifications, conferred on each house

Library of Congress

Adam Clayton Powell, Jr., speaks to reporters after the House Democratic Caucus on January 9, 1967, removed him as chairman of the Education and Labor Committee. In March the full House adopted a resolution excluding Powell from the 90th Congress. The Supreme Court later ruled that the House had acted unconstitutionally.

"certain powers which are not legislative but judicial in character," including the power "to render a judgment which is beyond the authority of any other tribunal to review."

Powell: Added Qualifications Barred

One of the stormiest episodes in congressional history was the precedent-shattering case of Rep. Adam Clayton Powell, Jr., D-N.Y. It was Powell's exclusion from the House that led to the 1969 Supreme Court decision prohibiting Congress from adding to the constitutional qualifications for membership in Congress.

In 1937 Powell succeeded his father as pastor

of the Abyssinian Baptist Church in Harlem, one of the largest congregations in the country. The new pastor was elected to the 79th Congress in 1944 with the nomination of both the Democratic and Republican parties. He took his seat with the Democrats, was reelected regularly by large majorities, served as chairman of the House Committee on Education and Labor from 1961 to 1967, and was considered by many observers the most powerful black in the United States. Throughout his legislative career, he retained his pastorate.

Powell's troubles stemmed in part from his flamboyant personality and his apparent disregard for the law. On the eve of Powell's 1952 reelection bid, the Internal Revenue Service said that he had underestimated his 1945 income tax by $2,749. A 1960 trial for criminal tax evasion resulted in a hung jury, and Powell eventually paid $27,833 in back taxes and penalties. Meanwhile he lost two suits brought by a widow in his district, Esther James, whom he had described in a television interview as a "bag woman" or graft collector for New York City police. While in legal difficulties Powell was held in contempt of court on four occasions.

In the 1950s and the early 1960s, Powell repeatedly went on costly pleasure trips at government expense. In addition, he incurred criticism for taking a staff member, Corinne A. Huff, on many trips to Bimini Island in the Bahamas. Out of government funds, he paid his wife $20,578 a year as a clerk while she lived in Puerto Rico. She was ordered dropped from the payroll in 1967.

The preceding year Powell was stripped by his committee colleagues of his powers as chairman of the House Education and Labor Committee. He had angered committee Democrats by long absences that delayed House action on President Johnson's antipoverty bill. By a vote of 27 to 1, the committee September 22, 1966, adopted new rules, one of which provided that if the chairman failed to bring a bill to the floor, one of the six subcommittee chairmen could do so.

The House Democratic Caucus on January 9, 1967, removed Powell from his committee chairmanship for the duration of the 90th Congress. This was the first time since 1925 that a committee chairman had been deposed in either house of Congress. Powell, who attended the caucus, called the action "a lynching, northern style." A day later, Powell was embroiled in a challenge to his seat in the House.

When members of the House convened January 10, 1967, a resolution submitted by Morris K. Udall, D-Ariz., proposed that Powell be sworn in, pending the result of a sixty-day investigation of his conduct by a select committee. Udall contended that stripping Powell of his chairmanship was punishment enough because his malfeasance was based on his misuse of that position. But the resolution was rejected on a 126-305 vote.

The House then adopted a resolution offered by Minority Leader Gerald R. Ford, R-Mich., which denied Powell his seat pending an investigation. The vote was 363 to 65.

House Judiciary Committee Chairman Emanuel Celler, D-N.Y., was chairman of the select committee appointed to investigate Powell's qualifications for his seat. The committee conducted hearings beginning February 8, 1967. Its report, submitted February 23, included a recommendation, unprecedented in congressional history, that Powell be fined. The committee proposed that he be sworn in; that his seniority be based on the date of his swearing in; that he be censured for "gross misconduct" through misuse of funds of the Committee on Education and Labor, refusal to pay the judgment against him, and noncooperation with House investigating committees; and that he be fined $40,000, to be paid to the clerk of the House in the form of a monthly deduction of $1,000 from Powell's salary, in order to "offset any civil liability of Mr. Powell to the United States."

The House on March 1, 1967, rejected the committee's proposals and adopted instead a resolution excluding Powell from the 90th Congress. On the select committee's proposals, the vote was 202 in favor, 222 against; on the exclusion resolution, 307 in favor, 116 against.

It was the first exclusion since Wisconsin Socialist Victor L. Berger was barred in 1919 and 1920. The House barred Berger, who had served one term in 1911-13, because he had been found guilty of sedition by publishing antiwar statements. But after the Supreme Court reversed his conviction he was elected again and served three more terms beginning in 1922.

Powell was the only other person excluded from the House or Senate in the twentieth century. As in his ouster from his committee chairmanship, Powell ascribed his downfall to racism. That racial feeling played a part in the vote to exclude Powell seemed probable. Celler said on television and on the House floor that he saw "an element of racism in the vote." Arlen J. Large, a Washington correspondent, wrote in the *Wall Street Journal,* March 22, 1967: "Disclaimers of race as a factor in Mr. Powell's exclusion don't jibe with the nearly solid anti-Powell votes of Southern congressmen, reflecting the bitterly worded letters from white voters back home."

In his appearances before the select committee, Powell responded only to questions relating to the constitutional requirements for House membership—his age, citizenship, and inhabitancy. These were the only questions that the House could properly inquire into, Powell and his lawyers claimed. Upon his exclusion, Powell filed suit.

Central Issues

Until the Powell case, Congress had acted from time to time as if it were entitled to add qualifications as well as to wink at failure to meet them.

Alexander Hamilton in No. 60 of *The Federalist* wrote: "The qualifications of the persons who may ... be chosen are defined and fixed in the Constitution, and are unalterable by the legislature."

Later authorities, including a House committee in 1900 considering the seating of a Mormon convicted of polygamy, argued that the Constitutional Convention intended to empower Congress to add qualifications. The committee concluded that if the Convention meant to restrict qualifications to the three in the Constitution, it would have phrased them affirmatively. For example, the Framers would have written: "Every member of the House of Representatives shall be of the age of twenty-five years at least," rather than deliberately using the supposedly more flexible negative phrasing of Article I, Section 2: "No Person shall be a Representative who shall not have attained to the Age of twenty five Years...."

The qualifications issue was a dilemma. If Congress followed only the three requirements, it had to seat individuals regarded as obnoxious. If it excluded such individuals, it could be charged with exceeding its powers.

The Civil War turmoil focused the debate. Both houses added a qualification for membership in 1862 known as the "Ironclad Oath Law" or the "Test Oath Law." It required members to swear, before taking the oath of office, that they had never voluntarily borne arms against the United States or aided, recognized, or supported a jurisdiction hostile to the United States. This law remained in effect until the Fourteenth Amendment was ratified in 1868.

Cases in which House proceedings on exclusion ended in admission of the representative-elect evoked various memorable exchanges on the floor. An example is the case of John C. Conner, D-Texas, who was accused of having whipped black soldiers under his command in 1868 and of having boasted in 1869 that he would escape conviction by a military court by bribing witnesses. James A.

Garfield, R-Ohio, speaking in the House on March 31, 1870, raised a constitutional question on this case: "Allow me to ask . . . if anything in the Constitution of the United States . . . forbids that a 'moral monster' shall be elected to the Congress?" Ebon C. Ingersoll, R-Ill., replied: "I believe the people may elect a moral monster to Congress if they see fit, but I believe that Congress has a right to exclude that moral monster from a seat if they see fit." A resolution allowing Conner to take his seat was adopted the same day.

Against that background, the central issues in the Powell case were:

- Could the House add to the Constitution's three qualifications for House membership: age, citizenship, and residency?
- Did the courts have the power to examine the actions of the House? U.S. District Judge George L. Hart, Jr., ruled April 7, 1967, that he had no jurisdiction in the case and dismissed the suit.

The U.S. Court of Appeals for the District of Columbia on February 28, 1968, affirmed Hart's action. The Court of Appeals stated that the case involved a political question, which, if decided, would constitute a violation of the separation of powers and produce an embarrassing confrontation between Congress and the courts.

Supreme Court Ruling

While the case was before the Supreme Court, the next Congress seated Powell, who had been re-elected again in 1968. But the court decided that the issues, including Powell's claim for back pay, required settlement. By a 7-1 vote on June 16, 1969, the Supreme Court reversed the lower court. Chief Justice Earl Warren, delivering the opinion, said the House had improperly excluded Powell because he met the constitutional requirements of age, residence, and citizenship.

On the question of the lower court's jurisdiction, Warren acknowledged that five members of Congress who were defendants (the Speaker of the House, the majority and minority leaders, and the ranking members of the committee that investigated Powell) were immune under the speech or debate clause of the Constitution. However, three other defendants, functionaries of the House who had withheld Powell's pay and denied him such perquisites as an office and staff, were liable for action, the Court said. A claim for back pay was sent back to a lower court but Powell never pursued the matter.

His district reelected Powell in a special election April 11, 1967, but he did not apply to the House to be seated while appealing his exclusion to the courts. Reelected in 1968, Powell was sworn in and seated but subjected to loss of seniority and fined $25,000. In the voting on the resolution imposing these penalties, there were 254 yeas, 158 nays.

Although he had won the right to be seated, Powell rarely attended Congress, preferring instead his retreat in Bimini. In 1970 Charles B. Rangel successfully challenged Powell in the Democratic primary and went on to win the general election. Powell died in Miami, Florida, April 4, 1972.

CHAPTER 2

Expulsion:

The Ultimate Sanction

Congress basically has two ways to punish members for serious misbehavior—expulsion or censure. Of the two, expulsion is the far more severe and direct. Simply put, the expelled member is out. And, as in baseball, when you're out, you're out.

Although the House and even the Senate are not considered exlusive clubs so much as they once were, being thrown out is still humiliating to the person who experiences it. Understandably, both chambers rarely resort to this form of punishment.

Censure, on the other hand, can be softened to make it more palatable both to the offender and to the colleagues meting out the punishment. Various circumlocutions, such as "reprimand" or "denounce," have been used to disguise what is essentially a censure. *(See Chapter 3.)*

Fifteen senators have been expelled, one in 1797 and fourteen during the Civil War. One of the latter actions was reversed after the expelled senator had died. Formal expulsion proceedings in the Senate have been instituted nine times since the Civil War, always without success. *(Senate expulsion proceedings, table, Appendix, p. 168)*

In the House, only four members have been expelled, three in 1861 and one in 1980. Nine representatives have been censured as a lesser form of punishment during expulsion proceedings against them. *(House expulsion proceedings, table, Appendix, p. 167)*

In both chambers, embattled members have resigned rather than risk expulsion or other punishment.

GROUNDS FOR EXPULSION

The Abscam investigation of 1980, in which FBI agents posing as Arab sheiks or businessmen offered bribes to members of Congress, resulted in the first ouster of a member for corruption. Until then the only grounds on which a member had been expelled was conspiracy against a foreign country (the 1797 case in the Senate) and support of a rebellion (the Civil War cases of fourteen senators and three representatives).

Other cases dealing with corruption had been unsuccessful, as had others concerned with the killing of a representative in a duel, the assaulting of a senator or a representative, treasonable or offensive utterances, sedition, and Mormonism.

Prior Offenses

The most important question raised about the power to expel has been whether a member may be ousted for offenses committed before the person was elected.

John Quincy Adams, while serving in the Senate before he became president, submitted a committee report supporting the Senate's power to expel a member for preelection conduct that came to light after he had taken his seat. The case was that of John Smith, D-Ohio, who allegedly had been connected with Aaron Burr's conspiracy to separate several of the western states from the Union. Adams's committee, in its report of December 31, 1807, said:

> When a man whom his fellow citizens have honored with their confidence on the pledge of a spotless reputation has degraded himself by the commission of infamous crimes, which become suddenly and unexpectedly revealed to the world, defective, indeed, would be that institution which should be impotent to discard from its bosom the contagion of such a member.

The expulsion case against Smith was lost by a single vote on April 9, 1808, when 19 yeas, not enough to make up the required two-thirds, were cast for expulsion, against 10 nays. (Smith's counsel was Francis Scott Key, who later wrote the poem that became the national anthem.)

Later Congresses that debated proposals to unseat members repeatedly took up the question of whether acts committed prior to the member's election furnished legitimate grounds for expulsion.

Incompatible Office

The Constitution, in Article I, Section 6, provides: "[N]o Person holding any Office under the United States, shall be a Member of either House during his Continuance in Office." When a senator or representative has accepted appointment to another "Office under the United States," the member has jeopardized but not always lost the privilege of remaining in Congress, depending on the type of office the member accepted and the attitude of the chamber in which he or she was serving. If a congressional seat is forfeited by acceptance of another office, the person is not considered to have been expelled; the seat is treated as having been vacated.

Cases arising in the Civil War and subsequent wars in which members of Congress served in the armed forces generally did not result in vacating of their seats. In the Spanish-American War, a House committee recommended vacating the seats of four representatives who had accepted U.S. Army commissions. "No mere patriotic sentiment," it said, "should be permitted to override the plain language of the fundamental written law." On March 2, 1899, the House, by a vote of 77 yeas and 163 nays, declined to consider the proposed resolution.

Members of both chambers have been appointed to serve as commissioners to negotiate peace and arbitrate disputes, as members of "blue ribbon" boards of inquiry, and so forth, without losing their seats in Congress. The House in 1919 authorized members who had been absent on military service to be paid their salaries minus the amount they were paid for military service.

During the Vietnam War, Judge Gerhard A. Gesell of the U.S. District Court for the District of Columbia ruled on April 2, 1971, that the 117 members who held commissions in military reserve units were violating the incompatible-office clause. The decision reached the Supreme Court, which ruled June 25, 1974, that the plaintiffs—current and former reservists opposed to the war—did not have legal standing to make the challenge. *(Schlesinger v. Reservists Committee to Stop the War,* 418 U.S. 208)

Civil War Cases

After the Senate's expulsion of William Blount, Ind-Tenn., in 1797 for conspiracy to incite members of two Indian tribes to attack Spanish Florida and Louisiana, the only successful expulsion cases were those resulting from the Civil War.

On January 21, 1861, Jefferson Davis, D-Miss., like a number of other southern senators before and after that date, announced his support of secession. He withdrew from the Senate and became president of the Confederacy a month later. On March 14, 1861, ten days after Abraham Lincoln's inauguration, the Senate adopted a resolution ordering that because the seats of these southerners had "become vacant, . . . the Secretary be directed to omit their names respectively from the roll." Although Davis and the five other southern senators had left voluntarily, they had not formally resigned. Hence the Senate's action resembled expulsion, but it was not in fact a true expulsion. Both chambers later expelled other rebellion supporters in actions that historians count as definite expulsions.

Senate. On a single day, July 11, 1861, the Senate expelled ten members—two each from Arkansas, North Carolina, Texas, and Virginia, and one each from South Carolina and Tennessee, for failure to appear in their seats and for participation in secession. The vote was 32 in favor of expulsion, 10 against. John C. Breckinridge, D-Ky., who had been vice president of the United States from 1857 to 1861, was expelled December 4, 1861, by the following resolution: "Whereas John C. Breckinridge, a member of this body from the State of Kentucky, has joined the enemies of his country, and is now in arms against the Government he had sworn to support: Therefore, Resolved, That said John C. Breckinridge, the traitor, be, and he hereby is, expelled from the Senate." On this resolution the vote was 37 to 0.

Library of Congress

Sen. John C. Breckinridge, D-Ky., who joined the Confederate army in September 1861, was expelled by the Senate on December 4 of that year.

Of the ten July 11 expulsions, one was later annulled posthumously. In 1877 the Committee on Privileges and Elections reviewed the expulsion of William K. Sebastian, D-Ark., decided that the Senate had a right to reverse its earlier action, and recommended that it do so. The Senate on March 3, 1877, voted for reversal, adopting the committee's view that the original action against Sebastian had been "occasioned by want of information, and by the overruling excitement of a period of great public danger." Sebastian, who remained loyal to the Union throughout the war, had been dead twelve years when his expulsion was reversed.

In 1862 the Senate expelled three senators, all for disloyalty to the government: Missouri Democrats Trusten Polk and Waldo P. Johnson and Indiana Democrat Jesse D. Bright. Polk was accused of stating in a widely published letter his hopes that Missouri would secede from the Union. Johnson reportedly held similar feelings and did not appear to take his Senate seat. Bright was charged with treason for giving an arms salesman a letter of introduction to Confederate president Davis.

House.   On July 13, 1861, the House expelled a member-elect, John B. Clark, D-Mo., who had not yet taken the oath. After a brief debate on Clark's entrance into the Confederate forces, and without referring the case to a committee, the House adopted the expulsion order by slightly more than a two-thirds vote, 94 to 45.

Two other representatives were expelled in December 1861: John W. Reid, D-Mo., for taking up arms against the country, and Henry C. Burnett, D-Ky., for open rebellion against the federal government.

TWENTIETH-CENTURY SENATE CASES

No senators have been expelled since the Civil War, but World War I brought the first of several attempts in modern times to dismiss members for disloyalty or, more commonly, for corruption. All failed, but one such effort in 1981 resulted in the resignation of the senator under fire.

In the World War I instance, Sen. Robert M. La Follette, R-Wis., spoke at St. Paul, Minnesota, September 20, 1917, decrying American participation in the fighting. On the basis of that speech, Minnesota's Public Safety Commission petitioned the Senate to expel La Follette for sedition. The Senate by a 50-21 vote dismissed the petition on January 16, 1919.

In 1932-34 the two senators from Louisiana, Democrats Huey P. Long and John H. Overton, were accused of fraud and corruption in connection with their nomination and election. The Commit-

tee on Privileges and Elections investigated but eventually asked to be taken off the cases. The Senate did so on June 16, 1934, in effect burying expulsion resolutions that had been introduced.

Charges of corruption against William Langer, then a senator-elect from North Dakota, prompted an effort to block his admission or to expel him should he be seated. On March 27, 1941, the Senate first rejected a resolution, 37-45, stating that the case did not fall within the constitutional provisions for expulsion. It then rejected, 30-52, a resolution declaring that Langer was not entitled to his seat.

Resignation of Senator Williams

Harrison A. Williams, Jr., D-N.J., the only senator caught in the FBI's Abscam net, was convicted May 1, 1981, of accepting stock in a titanium mining company in return for his promise to get government contracts for the mine's output. On August 24 the Senate Ethics Committee unanimously recommended that the Senate expel Williams. After numerous delays, the Senate began debate on the committee's resolution March 3, 1982. On March 11, when it was clear to all that more than two-thirds of the senators would vote for expulsion, Williams resigned his Senate seat. *(Abscam prosecutions, Chapter 6, p. 63)*

House Expulsion of Myers

The Abscam scandal also produced the first expulsion of a House member since the Civil War. Michael J. "Ozzie" Myers, D-Pa., one of six representatives convicted as a result of the operation, became the fourth person in history to be ousted from the House. He was expelled October 2, 1980, on a 376-39 vote. Videotapes made by the FBI had shown Myers accepting a bribe of $50,000 in cash and boasting of his familiarity with Philadelphia officials and the Mafia.

Williams: Fourth Senator Convicted in Office

Harrison A. Williams, Jr., D-N.J., implicated in the Abscam scandal in 1981, was the fourth senator convicted of criminal wrongdoing while in office. The previously convicted sitting senator was Truman H. Newberry, R-Mich., who was found guilty in March 1920 of election irregularities. The Supreme Court reversed Newberry's conviction in May 1921, but he resigned in November 1922 after realizing that, despite the Court's finding, "his position could never be other than uncomfortable," according to *Senate Election, Expulsion, and Censure Cases* (S Doc 92-7).

The other two convicted sitting senators were:

- John H. Mitchell, R-Ore., convicted in July 1905 on charges of accepting compensation for services rendered before a U.S. department. He died in late 1905 while his conviction was on appeal.
- Joseph R. Burton, R-Kan., convicted in November 1905 for allegedly using the mails for fraudulent purposes and accepting compensation for services rendered before a U.S. department. Burton resigned in June 1906 after the Supreme Court upheld his conviction, and he served five months in prison.

Indicted but Not Convicted

Four other senators were charged with criminal offenses while in office but not convicted. They were:

- John Smith, D-Ohio, indicted in 1806 along with Vice President Aaron Burr for treason. He was acquitted.
- Charles H. Dietrich, R-Neb., indicted in December 1903 on bribery and conspiracy charges in connection with the appointment of a postmaster and the leasing of a post office. The charges were dropped on a technicality in January 1904.
- Burton K. Wheeler, D-Mont., indicted in April 1924 on a bribery charge. Wheeler was acquitted.
- Edward J. Gurney, R-Fla., indicted in April 1974 for alleged election law violations. The indictment was dismissed in May 1974. Gurney was again indicted in July 1974, this time on charges of perjury and soliciting bribes. He was acquitted on the bribery solicitation charge in August 1975 and on the perjury charge in October 1976.

HOUSE LEADERSHIP RESIGNATIONS

Throughout the history of Congress, senators and representatives in danger of being expelled or censured have resigned to escape the penalty. As in the case of Williams in the Senate, two House members convicted in the Abscam scandal resigned to avoid expulsion proceedings: John W. Jenrette, Jr., D-S.C., and Raymond F. Lederer, D-Pa. Others implicated did not seek reelection or were defeated.

The 1980s also saw two of the top leaders of the House surrender their seats to head off possible punishment for financial activities then under investigation.

Coelho

A *Newsweek* story in 1987 alleged that Democratic Majority Whip Tony Coelho, D-Calif., might have violated House rules and federal law in his dealings with a Texas savings and loan. At issue was Coelho's use of the company's yacht for eight fund raisers in 1986, when he headed the Democratic Congressional Campaign Committee. *Newsweek* put the events' cost at $25,184; federal law prohibited political committees from receiving more than

Wright: First Speaker Deposed But Not the First Under Fire

Although he was the first House Speaker forced out of office at midterm, Jim Wright of Texas was not the first to be embroiled in a controversy that attracted national attention and disrupted congressional leadership.

In the closest parallel, the House in 1910 nearly deposed Speaker Joseph G. Cannon of Illinois for his heavy-handed use of power. The revolt against Cannon, a Republican, exploded in response to his spectacular use of the Speaker's powers to reward friends and punish foes. Cannon freely wielded his authority to control who sat on which committee, which bills went to the floor, and who would be recognized to speak.

Democrats made common cause with insurgent Republicans on March 16, 1910, and defeated Cannon on a procedural question that was, in effect, a referendum on his leadership. The insurgents went on, three stormy days later, to ram through rules changes that stripped the Speaker of his right to make committee assignments and of his control of the Rules Committee.

Cannon refused to resign as Speaker, but he invited a vote on deposing him. Pandemonium broke loose on the House floor, judging from the notation in the *Congressional Record:* "Great confusion in the Hall."

A resolution declaring the Speaker's office vacant was put to a vote—the only time such a vote has been taken—but Cannon survived, 155-192. It suited the political purposes of some to keep Cannon in office: That made it easier to run against "Cannonism" in the 1910 elections. He lost the speakership after Democrats won a majority of House seats for the first time since 1895.

In the early nineteenth century, Speaker Nathaniel Macon also came close to being deposed. Macon, one of Thomas Jefferson's most devoted loyalists, was rewarded for his fealty with Jefferson's support during his election as Speaker in 1801.

But Macon later allied himself with a bitter foe of the president's, John Randolph, who broke with Jefferson over a plan to acquire Florida. Jefferson retaliated against Macon by opposing his re-election as Speaker in 1805. Jefferson's effort failed, but it was a close enough decision that Macon chose not to seek another term as Speaker.

Some Speakers have been tainted by scandal after they left office. John White, one of the more obscure Speakers (1841-43), came under fire for one of the last speeches he gave before leaving the House in 1845 to take a judgeship in Kentucky. After it was disclosed that a particularly eloquent

---

$15,000 from one source.

If Coelho had personally accepted gifts of more than $100 in total value, he would have violated the House's gift rule. Coelho declined to comment on the *Newsweek* story.

No investigation was launched into the allegations, despite calls from conservatives for a probe. But in 1989 Coelho resigned from Congress rather than face a protracted ethics investigation of his personal finances in the wake of a controversy surrounding a "junk bond" deal. Coelho resigned effective June 15, 1989.

Wright

The House ethics committee opened a formal investigation of Speaker Jim Wright, D-Texas, on June 9, 1988. Wright had publicly invited such an inquiry after a longtime critic, Newt Gingrich, R-Ga., had been joined by the government-watchdog group Common Cause in urging an investigation.

Republicans, especially Gingrich, had been criticizing Wright since he became Speaker. Democrats generally closed ranks around the Speaker, saying that questions about his finances were a

speech he gave had been plagiarized from Aaron Burr, White committed suicide.

While James G. Blaine, R-Maine, was Speaker (1869-75), he was cleared of wrongdoing by a special committee appointed to look into the Crédit Mobilier scandal, in which promoters of the Union Pacific Railroad used stock to bribe members to support federal subsidies for the railroad. *(Crédit Mobilier scandal, Chapter 1, p. 7)*

But other allegations of graft surfaced in 1876, after Blaine left the Speaker's office due to a change of party control in the House. Blaine took to the House floor to read from letters that supposedly exonerated him. That quelled efforts to censure him, but the flap did not help his unsuccessful quest for his party's presidential nomination at the GOP convention just months later. Blaine was finally nominated in 1884, but he lost the election to Grover Cleveland.

A newspaper clipping prompted Speaker Henry Clay to defend himself on the floor in 1825. In a published letter, another member accused Clay of cutting a secret deal to support John Quincy Adams for president in exchange for an appointment as secretary of state. The scandal died quickly. Clay asked the House to name a special committee to look into the charges, but the member who had made the allegation refused to appear.

More recently, Speaker John McCormack, D-Mass., retired in 1971 after one of his top aides, Martin Sweig, was accused of using the Speaker's office and name for fraudulent purposes, without McCormack's knowledge. McCormack, in his seventies and under pressure from a restive younger generation of lawmakers, had other reasons for leaving the House when he did. *(Sweig activities, Chapter 8, p. 103)*

His successor as Speaker, Carl Albert of Oklahoma, was troubled by publicity about an alleged drinking problem.

When Thomas P. O'Neill, D-Mass., became Speaker in 1977, he immediately faced questions raised in connection with a newly disclosed bribery scandal involving South Koreans. The ethics committee in January 1977 began an investigation into allegations that as many as 115 members—Republicans and Democrats—had taken illegal gifts from South Korean agents. *(Korean lobbying scandal, Chapter 5, p. 58)*

Some people suggested that O'Neill, during a 1974 trip to Korea, had asked Korean rice dealer Tongsun Park to make contributions to House members and their wives. But other members were the principal target, and in July 1978 the committee issued a statement exonerating O'Neill. The panel said the only thing of "questionable propriety" the Speaker had done was to let Park pay for two parties in his honor.

Republican tactic to deflect attention from allegations of misconduct in the Reagan administration. But the call by Common Cause for an investigation made it difficult for Democrats, many of whom had strong ties to the nonpartisan organization, to dismiss the attacks on Wright as purely partisan.

Republican leaders in September filed another complaint seeking a second, unrelated inquiry into allegations that Wright improperly disclosed security secrets in comments he made relating to activities of the CIA in Nicaragua. The ethics panel did not rule on the complaint in the 100th Congress.

When the panel opened its preliminary investigation in June by unanimous vote after a marathon eight-and-a-half-hour session that extended into the night, it announced that it would investigate six allegations against Wright raised by Gingrich, Common Cause, and press accounts.

The six allegations concerned:

- A Gingrich allegation that Wright in 1979 lobbied U.S. and Egyptian officials on behalf of Neptune Oil Co., shortly after the company's president had given Wright the chance to

R. Michael Jenkins

Ethics charges ended the career of Speaker Jim Wright, D-Texas, who resigned from the House in 1989.

paign committees over the years. Wright had earned about $55,000 in royalties, at a 55 percent rate that critics called unusually high.

The panel also agreed to look into questions on whether the book deal violated House rules by channeling campaign funds to Wright's personal use. Wright denied that any campaign funds were used in publishing and promoting the book.

- The role of a Wright staff aide, Matthew Cossolotto, in helping to prepare the book. Press reports raised questions about whether Wright had violated House rules barring employees from being compensated with public funds for nonofficial, personal, or campaign activities.
- Questions that Wright might have violated House rules restricting members' acceptance of gifts by regularly staying, during visits to his district, in a Fort Worth apartment that until recently had been owned by the family of a business associate, Texas developer George Mallick, without paying monthly rent. Wright did pay $21.67 for each day of use—a per diem rate he said was based on market rates—and later bought the apartment.

House rules barred members from accepting more than $100 worth of gifts annually from anyone with an interest in legislation. Wright said the arrangement did not violate that rule because the apartment's owner, Mallick's son Steve, had "no direct interest in legislation."

- Questions about whether Wright exercised "undue influence" in dealing with officials of the Federal Home Loan Bank Board. Controversy centered around Wright's actions in late 1986, when he intervened with federal regulators for three fellow Texans—a real estate investor and two savings and loan executives. Wright insisted he was only going to bat for the interests of his constituents.

invest in an obviously lucrative gas well. Wright said his lobbying on behalf of a constituent was unrelated to the investment, which he said was not the risk-free venture Gingrich made it out to be.

- Claims by Gingrich, which he later acknowledged to be partially in error, that Wright tried to influence an Interior Department decision affecting Texas Oil & Gas Corp. in 1979, just months after buying stock in the company. Wright denied he ever owned stock in the company, although he acknowledged that Texas Oil & Gas drilled the gas well he had been invited to invest in.
- Questions raised both by Gingrich and Common Cause about the financial arrangements surrounding the publication and sale of a 117-page book by Wright, *Reflections of a Public Man,* which was sold primarily at political rallies and through bulk purchases by lobbyists. It was published by a Fort Worth associate, Carlos Moore, whose printing firm had done substantial business with Wright's cam-

The "preliminary inquiry" voted by the committee was a grand jury-like investigation, in which the panel would gather evidence and take testimony from witnesses. It offered Wright a chance to testify before the panel—an opportunity he had been seeking in the days before the committee action.

The preliminary inquiry was to lead to a staff report to the committee, with recommendations about whether to issue the equivalent of an indictment, known as a "statement of alleged violations," that would be followed by a trial-like phase of the investigation known as a disciplinary hearing. In a move to enhance the credibility of the inquiry, the ethics committee in July hired an outside attorney, Chicago trial lawyer Richard J. Phelan, to head it.

Wright testified for more than five hours September 14. But the panel did not finish its investigation by the end of the 100th Congress (1987-89), much to the disappointment of Wright's supporters.

After a ten-month investigation, the ethics committee April 17, 1989, formally charged Wright with accepting improper gifts from Mallick, a longtime friend and business associate who paid Wright's wife, Betty, an $18,000-a-year salary and gave her use of a company car and condominium—benefits the committee valued at a total of $145,000 over ten years.

The committee also alleged that bulk sales of Wright's book were intended as an "overall scheme to evade the House outside earned income limits."

Those allegations were spelled out in a statement of alleged violations, citing sixty-nine instances in five broad categories where the committee found "reason to believe" Wright violated House rules over the previous ten years.

The committee also announced it was continuing to investigate a previously undisclosed allegation concerning an oil-well deal that resulted in huge profits for Wright.

But the committee decided not to pursue half of the 116 possible rule violations identified by Phelan. Among those dropped were questions about Wright's investment in a lucrative oil well and allegations that he had been too heavy-handed in his dealings with federal thrift-industry regulators.

Procedural and legal delays pushed the next phase, the disciplinary hearing, into June. In the meantime, Wright was pummeled in the press with new allegations about his conduct, and negotiations to have key charges against him dismissed were unsuccessful.

Before leaving the House he gave a farewell speech on May 31 in which he portrayed himself as a victim of a partisan vendetta and denounced the "mindless cannibalism" of attacks on politicians' personal ethics. He announced that he would resign as Speaker, which he did on June 6, and would leave the House, which he did on June 30.

CHAPTER 3

Censure/Reprimand:
A Public Scolding

For offenses where expulsion is deemed too harsh, the Senate and House may punish their members by scolding them in a resolution of censure. Besides being milder, censure requires only a simple majority vote while expulsion requires a two-thirds majority. Censure also has the advantage of not depriving constituents of their elected senators or representatives. Grounds for disciplining members usually consist of a member's action during service in Congress. Both houses have sparingly used their power to penalize a member for prior offenses and have been shy about punishing misdeeds committed during a previous Congress.

For minor transgressions of the rules, the presiding officer of either chamber may call a member to order, without a formal move to censure. For example, on January 14, 1955, Russell B. Long, D-La., while presiding over the Senate, called Joseph R. McCarthy, R-Wis., to order after McCarthy questioned the motives of some senators who had voted on a resolution continuing an investigation of communists in government. Long said: "The statement of the junior senator from Wisconsin was that other senators were insincere. In making that statement, the senator from Wis-

consin spoke contrary to the rules of the Senate. . . . He must take his seat." Later on the same day, Long again called McCarthy to order.

In recent years, Congress has turned to alternative words when it wants to avoid the term *censure,* usually out of affection for the person being disciplined. In the Senate, the words *condemn* and *denounce,* have sometimes have been used instead of censure. In the House, the favored alternative term has been *reprimand,* which calls for somewhat less public humiliation than a formal censure. The Senate issued its first reprimand in 1991, against one of the so-called Keating Five senators.

Other punishments that fell short of expulsion have included denial of the member's right to vote, stripping of chairmanships, and imposition of fines.

In the entire history of Congress, the Senate has censured, condemned, or denounced nine senators and reprimanded one. The House has censured twenty-two representatives and reprimanded seven. *(Senate censure proceedings, Appendix, p. 169; House censure and reprimand proceedings, pp. 170 and 172)*

In the Senate, censure proceedings are carried out more moderately than they are in the House. The senator accused of wrongdoing, for example, is allowed to speak in self-defense.

The House treats the accused more harshly. It has often denied the privilege of speaking to an alleged offender. In most cases, a censured member is treated like a felon; the Speaker calls the person to the bar of the House and makes a solemn pronouncement of censure.

For example, Speaker Frederick H. Gillett, R-Mass., on October 27, 1921, directed the sergeant at arms to bring to the bar of the House Rep. Thomas L. Blanton, D-Texas, who was being disciplined for inserting indecent matter in the *Congressional Record*. The Speaker then made the following statement:

> Mr. Blanton, by a unanimous vote of the House—yeas, 293; nays, none—I have been directed to censure you because, when you had been allowed the courtesy of the House to print a speech which you did not deliver, you inserted in it foul and obscene matter, which you knew you could not have spoken on the floor; and that disgusting matter, which could not have been circulated through the mails in any other publication without violating the law, was transmitted as part of the proceedings of this House to thousands of homes and libraries throughout the country, to be read by men and women, and worst of all by children, whose prurient curiosity it would excite and corrupt. In accordance with the instructions of the House and as its representative, I pronounce upon you its censure.

CENSURE BY THE SENATE

Timothy Pickering, F-Mass., was the first member to be censured by the Senate. In December 1810 he had read aloud in the chamber secret documents relating to the 1803 convention with France for the cession of Louisiana. The Senate on January 2, 1811, adopted the following resolution of censure:

> Resolved, That Timothy Pickering, a Senator from the State of Massachusetts, having, . . . whilst the Senate was in session with open doors, read from his place certain documents confidentially communicated by the President of the United States to the Senate, the injunction of secrecy not having been removed, has, in so doing, committed a violation of the rules of this body.

Twenty senators voted for the resolution; seven, against it.

Benjamin Tappan, D-Ohio, was similarly censured on May 10, 1844, when the Senate adopted a two-part resolution concerning his release to the press of confidential material relating to a treaty for the annexation of Texas. The first part, adopted 35 to 7, censured Tappan for releasing the documents in "flagrant violation" of the Senate rules. The second, adopted 39 to 3, accepted Tappan's apology and said that no further censure would "be inflicted on him."

Threatened violence was involved in the next censure case in the Senate. On the Senate floor April 7, 1850, Thomas H. Benton, D-Mo., made menacing gestures and advanced toward Henry S. Foote, U-Miss., while Foote was making a speech. Foote drew a pistol from his pocket and cocked it. Before any damage was done, other senators intervened and restored order. A committee appointed to consider the incident said in its report, July 30, that what the two men had done was deplorable. The committee recommended that Foote be censured, but the Senate took no action. This was the only Senate case in which an investigating committee's recommendation of censure was not adopted.

More than half a century later, on February 22, 1902, while the Senate was debating Philippine affairs, Benjamin R. Tillman, D-S.C., questioned the integrity of John L. McLaurin, D-S.C. When

McLaurin branded the statement as "a willful, malicious, and deliberate lie," Tillman advanced toward McLaurin and they engaged in a brief fistfight. After they had been separated, the Senate by a vote of 61 to 0 declared them to be "in contempt of the Senate" and referred the matter to the Committee on Privileges and Elections. The committee on February 27 recommended censure and the Senate adopted the resolution by a vote of 54 to 12.

The Senate censured Hiram Bingham, R-Conn., in 1929 for placing a lobbyist on the payroll. Bingham had hired Charles L. Eyanson, a secretary to the president of the Connecticut Manufacturers' Association, to assist him with tariff legislation. Sen. George W. Norris, R-Neb., introduced a resolution declaring that Bingham's action was "contrary to good morals and senatorial ethics." During consideration of the resolution on November 4, 1929, the Senate added language stating that Bingham's actions were "not the result of corrupt motives." The resolution was then adopted by a vote of 54 to 22, with eighteen senators (including Bingham) not voting.

McCarthy: Brought "Senate into Dishonor"

The sixth member of the Senate to be censured—"condemned" was the actual language used by the Senate—was Joseph R. McCarthy, R-Wis. Proceedings on this case began in the 82nd Congress (1951-52) and were concluded in the 83rd (1953-54). William Benton, D-Conn., in August 1951 offered a resolution calling on the Committee on Rules and Administration to investigate, among other things, McCarthy's participation in the defamation of Millard E. Tydings, D, during the Maryland senatorial campaign, to determine whether expulsion proceedings should be instituted against McCarthy.

On April 10, 1952, McCarthy submitted a resolution calling for investigation by the same committee of Benton's activities as assistant secretary of state, campaign contributions Benton had received, and other matters. The Rules Committee's Privileges and Elections Subcommittee, after conducting an investigation, submitted an inconclusive report on January 2, 1953.

In the spring of 1954 the Senate Permanent Investigations Subcommittee conducted hearings on mutual accusations of misconduct by McCarthy and U.S. Army officials. Sen. Ralph E. Flanders, R-Vt., on July 30 introduced a resolution to censure McCarthy. Among Flanders's reasons for pressing censure were McCarthy's refusal to testify before the Rules subcommittee in 1952, refusal to repudiate the "frivolous and irresponsible" conduct of Investigations Subcommittee Counsel Roy M. Cohn and consultant G. David Schine on their 1953 subversion-seeking trip to Europe, and "habitual contempt for people." The Senate on August 2 adopted, by a vote of 75 to 12, a proposal to refer Flanders's censure resolution to a select committee. Three days later, Vice President Richard Nixon appointed the select committee.

The Select Committee to Study Censure Charges held hearings from August 31 to September 13, 1954. The committee, after rejecting McCarthy's contention that the Senate cannot punish a member for what he did in a previous Congress, on September 27 submitted a forty-thousand-word report unanimously recommending that the Senate censure McCarthy. After an election campaign recess the Senate reconvened November 8 to consider the censure proposal. Proceedings in the next few weeks led to modifications of the proposal and substitution of the word "condemned" for "censured." Historians nonetheless count the rebuke as a censure. *(Text of final resolution on McCarthy, p. 30)*

The Senate adopted the resolution of condemnation on December 2 by a vote of 67 to 22. Republicans split evenly, twenty-two favoring and twenty-two opposing. All forty-four Democrats,

McCarthy's Rough Investigative Tactics
His Rocket to Fame—and Disgrace

The controversial hearings that produced the term *McCarthyism* also culminated in the 1974 Senate censure of the word's namesake, Wisconsin Republican Joseph R. McCarthy. As a subcommittee chairman, McCarthy carried out hearings in an abrasive and aggressive manner. He investigated varied subjects, but his main focus was a purported Communist subversion of the U.S. government, including the armed forces, and the United Nations.

McCarthy tangled with the press, Harvard University, and fellow senators. Long before the stormy hearings got under way, the senator had become a controversial public figure. The period that was later called the McCarthy era began in 1950. On February 9 he delivered a speech before the Ohio County Women's Republican Club in Wheeling, West Virginia. According to the Wheeling *News Register* and the Wheeling *Intelligencer,* the senator said at one point: "While I cannot take the time to name all the men in the State Department who have been named as members of the Communist party and members of a spy ring, I have here in my hand a list of 205 that were known to the secretary of state as being members of the Communist party and who, nevertheless, are still working and shaping policy in the State Department." The number varied in later versions of the speech, and the text that was read into the *Congressional Record* omitted the paragraph referring to the list of 205 Communists.

The Foreign Relations Committee set up a special subcommittee headed by Millard E. Tydings, D-Md., to investigate McCarthy's charges. The subcommittee, in one of the most bitterly controversial investigations in the history of Congress, held thirty-one days of hearings between March 8 and June 28, 1950. During the sessions, McCarthy charged ten individuals with varying degrees of Communist activity. One was Professor Owen J. Lattimore of Johns Hopkins University, who in the summer of 1950 published a book, *Ordeal by Slander,* defending his record against McCarthy's accusations of disloyalty.

The investigation was a major issue in the 1950 elections. Charges of "softness" toward communism were widely credited with Tydings's defeat. On August 6, 1951, after a Senate Rules and Administration Committee report had criticized McCarthy's part in the Maryland election, William Benton, D-Conn., led a move to expel McCarthy, who in turn demanded an investigation of Benton. The result was a simultaneous investigation of both men by an elections subcommittee. By the time the subcommittee reported, Benton had lost the 1952 election; his defeat was widely attributed to his feud with McCarthy.

The election gave Republicans a majority in both chambers in 1953, and McCarthy became chairman of the Senate Government Operations Committee and its Permanent Investigations Subcommittee. After the first year of McCarthy's chairmanship, the subcommittee claimed in its annual report that its exposures had caused the removal of "Fifth Amendment Communists" from federal jobs and defense plants, the removal of incompetent and undesirable persons from federal employment, and indictment of several witnesses.

Army-McCarthy Dispute

McCarthy became involved during the first half of 1954 in a controversy with high officials of the army and, by extension, with the Eisenhower administration itself. At issue was the question of whether McCarthy and his staff had used improper means to secure preferential treatment for a former subcommittee consultant, G. David Schine, who had been drafted. Also involved was a charge that the army had tried to pressure McCarthy into calling off his investigation of alleged Communists in the army.

Both sides filed charges. To investigate them, the subcommittee held hearings with Sen. Karl E. Mundt, R-S.D., as acting chairman. McCarthy resigned temporarily from subcommittee membership. The subcommittee in effect began an investigation of its own activities.

The thirty-five days of hearings from April 22 to June 17 attracted, during 187 hours of television coverage, as many as twenty million viewers at peak periods. In addition to the principals charged and the subcommittee members, the drama featured, as the main interrogators, special army counsel Joseph N. Welch and special subcommittee counsel Ray H. Jenkins. In a report the subcommittee issued August 31, the Republican majority concluded that the charge of "improper influence" by McCarthy on behalf of Schine "was not established," but that subcommittee counsel Roy M. Cohn had been "unduly aggressive and persistent" on Schine's behalf.

The Republicans said also that Army Secretary Robert T. Stevens and counsel John G. Adams had tried "to terminate or influence" investigations. The Democratic minority asserted that McCarthy had "fully acquiesced in and condoned" the "improper actions" of Cohn, who in turn had "misused and abused the powers of his office and brought disrepute to the committee." The minority report said also that Stevens merited "severe criticism" for "an inexcusable indecisiveness and lack of sound administrative judgment."

Censure

On June 11, 1954, while the Army-McCarthy hearings were in progress, Ralph E. Flanders, R-Vt., initiated a six-month controversy over the Senate's official attitude toward McCarthy's actions. He introduced a resolution to remove McCarthy from the chairmanship of the Government Operations Committee and any of its subcommittees, and to prohibit him from reassuming such posts unless he answered questions raised in 1952 by the elections subcommittee.

AP/Wide World Photos

After Senate Majority Leader William F. Knowland, R-Calif., voiced opposition, Flanders on July 30 introduced a substitute resolution, charging McCarthy with "personal contempt" of the Senate. These resolutions were referred to a Select Committee to Study Censure Charges. After nearly two weeks of hearings, the committee on September 27 unanimously recommended that the Senate censure McCarthy for his conduct in the Benton-McCarthy investigation in 1952 and toward Army Brig. Gen. Ralph W. Zwicker. At a Permanent Investigations Subcommittee hearing in 1954, McCarthy had told Zwicker that he was "not fit to wear that uniform" and implied that Zwicker did not have "the brains of a five-year-old."

The Senate adopted a substitute resolution, 67-22, on December 1, 1954, that "condemned" McCarthy on several counts. McCarthy lost his committee and subcommittee chairmanships when control of Congress passed to the Democrats in January 1955. His activities no longer attracted any notable attention. He died a few years later on May 2, 1957.

Senate Condemnation of Joseph R. McCarthy

Resolution relating to the conduct of the Senator from Wisconsin, Mr. McCarthy. [S Res 301, 83rd Cong., 2nd sess., adopted December 2, 1954.]

Section 1. Resolved, that the Senator from Wisconsin, Mr. McCarthy, failed to cooperate with the Subcommittee on Privileges and Elections of the Senate Committee on Rules and Administration in clearing up matters referred to that Subcommittee which concerned his conduct as a Senator and affected the honor of the Senate and, instead, repeatedly abused the Subcommittee and its Members who were trying to carry out assigned duties, thereby obstructing the constitutional processes of the Senate, and that this conduct of the Senator from Wisconsin, Mr. McCarthy, is contrary to Senatorial traditions and is hereby condemned.

Section 2. The Senator from Wisconsin (Mr. McCarthy), in writing to the chairman of the Select Committee to Study Censure Charges (Mr. Watkins) after the Select Committee had issued its report and before the report was presented to the Senate charging three members of the Select Committee with "deliberate deception" and "fraud" for failure to disqualify themselves;

In stating to the press on November 4, 1954, that the special Senate session that was to begin November 8, 1954, was a "lynch party";

In repeatedly describing this special Senate Session as a "lynch bee" in a nationwide television and radio show on November 7, 1954;

In stating to the public press on November 13, 1954, that the chairman of the Select Committee (Mr. Watkins) was guilty of "the most unusual, most cowardly thing I've ever heard of" and stating further: "I expected he would be afraid to answer the questions, but didn't think he'd be stupid enough to make a public statement"; and in characterizing the said Committee as the "unwilling handmaiden," "involuntary agent," and "attorneys-in-fact" of the Communist party and in charging that the said Committee in writing its report "imitated Communist methods—that it distorted, misrepresented, and omitted in its efforts to manufacture a plausible rationalization" in support of its recommendations to the Senate, which characterizations and charges were contained in a statement released to the press and inserted into the *Congressional Record* of November 10, 1954, acted contrary to Senatorial ethics and tended to bring the Senate into dishonor and disrepute, to obstruct the constitutional processes of the Senate, and to impair its dignity.

And such conduct is hereby condemned.

---

together with Wayne Morse, R-Ore., voted for the resolution. In January 1955, when control of Congress passed to the Democrats, McCarthy lost his committee and subcommittee chairmanships. His activities thereafter attracted less public attention, and he died May 2, 1957.

Dodd: Used Office "to Obtain . . . Funds"

House Speaker Sam Rayburn, D-Texas, often said that the ethics of a member of Congress should be judged not by his peers but by the voters at reelection time. By the mid-1960s it had become clear that neither Congress nor the public felt this was enough.

In 1964 the Senate was jolted by publicity over charges that Robert G. "Bobby" Baker had used his office as secretary to the Senate majority to promote his business interests. To allay public misgivings, the Senate on July 24 of that year established a Select Committee on Standards and Conduct with responsibility for investigating "allegations of improper conduct" by senators and Senate employees. In September, however, the

Senate assigned jurisdiction over the Baker case to the Rules and Administration Committee. *(Baker case, Chapter 8, p. 102)*

The new select committee's first inquiry, begun in 1966, concerned the Dodd case. On January 24, 1966, and later dates, columnists Drew Pearson and Jack Anderson accused Sen. Thomas J. Dodd, D-Conn., of having (1) used for personal expenses funds contributed to him to help meet the costs of his campaign for reelection in 1964, (2) double-billed the government for travel expenses, and (3) improperly exchanged favors with Julius Klein, a public relations representative of West German interests. On the last charge, the columnists said that Dodd had gone to Germany to intercede with Chancellor Konrad Adenauer in behalf of Klein's accounts, although the trip was supposedly made on Senate business.

Dodd on February 23, 1966, requested the Select Committee on Standards and Conduct to investigate his relationship with Klein. The committee conducted hearings on all three of the Pearson-Anderson charges in June-July 1966 and March 1967. Dodd testified in his own defense. On the first charge, Dodd said he "truly believed" the proceeds from the testimonial dinners "to be donations to me from my friends." The second charge, he said, stemmed from "sloppy bookkeeping" by Michael V. O'Hare, who had been an employee of Dodd. O'Hare and other former Dodd employees reportedly had taken documents from Dodd's files and made copies of them available to the committee. In the course of the hearings, Dodd called O'Hare a liar. On charge three, Dodd denied that he had been a mere errand boy for Klein on the trip to Europe.

The committee on April 27, 1967, submitted its report on the Dodd case. It recommended that Dodd be censured for spending campaign contributions for personal purposes and for billing seven trips to both the Senate and private organizations. The committee dropped the third charge, saying

that while Dodd's relations with Klein were indiscreet, there was not sufficient evidence of wrongdoing.

Voting on the committee's recommendations, June 23, 1967, the Senate censured Dodd on the first charge, by a vote of 92 to 5, but refused by a vote of 45 yeas to 51 nays to censure him on the second charge. The resolution as adopted recorded the judgment of the Senate that Dodd

> for having engaged in a course of conduct . . . from 1961 to 1965 of exercising the influence and favor of his office as a United States Senator . . . to obtain, and use for his personal benefit, funds from the public through political testimonials and a political campaign, deserves the censure of the Senate; and he is so censured for his conduct, which is contrary to accepted morals, derogates from the public trust expected of a Senator, and tends to bring the Senate into dishonor and disrepute.

Dodd declined to seek the Democratic nomination for senator from Connecticut in 1970 but ran in the general election as an independent. He placed third, with 24 percent of the votes, while the Democratic nominee lost to Republican Lowell P. Weicker, Jr., 34 percent to 42 percent. Dodd died May 24, 1971. His son, Christopher J. Dodd, D-Conn., was elected to the House in 1974 and served there until his election to the Senate in 1980.

Talmadge: "Gross Neglect of Duty"

Twelve years after the censure of Thomas Dodd, the Senate voted to discipline Georgia veteran Herman E. Talmadge, D, for financial misconduct. Talmadge was formally "denounced"—a punishment regarded as virtually synonymous with censure.

In 1978 both a federal grand jury and the Senate Ethics Committee (by then a permanent,

Steve Karafyllakis

In 1979 the Senate voted to discipline Sen. Herman E. Talmadge, D-Ga., for financial misconduct. Talmadge was formally "denounced"—a punishment regarded at the time as slightly less severe than censure. Many senators gave testimony to Talmadge's long service in the Senate.

standing committee) began investigating reports of financial irregularities by Talmadge that first arose during his divorce proceedings. The charges, reported extensively by the *Washington Star,* stemmed principally from Talmadge's ex-wife, Betty, and his former administrative assistant Daniel Minchew, a member of the Interstate Commerce Commission. Campaign expenses and office accounts were the focus of the investigations.

Financial information made public during his bitterly contested divorce settlement disclosed that Talmadge had written only one check to "cash" during the entire period 1970-76. Talmadge said he was able to live without cashing checks because he accepted small amounts of cash from his constituents, friends, and supporters throughout his pub-

lic career. He also admitted to accepting meals, lodging, and most of his clothes.

"Wherever I go [in Georgia], people entertain me, lodge me, give me small amounts of money," Talmadge told the *Star* in May 1978.

Talmadge also acknowledged that he had not reported the money, goods, or services as "income" or as campaign contributions because they were "gifts." A spokesman said the senator was unable to remember a single individual who had given him such gifts of cash and goods.

During a one-day appearance before the Ethics Committee in 1979, Betty Talmadge told the committee that her husband had for years kept a roll of cash, most of it in hundred dollar bills, in his overcoat pocket in a closet of their Washington residence. Talmadge denied that.

At the committee hearings, which began April 30, 1979, Talmadge delivered an unsworn statement that called the bulk of the charges against him "trivial" and "petty" and said the remaining, serious charges were untrue or due to negligence. For example, the failure in his initial 1974 campaign report (a year when he was reelected) to list campaign receipts and expenditures was due to "confusion" by his staff, he said.

Although he was reimbursed "around $12,000" by his campaign committee in January 1975 for his 1974 expenses—a total not reported to the Federal Election Commission until 1978—Talmadge told the Ethics panel that "there is not the slightest basis for concluding that those errors were due to anything but inadvertence and confusion."

Talmadge said the fact that he repaid the Senate more than $37,000 in 1978 for expenses that were claimed in prior years, but were not reimbursable under Senate rules, should put that charge to rest. He laid the improper claims to his staff. Talmadge reserved his harshest words for former aide Minchew, whom he called "a proven liar, cheat, and embezzler."

In June Minchew testified for eight days before

the committee. He said his role in laundering campaign contributions and Senate expense funds through a secret Washington bank account was to provide the senator with "insulation" and "deniability" in case the scheme ever was uncovered. By the end of his testimony, several committee members and the special counsel expressed doubts of Minchew's credibility, which was shaken by questioning from Talmadge's attorney.

On October 3 the Ethics Committee recommended that the Senate denounce Talmadge for financial misconduct. It said Talmadge's conduct "is reprehensible and tends to bring the Senate into dishonor and disrepute and is hereby denounced."

The committee skirted the question of Talmadge's direct involvement in the financial misconduct. Instead, it said "Talmadge either knew, or should have known, of these improper acts and omissions, and, therefore, by the gross neglect of his duty to faithfully and carefully administer the affairs of his office, he is responsible for these acts and omissions." Talmadge called the committee's action "a personal victory" and said the findings "support my basic contention . . . that I was negligent in the oversight of my office, but that I have committed no intentional wrongdoing."

The committee said that Talmadge:

- Improperly collected $43,435.83 in reimbursements after submitting false, unsigned expense vouchers from 1973 to 1978;
- Filed inaccurate reports and failed to file other reports in a timely fashion in accounting for the use of funds during his 1974 Senate race;
- Filed "inaccurate" Senate financial disclosure reports for 1972 through 1977;
- Failed to report more than $10,000 in campaign contributions deposited in the secret Washington bank account.

The committee said that allegations of improper conduct by Talmadge in real estate transactions were "without foundation." It also said that charges of nonpayment of gift taxes were "not substantiated."

On October 11, 1979, the Senate voted 81-15 to denounce Talmadge as recommended by the committee. Despite the overwhelming vote, many senators gave testimonials to Talmadge's service in the Senate, where he was fifth in seniority, chairman of the Agriculture and Forestry Committee, and ranking Democrat on the Finance Committee.

In May 1980 the Justice Department announced it had completed its investigation of Talmadge's financial affairs and decided not to seek an indictment. The senator lost his 1980 try for reelection.

Durenberger: "Reprehensible" Conduct

In 1990 another senator was denounced. On July 25 the Senate voted 96-0 to denounce Dave Durenberger, R-Minn., for conduct it called "clearly and unequivocally unethical." The charges against Durenberger focused mainly on a 1985-86 book deal the senator had with a Minnesota publishing company and on Senate reimbursement Durenberger received for rent he paid on a Minneapolis condominium from August 1983 to November 1989.

More than a year after it opened its investigation, and five months after it first met with Durenberger about the case, the Ethics Committee on July 18 unanimously called for Durenberger to be formally denounced for his financial dealings. The panel went beyond the recommendation of special counsel Robert S. Bennett—who also handled the committee's investigation of Senator Williams in 1982—by calling for Durenberger to pay more than $124,000 in restitution.

The Ethics Committee's June 12-13 public hearings on the Durenberger case marked the first time in its twenty-six-year history that it had conducted business before television cameras.

Bennett's investigation produced twenty-three

R. Michael Jenkins

The Senate in 1990 formally denounced Dave Durenberger, R-Minn., for his financial dealings. Shown here are Durenberger (center) with his attorney and chief of staff at the Ethics Committee hearing.

volumes of evidence, the result of 198 subpoenas for internal documents, 240 interviews with witnesses, numerous depositions, and at least 75 affidavits. Bennett's prosecutorial style in this and the so-called Keating Five cases itself became part of those controversies. *(Bennett's style, box, p. 124)*

Bennett focused on the book deal with Piranha Press and the Minneapolis condominium. Piranha Press was a company owned by Gary L. Diamond, a friend of Durenberger's who also published trade journals for the restaurant and hospitality industries. He published two books by Durenberger: *Neither Madmen Nor Messiahs,* a collection of white papers on defense policy, in 1984; and *Prescription for Change,* a collection of speeches about health care, in 1986. The only other book

Diamond had published, Bennett said, was about wrestling holds.

Piranha Press paid Durenberger $100,000 in quarterly installments of $12,500 that began in 1985 and ended in early 1987 in return for his making 113 appearances to promote the book. Bennett contended that the arrangement "was little more than a pretext to sanitize what were honestly honoraria payments."

Bennett traced the deal to Durenberger's need to replace lost honoraria income. The senator reported $92,750 in honoraria in 1983, the last year the Senate permitted members to collect unlimited speech fees. Subsequent Senate rules capped Durenberger's honoraria income at $22,530 in 1985 and $30,040 in 1986, the years of the book deal.

In those two years, Durenberger made traditional honoraria speeches until he reached the limit. At that point, speeches would be designated as "Piranha Press events," Bennett said.

The senator's attorney, Michael C. Mahoney of Minneapolis, asked the Federal Election Commission to rule on the nature of the publishing agreement. The FEC ruled that Durenberger's stipend from Piranha was acceptable—a ruling Durenberger would repeatedly use as a shield. The request for the opinion, however, never mentioned what Bennett said were three crucial facts: Durenberger's contract called for the groups he addressed to pay the publisher a fee; the appearances stemmed from requests for speeches, not book promotions; and the promotional events were identical to traditional honorarium events.

Groups wanting to hear Durenberger were referred by his staff to Mahoney, the agent for Piranha Press. With a call or a letter, Mahoney would tell the organizations that Durenberger's appearance was a book promotion. "What were honoraria events one day magically became book promotion events the next," Bennett said.

Never in the 113 times Durenberger appeared for Piranha did an organization actually ask Durenberger to promote his book, Bennett said. Some organizations and constituencies important to the senator objected to the arrangement.

"This very hungry fish, Piranha Press, was allowed to engage in a feeding frenzy on responsible organizations who thought they were sponsoring traditional honorarium events," Bennett said. "And unfortunately, the evidence shows that Senator Durenberger . . . allowed himself and the stature of his office to be used as the bait, and he got $100,000 for his trouble."

Bennett depicted Durenberger's handling of his Minneapolis condominium as a "search for loopholes." It began in 1983, when Durenberger decided he could not afford two residences—a house in McLean, Virginia, and the one-bedroom condominium. Owning the Minneapolis condo where he

stayed also prevented the Senate from reimbursing him for living expenses on his frequent trips to Minnesota.

Durenberger took two steps in 1983 to change this situation. First, he changed his legal residence to his parents' address in Avon, Minnesota. Second, he sought to change the ownership of the condo to a partnership with Roger Scherer, a friend and political backer who owned another condo in the same building.

From August 1983 until mid-November 1989, Durenberger collected $40,055 from the U.S. Treasury for per diem expenses while staying at the condo. After receiving the ruling from the Senate Rules Committee in January 1990, Durenberger reimbursed the Treasury for $11,005 in expenses paid. The committee ruled that Durenberger's resident city for the purposes of reimbursement was Minneapolis, not Avon, during these periods.

Before seeking reimbursement for staying in the condo, Durenberger said, his staff consulted the Senate's Rules and Ethics committees, which raised no objections at the time.

The denouncement said that Durenberger's conduct "has been reprehensible and has brought the Senate into dishonor and disrepute." He was ordered to repay more than $124,000 in restitution, including $29,050 plus interest for reimbursements he received for the cost of staying in his Minneapolis condominium. That sum was owed on top of $11,005 Durenberger already had repaid in early 1990, based on an incomplete calculation by the Senate Rules Committee. The Senate also required Durenberger to give charities an amount equal to the honoraria he allegedly obtained improperly, approximately $95,000.

Though Durenberger had called denouncement too harsh a penalty, he did not challenge the sanction or the version of events Ethics Committee Chairman Howell Heflin, D-Ala., presented to the Senate. "Today is an ending, and it is a begin-

Assault on Sumner

Charles Sumner of Massachusetts, in a Senate speech May 20, 1856, denounced in scathing language supporters of the Kansas-Nebraska Act of 1854, which repealed the Missouri Compromise of 1820 and permitted the two new territories to decide whether slavery would be allowed there.

Two days later, while Sumner was seated at his desk on the Senate floor after the day's session had ended, he heard his name called. Looking up, he saw a tall stranger, who berated him for his speech and then struck him on the head repeatedly with a heavy walking stick, which was broken by the blows. Sumner fell bleeding and unconscious to the floor. He was absent from the Senate, because of the injuries suffered in the assault, for three and a half years, until December 5, 1859.

The attacker was Rep. Preston S. Brooks, SRD-S.C., nephew of one of those whom Sumner had excoriated—Sen. A. P. Butler, SRD-S.C. Expulsion proceedings against Brooks failed, on a strictly party vote. He resigned his House seat July 15, 1856, but was elected to fill the vacancy caused by his resignation.

Rep. Laurence M. Keitt, D-S.C., was censured by the House on July 15, 1856, for having known of Brooks's intention to assault Sumner, for having taken no action to discourage or prevent the assault, and for having been "present on one or more occasions to witness the same." Keitt resigned July 16, 1856, and was elected to fill the vacancy caused by his resignation. A resolution similar to the one censuring Keitt but directed against Rep. Henry A. Edmundson, D-Va., failed of adoption July 15, 1856.

ning," Durenberger said. "For past mistakes, I ask your forgiveness. For future challenges, I need your friendship."

The only senator to rise in Durenberger's defense was Rudy Boschwitz, a fellow Minnesota Republican. Boschwitz contended, as Durenberger had in committee hearings, that the senator had relied on lawyers' advice before going ahead with the questionable book and real estate deals.

Durenberger did receive some solace from the debate. Several colleagues, including Republican leader Bob Dole of Kansas, offered paeans to the legislative style that had made him one of the Senate's rising stars.

Boschwitz and Durenberger voted present when the roll was called. Two senators were absent. After the vote, Durenberger pledged to bring new vigor to his work. He said in a news conference that he had not decided whether to run for reelection in 1994. But his lone defender, Boschwitz, was a surprise loser in the 1990 election.

CENSURE BY THE HOUSE

The House in 1789 adopted a rule that, as amended in 1822 and 1880, is still in effect (Rule 14, Section 4). It reads: "If any member, in speaking or otherwise, transgress the rules of the House, the Speaker shall, or any member may, call him to order; . . . and if the case require it, he shall be liable to censure or such punishment as the House may deem proper." By 1992 this censure clause had been invoked thirty-six times, and censure had been voted twenty-two times, two-thirds of them in the 1860s and 1870s. Grounds for censure included assault on a fellow member of the House, insult to the Speaker, treasonable utterance, corruption, and other offenses. In the twentieth century, five representatives have been censured. *(House censure proceedings, table, Appendix, p. 170)*

The first censure motion in the House was introduced following a physical attack in January 1798 by Matthew Lyon, Anti-Fed-Vt., on Roger Griswold, F-Conn., who had taunted Lyon on his allegedly poor military record. The censure motion failed. In the following month, Lyon and Griswold engaged in an affray with tongs and cane. Both fracases occurred on the House floor. Following the second incident, a motion was introduced to censure both members. The motion failed.

The first formal censure by the House was imposed in 1832 on William Stanbery, JD-Ohio, for saying, in objection to a ruling by the chair, "The eyes of the Speaker [Andrew Stevenson, D-Va.] are too frequently turned from the chair you occupy toward the White House." There were 93 votes for censuring Stanbery; 44 were opposed. Censure for unacceptable language or offensive publication was imposed in seven other cases. For example, John W. Hunter of New York was censured on January 26, 1867, for saying, about a statement made by a colleague, "So far as I am concerned, it is a base lie."

In 1842 censure was considered and rejected in the case of one of the most distinguished representatives in American history, John Quincy Adams, a former president of the United States. Adams had presented to the House, for forty-six of his constituents, a petition asking Congress to dissolve the Union and allow the states to go their separate ways. A resolution proposing to censure him for this act was worded so strongly that Adams asserted his right, under the Sixth Amendment to the Constitution, to a trial by jury. He succeeded in putting his opponents on the defensive, and the resolution was not put to a vote.

Lovell H. Rousseau, R-Ky., during the evening of June 14, 1866, assaulted Josiah B. Grinnell, R-Iowa, with a cane in the portico on the East Front of the Capitol. On the House floor, earlier in the month, Grinnell had imputed cowardice to Rousseau. A committee appointed to report on the case recommended that Rousseau be expelled. The House rejected that recommendation, but on July 17, 1866, it voted that he "be summoned to the bar of this House, and be there publicly reprimanded by the Speaker for his violation of its rights and privileges." Despite its use of the term *reprimand*,

Censure for Dueling Withheld

The killing of one representative by another in a duel in 1838 went uncensured by the House. Rep. Jonathan Cilley, JD-Maine, had made statements on the floor reflecting on the character of James W. Webb, prominent editor of a New York City newspaper that was a Whig organ. When Webb sent Cilley a note by the hand of Rep. William J. Graves, Whig-Ky., demanding an explanation of the statements, Cilley refused to receive the note. Further correspondence led to a challenge by Graves and agreement by Cilley to a duel with rifles.

The duel took place on February 24, 1838, on the Marlboro Pike in Maryland, close to the District of Columbia. Graves and Cilley each fired twice, with no result. In the third volley, Cilley was shot fatally in the abdomen.

Four days later, the House appointed a committee to investigate the affair. A majority recommended on April 21 that Graves be expelled from the House and that the seconds in the duel, Rep. Henry A. Wise, W-Va., and George W. Jones (a member of the Tennessee House of Representatives who served in the national House of Representatives, 1843-59), be censured. One of the minority group on the committee, Rep. Franklin H. Elmore, SRD-S.C., observed that dueling by members had been frequent and generally had gone unnoticed by the House. A motion to table the committee's report and print the testimony was agreed to May 10, and an attempt on July 4 to take up the report was unsuccessful. Graves was not expelled and Wise and Jones were not censured.

the resolution was consistent with censure procedure and House documents described the action as "a censure resolution." The order was carried out July 21, despite Rousseau's announcement that he had sent his resignation to the governor of Kentucky.

Corruption was the basis for censure or proposed censure in a number of cases. The House on February 27, 1873, by a vote of 182 to 36, censured Oakes Ames, R-Mass., and James Brooks, D-N.Y., for their part in a financial scandal involving Crédit Mobilier stock given to members of Congress. Three years later, Speaker James G. Blaine, R-Maine, was accused of involvement in that scandal as well as of receiving excessive payments from the Union Pacific Railroad Co. for bonds sold to the company. Two months before the convention at which Blaine hoped to be chosen the Republican candidate for president, he spoke in the House on the charges against him. By selective reading of a series of allegedly incriminating letters, Blaine managed to confuse the evidence sufficiently to rout the proponents of censure. *(Crédit Mobilier scandal, Chapter 1, p. 7)*

In one instance, the House rescinded part of a censure resolution. During debate on a bill in 1875, John Y. Brown, D-Ky., referred to Benjamin Butler, R-Mass., as "outlawed in his own home from respectable society; whose name is synonymous with falsehood; and who is the champion, and has been on all occasions, of fraud; who is the apologist of thieves; who is such a prodigy of vice and meanness that to describe him would sicken imagination and exhaust invective."

Brown was censured February 4, 1875, for that insult and for lying to the Speaker in order to continue his insulting speech. But a year later, on May 2, 1876, the House agreed to rescind that portion of the censure resolution condemning Brown for lying to the Speaker. The charge of insulting another member remained, however.

Diggs

The late 1970s produced the first committee-approved censure resolutions in the House in more than fifty years. The first member censured since 1921 was Charles C. Diggs, Jr., D-Mich., who

AP/Wide World Photos

Rep. Charles C. Diggs, Jr., D-Mich., was censured by the House July 31, 1979. Diggs, who faced expulsion, had been convicted in 1978 of criminal charges of diverting congressional employee salary funds to his personal and official use.

was publicly chastised July 31, 1979, for misuse of his clerk-hire funds. The House rejected an attempt to expel him.

Diggs had been convicted October 7, 1978, on twenty-nine felony counts centering on charges that he illegally diverted more than $60,000 of his congressional employees' salaries to his personal and official use.

When Congress convened January 9, 1979, House Republicans announced they would seek to expel Diggs as a convicted felon. The ethics committee (formally the Committee on Standards of Official Conduct) began an investigation but moved too slowly to satisfy Newt Gingrich, a freshman Republican from Georgia.

Gingrich told Diggs in a February 22 letter that he would move for expulsion if Diggs chose to vote. House rules said that convicted members should not vote unless they were reelected after their conviction—as Diggs was in November 1978.

On the House floor February 28 Diggs voted "yea" on a bill to increase the public debt limit. The next day Gingrich offered a resolution to expel Diggs. Majority Leader Jim Wright, D-Texas, immediately moved to refer the resolution to the ethics committee, and this carried, 322-77.

The committee filed formal charges against Diggs for violating House rules and negotiated with him for an admission of guilt. On June 27 Diggs wrote to the committee admitting to some of the charges. He agreed to be censured in return for the committee's ending its investigation. Diggs admitted he had padded his office payroll and accepted kickbacks from five current and former employees. He said his personal gain from the kickbacks totaled $40,031.66. Diggs offered to repay the sum with interest. Diggs said he thought the agreement with the committee would help his pending appeal of his conviction. (It did not. The appeal was turned down by the Supreme Court in June 1980, and Diggs resigned from Congress the next day and began serving his three-year jail sentence.)

In recommending censure rather than expulsion, the committee explained in its July 19 report that it had "considered his admission of guilt of serious offenses against the House rules, his apology to the House therefor, his agreement to make restitution of substantial amounts by which he was unjustly enriched, and the nature of the offenses charged."

On July 30, 1979, the House tabled—and thus killed—by a 205-197 vote a Republican move to force a vote on expulsion. The next day censure of Diggs was approved by a vote of 414-0, with four members voting present.

Wilson

Rep. Charles H. Wilson, D-Calif., was censured June 10, 1980, for financial misconduct. The action came just a week after Wilson lost his bid for renomination in the June 3 California primary. The House approved the resolution on a voice vote after rejecting 97-308 a move to reduce the punishment to a reprimand. Following the vote, Wilson was called to the front of the chamber, where Speaker Thomas P. O'Neill, Jr., D-Mass., read the censure resolution to him. Wilson then turned and quickly left the chamber.

It was the second time in two years that the House had disciplined Wilson. He had been reprimanded in October 1978 after he first denied—and then acknowledged—receiving wedding gifts, including $600 in cash, from South Korean businessman Tongsun Park. *(Wilson reprimand, p. 41)*

In the censure case, the House found Wilson guilty of improperly converting almost $25,000 in campaign funds to his personal use and accepting $10,500 in gifts from an individual with a direct interest in legislation. The individual, who allegedly paid kickbacks to Wilson after being placed on his payroll, was Lee Rogers, president of a Los Angeles mail order company called the American Holiday Association.

At ethics committee hearings a committee lawyer produced a letter in which Wilson boasted to Rogers that his "strong opposition" had killed a bill in subcommittee. "You may be certain that I will work with you to see it stays buried in the subcommittee," Wilson wrote.

The House action ended Wilson's chairmanship of a postal subcommittee. House Democrats had voted in May to automatically deprive censured members of their chairmanships.

Studds, Crane

The 1980s brought the first censures arising from House members' sexual conduct. Daniel B. Crane, R-Ill., and Gerry E. Studds, D-Mass., became the twenty-first and twenty-second censured represen-

Paul Conklin

Sue Klemens

Reps. Gerry E. Studds, D-Mass. (left), and Daniel B. Crane, R-Ill., were censured in 1983 after the House ethics committee asserted that both had had sexual relationships with teenage pages.

tatives. Others involved in sex-related scandals received lesser punishments.

The House's action capped a year-long investigation by the ethics panel into allegations of sexual misconduct and drug use by members and congressional pages. The investigation was led by special counsel Joseph A. Califano, Jr., who served as secretary of health, education, and welfare in the Carter administration.

On July 14, 1983, the committee issued its report on the investigation, along with separate reports on Studds and Crane. The committee asserted that both Studds and Crane had had sexual relationships with teenage pages and thus had committed a "serious breach of duty owed by the House and its individual members to the young people who serve the House as its pages."

The panel reported that in 1973 Studds had a sexual relationship with a seventeen-year-old male page, who might have been sixteen at the time the relationship began. In addition, the committee said

Studds made sexual advances on two other male pages in 1973. Studds told his House colleagues July 14 that he was homosexual.

Crane, the panel said, had a sexual relationship with a seventeen-year-old female page in 1980. Since the legal age of consent in the District of Columbia was sixteen, the panel accused neither Studds nor Crane of a crime. Nevertheless, the panel felt that any sexual relationship, consensual or not, between a member and a page constituted improper sexual conduct.

In choosing an appropriate penalty for Studds and Crane, Califano cited as precedents the two most recent cases of severe discipline, the censure of Charles Wilson and the expulsion of Michael Myers. Califano concluded, "Measured against the precedents, neither expulsion nor censure is warranted." He recommended a reprimand, and the committee agreed by an 11-1 vote.

In the House debate on the ethics committee's recommendation, Gingrich argued that a reprimand was too mild. "With no malice toward any individual," he said, "I cannot see how a reprimand is in any way adequate." Gingrich wanted the two expelled.

House Minority Leader Robert H. Michel, R-Ill., moved to change the recommendation from reprimand to censure. Michel said he sensed that members wanted a more severe punishment.

Michel's motion in Crane's case was agreed to 289-136. The censure resolution then was adopted 421-3. In Studds's case, Michel's motion was agreed to 338-87, and the House voted to censure Studds by a 420-3 vote. Crane voted for his own censure. Studds voted "present" when the House voted on his censure.

Crane faced his silent colleagues as Speaker O'Neill read the resolution of censure to him. Studds faced the Speaker, hands clasped behind him, as his censure was read.

Studds was reelected in 1984 and again 1986, 1988, and 1990; Crane lost his next reelection bid.

In light of the incidents, Congress revised the page system to tighten control over the pages' housing and schooling.

REPRIMAND IN THE HOUSE

The distinction, if any, between *censure* and *reprimand* has long been a subject of discussion. House ethics committee chairman John J. Flynt, Jr., D-Ga., said in 1976 that he saw no real difference between the two terms. The major difference seems to be one of procedure. As noted in the House censure cases above, the censured member must stand in the well of the House and be publicly admonished by the Speaker. A reprimand resolution may be just as strongly worded, but the targeted member need not be present to hear it.

The Senate followed a similar procedure in its first reprimand, in 1991. *(Senate Reprimand of Cranston, p. 44)*

Sikes

Chairman Flynt's 1976 remark came after his committee recommended a reprimand for Robert L. F. Sikes, D-Fla., for failing to disclose financial holdings in defense business and a conflict of interest. Sikes was the first member of Congress investigated by the House Committee on Standards of Official Conduct, which had been established as a permanent ethics committee eight years earlier.

He was charged with failing to disclose his investments in a defense contractor, Fairchild Industries, in a bank he helped to establish on a naval base in his district, and in Florida land parcels that he tried to upgrade in value through legislation.

The complaint against Sikes was filed by the public affairs lobby Common Cause and forwarded to the committee by forty-four representatives—an unprecedented action at the time.

On July 29 the House approved the reprimand by a vote of 381-3. The following January the House Democratic Caucus voted 189-93 to unseat Sikes as chairman of the Appropriations Subcommittee on Military Construction.

McFall, Roybal, Wilson

The House ethics committee conducted highly publicized hearings in 1977-78 into reports of congressional lobbying by agents of the South Korean government and of lavish gifts to representatives by Korean businessman Tongsun Park. The investigations ended with slaps on the wrist to three California Democrats—John J. McFall, Edward R. Roybal, and Charles Wilson. The committee charged McFall and Roybal with failing to report campaign contributions from Park. Wilson was accused of failing to report, on a committee questionnaire, wedding gifts from Park that included $600 in cash. The recommended punishment was a reprimand for McFall and Wilson and censure for Roybal because the committee concluded he had lied to it.

AP/Wide World Photos

Rep. George V. Hansen, R-Idaho, was the first member of Congress to be convicted for failing to comply with financial disclosure rules—a federal felony offense. After he was fined and sentenced, Hansen was reprimanded by the House July 31, 1984.

On the House floor October 13, 1978, the resolution to censure Roybal was rejected on a 219-170 vote and he was reprimanded instead, as were McFall and Wilson. Several Roybal supporters suggested that as a Hispanic he was a victim of bias. *(Korean lobbying scandal, p. 58)*

Two years later the House censured Wilson for financial misconduct in another matter. *(Wilson censure, p. 39)*

Hansen

The House July 31, 1984, reprimanded George V. Hansen, R-Idaho, for failing to disclose financial dealings as required under the 1978 Ethics in Government Act (PL 95-521). Hansen's conviction and reprimand stemmed from his failure to report nearly $334,000 in loans and profits between 1978 and 1981. After being convicted April 2 on federal

felony charges, he had been sentenced June 15 to between five and fifteen months in prison and fined $40,000.

The vote for a reprimand was 354-52 with six members voting present. Leaders of the House ethics committee, which had recommended the reprimand by an 11-1 vote, used a parliamentary tactic to block a House vote to change the penalty to a censure or to include other House members.

During the debate, a defiant Hansen maintained his innocence, insisting that Reagan administration officials and other members of Congress had been caught in questionable financial reporting snags similar to his.

Hansen's 1984 conviction was not his first legal problem. In 1975 he pleaded guilty to two misdemeanor charges of filing late and false campaign finance reports from his 1974 House primary. He received a two-month prison sentence that was suspended and instead paid a $2,000 fine.

Hansen appealed his felony conviction, the first ever under the 1978 law. On March 3, 1986, the Supreme Court refused to review his conviction. The decision freed federal prosecutors to force Hansen to serve his prison sentence and pay the $40,000 fine.

The seven-term representative was narrowly defeated in his 1984 reelection bid.

Murphy

Accepting the recommendation of its ethics committee, the House December 18, 1987, voted 324-68 to reprimand Austin J. Murphy, D-Pa., for diverting government resources to his former law firm, for allowing another member to vote for him on the House floor, and for keeping a "no-show" employee on his payroll.

Murphy claimed he had been made a scapegoat to fend off conservative Republicans who all year had lambasted the House ethics committee for being slow to act on charges of misconduct by some

Democratic members, silent or secretive about others, and hesitant to recommend sanctions when it did find violations of law or ethics codes.

Ethics panel member Vic Fazio, D-Calif., said on the floor, "We are not scapegoating anybody. We've taken heat before; we'll take heat again."

Frank

The ethics committee did indeed take heat again—this time for being too lenient—when it recommended a reprimand for Barney Frank, D-Mass., who was accused of improperly using his office to help a male prostitute. The House voted 408-18 for the reprimand on July 26, 1990, after a roiling, unusually partisan debate about how harshly to punish Frank.

Despite politicians' election-year jitters about ethics issues—heightened in a case involving homosexuality—the House turned back demands for more severe penalties after ethics chairman Julian C. Dixon, D-Calif., urged his colleagues to stand by the panel as their bulwark against political attacks. "We will throw no one to the wolves," Dixon said.

Members rejected, 38-390, a resolution to expel Frank. The intermediate penalty of censure was also turned down, largely along party lines, 141-287.

Frank did not contest the finding that he "reflected discredit upon the House" by using his status as a member of Congress to fix thirty-three parking tickets and by writing a misleading memorandum in behalf of Steve Gobie, a male prostitute with whom Frank associated in 1985-87.

Frank, who had publicly acknowledged his homosexuality in 1987, went to the well of the House near the end of debate to apologize for his misconduct. Attributing it to the strain of concealing his homosexuality at the time, Frank said, "I should have known better. I do now."

In the eyes of other members, more was at stake

R. Michael Jenkins

The House formally reprimanded Rep. Barney Frank, D-Mass., in 1990 for improperly using his office to help a male prostitute. Members turned back efforts to impose stronger sanctions.

than a colleague's behavior. "We are here to repair the integrity of the United States House of Representatives," said House GOP Whip Newt Gingrich of Georgia, who proposed upping the sanction to censure.

Dixon, indignant at challenges to his committee's unanimous verdict, cast the debate as a referendum on the ethics panel itself. He said, "This case boils down to, really, who do you trust?"

The political crosscurrents in the Frank investigation had been strong from the day the committee opened it in September 1989. The *Washington Times* a few weeks earlier had disclosed Frank's relationship with Gobie, a felon on probation. After buying sex from Gobie in 1985, Frank befriended him and paid him to help with household chores.

In its report filed July 20, the panel said it found no conclusive evidence that Frank knew Gobie was running a prostitution service out of his apartment until his landlady told him that she had seen suspicious activity in his absence.

But the panel criticized Frank for a misleading memo written in support of ending Gobie's probation. The memo included assertions that Gobie had met Frank through "mutual friends"—when in fact Frank had responded to Gobie's escort-service ad in a gay newspaper—and that Gobie was adhering to his probation requirements, when Frank knew Gobie was engaged in prostitution. Frank said candor on those two points would have revealed his own homosexuality.

Although the panel concluded that Frank had not improperly pressured probation officials, it said that the memo "could be perceived as an attempt to use political influence." The panel also ordered Frank to pay the inproperly waived parking tickets. Having agreed on those two areas of impropriety, many Democrats on the ethics committee had sought a light sanction—a letter of reproval—that would have avoided House action.

But members on and off the committee were concerned that Frank might get off too lightly. George "Buddy" Darden, D-Ga., said publicity surrounding Frank's case had "held the House up to a certain amount of public embarrassment. There's no other way to look at it."

On July 19 the committee unanimously agreed to the harsher punishment of reprimand after it became clear that the House would overturn the committee unless it sent something stronger to the floor.

From the beginning, it was all but certain that the effort to expel Frank would be rejected. Its chief advocate, William E. Dannemeyer of California, was regarded as an antigay zealot by some of his own Republican colleagues.

Anticipating the effort to censure Frank, a task force of Democrats sympathetic to him had worked for months to drum up support among his colleagues. Under House rules, a censured member could not hold a chairmanship for the rest of that Congress. Frank was chairman of a Judiciary subcommittee.

Frank's effort to avoid censure was strengthened among Democrats by Gingrich's role in opposing it. Many Democrats still resented Gingrich's part in the 1989 resignation of Speaker Jim Wright. Democrats were also annoyed that Gingrich was criticizing the same committee that he once praised for clearing his own name. The ethics committee in March dismissed formal complaints against Gingrich over his own financial dealings.

Republicans had tried but failed to persuade someone other than Gingrich to offer the censure motion. GOP leader Robert H. Michel of Illinois voted for censure but did not speak on the floor. In the end, only 12 Democrats, most of them southerners, joined 129 Republicans in supporting censure.

Despite the reprimand from his colleagues, Frank had little trouble winning reelection to a sixth term in November 1990. His most serious Republican opponent already had dropped out of the race.

SENATE REPRIMAND OF CRANSTON

Until the 1990s reprimand was purely a House device. But in late 1991 the Senate reprimanded Alan Cranston, D-Calif., one of five senators investigated for ties to convicted banker Charles H. Keating, Jr. Technically, the reprimand came from the Ethics Committee, but the panel said that it had acted "on behalf of and in the name of the Senate." *(Keating Five details, Chapter 10, p. 117)*

By reprimanding Cranston on the Senate floor, the committee established a new form of in-house punishment—one that the chamber had refused to create in earlier cases because it smacked of leniency. Up to then the Senate had only expulsion or censure. Although other words such as *condemn* or *denounce* sometimes would be substituted, any disciplinary resolution short of expulsion that went to the floor and was voted upon was considered by historians to be a censure. In either chamber, anything else—such as a chiding letter or public report—was an action taken by its ethics committee.

The Senate first considered using the word "reprimand" in 1902. In the midst of a hot debate over the Philippines, Benjamin R. Tillman got into a fistfight on the floor with his fellow South Carolina Democrat, John L. McLaurin. The Senate voted 61-0 to declare them "in contempt" and to refer the matter to a committee for further action. The panel considered a reprimand but concluded that "a reprimand would be too slight a punishment. . . . It is not sufficiently severe." The panel recommended censure, which the Senate approved 54-12.

In 1967, when the Senate was debating the resolution to censure Thomas Dodd for financial misconduct, Texas Republican John Tower introduced an amendment to substitute the word *reprimand.* The Ethics Committee chairman, John C. Stennis, D-Miss., told the Senate that his panel had done extensive research on the term and rejected it.

"I will put it in this way, as to what we found as to the meaning of *reprimand* in legislative parlance," said Stennis. "It just does not mean anything. It means what you might call a slap on the wrist. It does not carry any weight."

Jack Maskell, a Congressional Research Service lawyer who found these examples for a 1990

R. Michael Jenkins

Senators in late 1991 were required to watch colleague Alan Cranston, D-Calif., be reprimanded as they sat silently at their desks on the Senate floor, but they were not allowed to judge his behavior by voting. Cranston was reprimanded for his dealings with banker Charles H. Keating, Jr.

review of Senate discipline, said the Cranston action was unprecedented. "A committee reprimand seems to be something new," he said. "It's certainly not a censure. Historians will treat it as discipline by the committee, and it will be a new form of sanction."

Cranston spoke in his own defense after the committee action was reported to the full Senate on November 20. He accepted the rebuke but went on to complain bitterly that other senators had done the same or worse.

CHAPTER 4

Other Forms of Discipline:
Loss of Chair or Right to Vote

Senators or representatives who run afoul of the law or their chamber's ethics code also run the risk of being denied the right to vote on the floor or in committee. And those who head committees or subcommittees may have those chairmanships taken away from them.

As in most cases of procedural difference between the two chambers, House rules tend to be more explicit about when a member should be suspended or stripped of chairmanship. The Senate generally decides such questions on a case-by-case basis.

In *The Senate of the United States: A Bicentennial History,* Senate historian Richard A. Baker noted that

> The Senate's approach to matters of ethics and discipline provides a useful example of its uncommon ability to reconcile protection of its members and procedures with overriding requirements for justice and institutional integrity. This has been accomplished without rigid codes of conduct and centralized enforcement mechanisms. Although characteristically fluid and protracted, the process of setting and applying standards of conduct,

as with the broader legislative process, has functioned to achieve creditable results.

LOSS OF CHAIRMANSHIP

Beginning in 1980, forfeiture of House committee or subcommittee chairmanships became automatic in serious disciplinary cases. In the previous two decades this reduction of power and prestige had become an increasingly common form of punishment:

- Adam Clayton Powell, Jr., D-N.Y., was deposed as chairman of the Education and Labor Committee in 1967 before the House attempted to exclude him because of his controversial behavior. *(Powell case, p. 11)*
- Wayne L. Hays, D-Ohio, in mid-1976 gave up the chairmanship of both the Democratic Congressional Campaign Committee and the House Administration Committee after it was alleged that he had kept a mistress on the latter committee's payroll. Hays was pressured to resign the posts by the House Democratic leadership, and it was evident that the Democratic Caucus would have forced him to

Steve Karafyllakis

R. Michael Jenkins

The House Democratic Caucus May 29, 1980, passed a rule to take away automatically a committee or subcommittee chairmanship from any party member who was censured by the House, or indicted or convicted of a felony carrying a sentence of at least two years. House members who lost their chairmanships under the 1980 rule included (from left) Frank Thompson, Jr., N.J., and Harold E. Ford, Tenn.

- do so if he had not stepped aside voluntarily. Hays resigned from Congress September 1, 1976. *(Hays case, p. 89)*
- Robert L. F. Sikes, D-Fla., lost his Appropriations subcommittee chairmanship in 1977. *(Sikes reprimand, p. 41)*
- In January 1979 House Democratic leaders persuaded Charles C. Diggs, Jr., D-Mich., to resign as chairman of the House Foreign Affairs Subcommittee on Africa after his conviction for taking kickbacks. Diggs voluntarily gave up his chairmanship of the Committee on the District of Columbia. The House later censured him. *(Diggs censure, p. 38)*

Automatic Action

The House Democratic Caucus May 29, 1980, changed its rules to take away automatically a committee or subcommittee chairmanship from any party member who was censured by the House, or indicted or convicted of a felony carrying a sentence of at least two years. Although they held a majority in the House, Democrats backed the revision to head off the setting of a precedent by a censure resolution

then pending against Charles H. Wilson, D-Calif. They feared that letting the entire House vote on a chairmanship would rob the party caucuses of an important prerogative. When the House voted later in the year to censure Wilson, the reference to his chairmanship had been dropped from the resolution. But he automatically lost the position, as head of a postal operations subcommittee, under the new rule.

The previous year the caucus had turned down a proposal to allow the full caucus, rather than committee members alone, to vote on subcommittee chairmanships of members reprimanded by the House. Instead, the proposal applied only to members censured or convicted of a felony liable to a prison term of two years or more.

By the first session of the 102nd Congress (1991-93), five Democrats besides Wilson had been stripped of their chairmanships under the 1980 rule: Gerry E. Studds, Mass., John M. Murphy, N.Y., Frank Thompson, Jr., N.J., Harold E. Ford, Tenn., and Robert Garcia, N.Y.

Murphy and Thompson lost full committee chairmanships following their indictments in the FBI's 1980 Abscam investigation. Studds forfeited his chairmanship of the Merchant Marine and

Fisheries Subcommittee on Coast Guard and Navigation after his 1983 censure for sexual misconduct.

Ford had to give up chairmanship of the Ways and Means Subcommittee on Human Resources in 1987 after he was indicted on fraud and influence-buying charges. Garcia resigned from Congress in 1990 after he was convicted in connection with the Wedtech scandal. He had lost the chairmanship of the Banking Subcommittee on International Finance, Trade, and Monetary under the 1980 rule. Garcia's conviction was overturned but federal prosecutors planned to seek a new trial.

Senate Cases

Whether to allow a convicted or censured member to continue holding a chairmanship has come up less often in the Senate than in the House, because fewer senators have been involved in such serious disciplinary cases.

Although it was his position as chairman of the Senate Government Operations Committee and its Permanent Investigations Subcommittee that enabled Joseph R. McCarthy, R-Wis., to engage in character assassination and other abuses that led to his censure in 1954, McCarthy continued briefly in those positions after the censure vote. He lost the chairmanships a month later, in January 1955, when the Democrats took over control of the Senate.

The only senator implicated in the Abscam scandal, Harrison A. Williams, Jr., D-N.J., was chairman of the Labor and Human Resources Committee when the investigation came to light in 1980. But by the time he was convicted in 1981 he had no chairmanship to lose. Republicans had gained control of the Senate in the meantime.

SUSPENSION IN THE HOUSE

In 1972 the House began to formalize an unwritten rule that a member indicted for or convicted of a crime should refrain from voting on the House floor or in committee. Before that, no member had voluntarily refrained from voting since 1929 when, under indictment in the District of Columbia, Frederick N. Zihlman, R-Md., did not vote on the floor and temporarily turned over his chairmanship of the House Committee on the District of Columbia to the committee's ranking member.

The move to codify that unwritten rule was prompted by the case of John Dowdy, D-Texas, who was convicted December 31, 1971, of bribery, conspiracy, and perjury charges. While Dowdy appealed his conviction, the ethics committee reported a resolution May 3, 1972, stating that any House member convicted of a crime for which he could receive a sentence of two or more years in prison should not participate in committee business or House votes. The maximum sentence for the crimes Dowdy was convicted of was forty years in prison and a $40,000 fine.

Because the Rules Committee failed to act, the resolution was not enacted. But Dowdy, in a June 21, 1972, letter to Speaker Carl Albert, D-Okla., promised he would refrain from voting. He retired from the House at the beginning of 1973. Later that year a federal court cleared him of the conspiracy and bribery charges but left standing his conviction for perjury.

Not until April 16, 1975, did the House enact a resolution similar to the one proposed in 1972. Under the 1975 rule, the voluntary prohibition against voting would apply during an appeal of the conviction but would end on reversal or when the member was reelected subsequent to conviction, even if the verdict was upheld on appeal. The new rule was adopted by the House April 16, 1975, by a vote of 360-37. Later, it was incorporated in the House Code of Official Conduct. *(Senate, House ethics codes, Appendix pp. 174, 178)*

Representative Diggs took advantage of the rule's leniency in 1979 until he was censured on July 31 of that year. Diggs had been convicted of taking kickbacks in October 1978 but was reelected in November. He continued to vote in the House until the censure resolution passed.

The rule, still in effect in 1992 as Section 10 of House Rule 43, states:

A Member of the House of Representatives who has been convicted by a court of record for the commission of a crime for which a sentence of two or more years' imprisonment may be imposed, should refrain from participation in the business of each committee of which he is a member and should refrain from voting on any question at a meeting of the House, or of the Committee of the Whole House, unless or until judicial or executive proceedings result in reinstatement of the presumption of his innocence or until he is reelected to the House after the date of such conviction.

SUSPENSION IN THE SENATE

The celebrated fistfight that led to the censure of South Carolina's Democratic senators, Benjamin R. Tillman and John L. McLaurin, in 1902 also led to debate in committee about the Senate's right to suspend members who misbehave. Part of the debate centered on whether the suspension could be longer for one participant than the other. The final decision of the Senate was to censure both senators and suspend them for six days. But six days already had elapsed between the time of their fight and the Senate action, so the suspension had no effect. *(Tillman-McLaurin censure, p. 45)*

There was no criminal action in the Tillman-McLaurin incident, but at that time in the early 1900s it was the custom for indicted senators to voluntarily stay out from the Senate chamber and refrain from voting. The March 21, 1920, *New York Times,* for example, noted that Sen. Joseph

R. Burton, R-Kan., convicted in November 1905 on charges of accepting a fee for services rendered before a U.S. department, chose to remain outside the Senate chamber because a colleague had threatened to offer a motion to exclude him from the Senate if he tried to enter.

"To draw his salary as a senator," the *Times* account continued, "Mr. Burton entered the Senate cloakroom and merely stuck his head into the Senate chamber, thus technically complying with the rule requiring the presence of senators on at least one day of the session before they can draw their salaries."

The custom was reversed, however, after the April 1924 indictment of Sen. Burton K. Wheeler, D-Mont., on a bribery charge. Wheeler at the time headed a special committee investigating the failure of the Harding administration to prosecute federal officials suspected of influence-peddling in the Teapot Dome scandal. Wheeler maintained he had been framed by the very officials he was investigating.

Rather than stay off the floor, Wheeler demanded the right to speak to declare his innocence and to ask the Senate to investigate the charge. During the ensuing probe, he continued to vote.

Wheeler subsequently was cleared of any wrongdoing both by the Senate and by a federal jury. Since then, indicted senators have remained active in Senate affairs until they either were cleared or left the Senate and have continued to vote in committee and during Senate debates.

The question of suspension arose after Senator Williams's Abscam conviction in 1981. Ethics Committee Chairman Malcolm Wallop, R-Wyo., and Vice Chairman Howell Heflin, D-Ala., said they thought Williams would have to seek the Senate's permission to withhold his vote. Another member, Mack Mattingly, R-Ga., argued that until the committee had concluded its probe Williams "should not be afforded" the opportunity to vote. He called on Senate Democratic leaders to urge Williams not to vote. Williams, however, continued to do so.

CHAPTER 5

Influence Buying:

Lobbying Gone Wrong

As a protected form of free speech, lobbying is a largely unregulated activity. The lack of regulation and the important issues at stake invite abuse, and many unscrupulous groups and individuals have accepted the invitation.

There are always some persons or groups willing to offer bribes or illegal campaign gifts to influence the outcome of legislation, obtain federal contracts, or persuade regulators to look the other way. As a result, numerous senators or representatives have taken bribes or accepted gifts that placed them in a conflict-of-interest situation.

In the early years of the Republic the ties between legislators and private interests were quite direct. While Congress forbade bribery of judges in 1790, bribing a member was not illegal until 1853. In addition to making direct payments, outside interests could hire members to do their legal work. In the 1830s, when President Andrew Jackson was battling with the Bank of the United States, Sen. Daniel Webster of Massachusetts was one of the bank's biggest defenders. On December 21, 1833, Webster complained to bank President Nicholas Biddle: "My retainer has not been renewed or refreshed as usual. If it is wished that my relation to the Bank should be continued, it may be well to send me the usual retainers." The bank also seems to have made sizable loans to other officials, including James Monroe and Henry Clay.

In the mid-1800s the successes of financier-socialite Samuel Ward, self-proclaimed "King of the Lobby," triggered a congressional investigation. In the Crédit Mobilier affair in the Grant administration, twelve members of Congress were accused of taking stock in return for helping the Union Pacific railroad to get huge land grants. Lobbyists' image was so bad that William McKinley had to tell his friend and political mentor, Mark Hanna: "Mark, I would do anything in the world for you, but I cannot put a man in my cabinet who is known as a lobbyist."

The excesses of the time led to a series of sporadic reforms, beginning in 1907 with the banning of campaign contributions from banks and corporations. Recognizing that anyone had a right to seek help from Congress, reformers settled for forcing lobbyists to disclose what they did, principally in 1946 with the requirement that lobbyists register and make available to the public basic information about their activities.

Efforts to buy a legislator's vote or help usually are directed at a single individual to lessen the

Office of Tom Evans   AP/Wide World Photos   Office of Dan Quayle

Lobbyist Paula Parkinson shared a Florida vacation cottage in 1981 with Reps. Tom Evans, R-Del. (left), Dan Quayle, R-Ind. (right), and Tom Railsback, R-Ill. (not pictured). The Justice Department investigated the relationship between Parkinson and Evans after the congressman voted against a bill Parkinson opposed. No charges were filed.

chances of exposure. But occasionally a group scandal comes to light. Korean influence buying in the 1970s, for example, was the first to involve a bloc of members since the Crédit Mobilier affair. More recently, the "Keating Five" case concerned senators investigated for accepting campaign help from California savings and loan executives seeking intercession with federal regulators.

Most such cases involve money offered as bribes or illegal campaign contributions. This chapter deals only with those where the apparent motive of the donor was to influence legislation or buy goodwill with Congress on a large scale. Other types of offenses, which constitute the majority of criminal prosecutions of members of Congress, are treated separately in Chapters 6 (Money) and Chapter 7 (Danger Zones).

At least one lobby scandal of recent times aroused speculation that sex, not money, was the offered inducement. The case involved the relationship in 1981 between Rep. Tom Evans, R-Del., and lobbyist Paula Parkinson, who had briefly shared a vacation cottage in Florida with Evans, Rep. Tom Railsback, R-Ill., and Rep. Dan Quayle, R-Ind. The Justice Department investigated after Evans voted against a crop insurance

bill that Parkinson opposed, but no charges were brought. Parkinson later posed for *Playboy*.

The incident was recalled in 1988 when George Bush chose then-senator Quayle as his running mate, but Quayle repeated his earlier denials that he had any relationship with Parkinson.

As in this case, congressional scandals are highly publicized. And in the unregulated atmosphere in which lobbying operates, the threat of unwanted publicity is the greatest deterrent to unethical behavior by lobbyists and the men and women they seek to influence.

LOBBY DISCLOSURE: "MORE LOOPHOLE THAN LAW"

The frequent abuses of lobbying have led to periodic efforts by Congress to regulate the profession. Beginning with the 62nd Congress in 1911, federal lobbying legislation has been debated in practically every session. Yet by 1991 only one comprehensive lobbying regulation law and a handful of more specialized measures had been enacted. In many cases, congressional investigations of lobby corruption, in response to the public outcry over corruption, took the place of tightening the rules.

The principal method of regulation has been disclosure rather than actual control. The major laws affecting lobbying are these:

- **Foreign Agents Registration Act of 1938.** Enacted amid reports of Fascist and Nazi propaganda circulating in the United States before World War II and amended several times after that. Its history has had more to do with this country's struggle with internal security than with efforts to regulate lobbying.
- **Federal Regulation of Lobbying Act of 1946.** The one existing omnibus lobbying law was enacted as part of a broader Legislative Reorganization Act. Its vague language and subsequent court interpretations combined to circumscribe the effectiveness of the law's spending and lobbying disclosure provisions.
- **Campaign finance legislation.** The ability to promise support or opposition—and to back that up with campaign contributions—gave pressure groups one of the most effective devices in their efforts to influence Congress on legislation. Precisely for this reason, Congress tried on several occasions to limit campaign contributions made by corporations, organizations, and individuals in connection with federal elections. Some limits on gifts to congressional campaigns were passed but were struck down by the courts as unconstitutional.

Registration

The 1946 act did not in any way directly restrict lobbyists' activities. It simply required any person who was hired by someone else for the principal purpose of lobbying Congress to register with the secretary of the Senate and clerk of the House and to file quarterly financial reports so that the lobbyists' activities would be known to Congress and the public. Organizations that solicited or received money for the principal purpose of lobbying Congress did not necessarily have to register, but they did have to file quarterly spending reports with the clerk detailing how much they spent to influence legislation.

In 1954 the Supreme Court in *United States v. Harris* upheld the constitutionality of the 1946 act but narrowly interpreted its key aspects. Since then the measure has commonly been described as "more loophole than law."

One loophole opened by the decision involved collection or receipt of money. As interpreted by the Court, the law did not cover groups or individuals that spent money to influence legislation, unless they also solicited, collected, or received money for that purpose. Another loophole involved the term "principal purpose." A number of organizations—including the National Association of Manufacturers (NAM) for nearly thirty years—argued that the law did not apply to them because lobbying was not their main reason for collecting money. The Court also held that the law did not cover indirect or grass-roots lobbying to pressure Congress by influencing the public on legislation.

Another weakness was that the law applied only to attempts to influence Congress, not administrative agencies or the executive branch, which originated much legislation and which put into effect many regulations similar to legislation. (Lobbying activities by former executive branch officials were restricted somewhat by the 1978 Ethics in Government Act; 1989 legislation extended restrictions to former members of Congress and their staffs.)

The law also left it up to each group of lobbyists to determine what portion of total expenditures were to be reported as spending for lobbying. As a result, some organizations, whose Washington office budgets ran into the millions of dollars, reported only very small amounts spent on lobbying,

"Revolving Door" Slowed

Congress rewrote restrictions on lobbying by former executive branch officials—and, for the first time, applied such limits to its own members and staff— as part of the 1989 pay-and-ethics package. The provisions were an attempt to clamp down on the "revolving-door" problem—officials trading top government positions for high-paying jobs lobbying former colleagues on issues they previously oversaw.

Members of Congress were prohibited from lobbying in the legislative branch for a year after leaving office. In addition, former government officials were barred from using confidential information concerning trade and treaty negotiations to advise clients for a year.

Cabinet secretaries and other top White House officials were banned from lobbying any other senior executive branch officials for a year after leaving office, a broader restriction than one that had prohibited contacts with their own former office. Similar legislation cleared Congress in 1988 but was vetoed by President Ronald Reagan.

The revolving-door provisions resurfaced only in the closing weeks of the session, when congressional leaders saw an opportunity to gain a pay raise in exchange for accepting new restrictions on a host of ethics issues, including postemployment lobbying. But while tightening some limits, Congress rolled back others already in law that the administration said were leading key procurement officials to quit their jobs.

At the last minute, administration officials demanded that the president remain exempt from the lobbying restrictions. They argued that the bill might bar ex-presidents from offering advice to other administrations. Sponsors maintained that the bill would not prevent a former president from expressing his personal views, but agreed to go along.

Another price on the bill imposed at the last minute was an administration demand that Congress roll back controversial lobbying restrictions already in law. A 1988 law (PL 100-679) barred former federal employees from working on a procurement contract for two years if they played a role in awarding that contract.

Early in 1989 top-level employees in the National Aeronautics and Space Administration (NASA), the Defense Department, and other agencies began resigning in droves to avoid being covered. Guidelines to implement the law were issued May 11, but Congress, at the administration's request, passed new legislation that delayed imposition of the new rules.

House sponsors were willing to go along with a repeal of the 1988 law and several others that restricted lobbying by former Defense and Energy Department employees. However, Senate negotiators would not accept a full repeal, and lawmakers agreed to suspend the laws for a year to allow further review.

---

contending that the remainder was spent for general public information purposes, research, and other matters.

Finally, reinforcing all the other weaknesses was the lack of enforcement. The 1946 law did not designate anyone to investigate the truthfulness of lobbying registrations and reports or to compel anyone to register. In 1989 the president of the American League of Lobbyists noted that fewer than six thousand lobbyists were registered out of the forty-seven thousand lawyers, eleven thousand five hundred public affairs professionals, and numerous other consultants in Washington.

"Revolving-Door" Restrictions

The 1978 Ethics in Government Act barred top executive branch officials from representing anyone before their former agency for one year after leaving government, and it permanently barred officials from lobbying on issues they had been directly responsible for. A 1988 law restricted the ability of former Pentagon officers to be involved in working on procurement contracts for defense contractors. In 1988 legislation cleared to extend limitations on postemployment lobbying for the first time to former members of Congress and congressional staff, and to tighten the restrictions on executive branch officials.

President Ronald Reagan pocket-vetoed the bill, saying the restrictions were so tight they would discourage people from entering government service. But virtually identical provisions were enacted in 1989 as part of a broad ethics package. Under the law, members and officers of Congress were barred from lobbying the legislative branch for a year after they left office. High-ranking staff members were barred for a year after leaving congressional employment from lobbying the member, office, or committee for which they had worked. *(Ethics legislation, Chapter 11, p. 158)*

LOBBYING INVESTIGATIONS

Public opprobrium has been as strong a force as the law in keeping lobbyists in check. Congresses in which major scandals have led to public investigations have been more frequent than Congresses in which lobbying legislation was enacted. While hearings have been used to prepare the way for new regulations, more often they have been used to see what cleansing effect sunshine will have on those trying to influence policy behind closed doors.

One of the earliest investigations examined the practices of Col. Martin M. Mulhall, a lobbyist for the NAM. In 1913 Mulhall published a sensational account of his activities in a front-page article in the *New York World*. Among other disclosures, Mulhall said he had paid "between

$1,500 and $2,000" to Rep. James T. McDermott, D-Ill., for legislative favors.

A four-month inquiry by a select House committee found that many of Mulhall's allegations were exaggerated. The panel established that Mulhall had set up his own office in the Capitol, had paid the chief House page $50 a month for inside information, had received advance information on pending legislation from McDermott and House Republican leader John W. Dwight, N.Y., and had influenced the appointment of members to House committees and subcommittees. Six of seven House members implicated by Mulhall were exonerated. The seventh, McDermott, was disciplined but not expelled. He resigned in 1914 but won reelection to another two-year term in November of that year.

Defense "Hospitality" Probe

Seventeen members of the Senate and House acknowledged during the 94th Congress that they visited hunting lodges as guests of major defense contractors on one or more occasions. The dates of the visits were not all known, but most appeared to have been between 1970 and 1975. These members insisted there was nothing improper in their acceptance of such invitations, and some pointed out that many of the companies involved had offices or plants in their own states or districts.

Acceptance of any gift of "substantial value" from a company with an interest in legislation was expressly forbidden by House rules. The Senate at the time had no such regulation.

The Defense Department on October 22, 1975, sent letters to thirty-six military officers and four civilian officials in the Pentagon, admonishing them for "lack of judgment" in accepting similar hunting invitations from defense contractors.

Beginning in 1961 one of the contractors, the Northrop Corporation, engaged in an extensive program of activities, some of them illegal, designed to promote goodwill for the company's products at home and abroad. An illegal $150,000 contribution to the 1972 Nixon campaign was investigated by the Watergate special prosecutor, the Senate Select Committee on Presidential Campaign Activities, and the Securities and Exchange Commission. In addition, Northrop stockholders filed a class-action lawsuit and the company's accounting firm, Ernst & Ernst, undertook a special audit

The audit disclosed that the corporation had rented a goose-hunting facility on Maryland's Eastern Shore and that between 1971 and 1973 the lodge had been visited 120 times by the Northrop staff, 123 times by military personnel, 21 times by civilian Pentagon officials, 11 times by members of Congress, 85 times by congressional staffers, and 49 times by other persons. The audit also exposed the company's practice of allowing federal, state, and local officials to ride on the corporation's private aircraft if such flights were already scheduled for company business.

Investigations of Northrop's activities by the Joint Committee on Defense Production and the Senate Foreign Relations Subcommittee on Multinational Corporations during the summer and fall of 1975 showed that hunting facilities were used for similar purposes by other defense contractors, including Rockwell International Corp. and Remington Arms Co. Inc., a subsidiary of E. I. Dupont de Nemours & Co.

In hearings February 2-3, 1976, the Joint Committee on Defense Production investigated the scope and significance of such corporate favors to Pentagon officials. Committee Vice Chairman Sen. William Proxmire, D-Wis., accused the Defense Department of lax enforcement of its own conflict-of-interest regulations and said that it had been "less than zealous" in its probe of the widely reported hunting trips by Pentagon personnel. But the committee avoided any reference to members' participation in the same activity.

Conflict-of-Interest Rules. Executive Order 11222, promulgated by President Lyndon B. Johnson in May 1965, required each executive branch department and agency to adopt a code of ethical standards for its employees. The Civil Service Commission was charged with coordinating and approving each agency's regulations.

The executive order stipulated that the codes had to specify that no government employee could accept directly or indirectly any gift, favor, entertainment, or other item with a monetary value from any corporation that had a business relationship with the issuing agency. Civil Service Commission regulations spelling out the executive order permitted the acceptance of gifts only where they were "obvious family or personal relationships . . . when the circumstances make it clear that it is those relationships rather than the business of the persons concerned which are the motivating factors."

House Rule 43 forbade any member or employee to accept any "gift or substantial value, directly or indirectly, from any person, organization or corporation having a direct interest in legislation before the Congress." According to an aide to the House Committee on Standards of Official Conduct, "substantial value" was defined according to a State Department rule forbidding acceptance of gifts from another government of more than $55 in value. (The rule has since been tightened in conformity with ethics legislation.) *(Rule 43 text, Appendix, p. 178)*

At the time, the Senate had no such prohibition, but its Rule 42 required that "all gifts in the aggregate amount or value of $50 or more received by a senator from any single source during a year [other than campaign contributions] shall be reported" in the annual financial report required of all members. (The Senate more recently adopted Rule 35 governing acceptance of gifts, but further changes were expected during the 102nd Congress to conform with the 1989 Ethics Reform Act.) *(See*

Chapter 11. For text of Rule 35, see Appendix, p. 174.)

Contractors and Congress. Six senators, four of them serving on committees dealing with military or space legislation, acknowledged acceptance of hospitality from at least one major defense contractor:

- Howard W. Cannon, D-Nev., chairman of the Select Committee on Standards and Conduct and of the Armed Services Subcommittee on Tactical Air Power; member of the Aeronautical and Space Sciences Committee.
- Barry Goldwater, R-Ariz., ranking Republican on the Aeronautical and Space Sciences Committee and on the Armed Services Tactical Airpower Subcommittee.
- Frank E. Moss, D-Utah, chairman of the Aeronautical and Space Sciences Committee
- Herman E. Talmadge, D-Ga.
- John G. Tower, R-Texas, ranking Senate Republican on the Joint Defense Production Committee and member of the Armed Services Tactical Airpower Subcommittee.
- Lowell P. Weicker, Jr., R-Conn.

Cannon and Goldwater accepted flights on Northrop aircraft. Cannon also was a guest at Northrop's Maryland hunting facility. Moss and Talmadge were hunting guests of Rockwell, and Weicker accepted invitations to Remington Arms' lodge.

Tower acknowledged receiving "hospitality" from Rockwell, but an aide said Tower could not recall the circumstances. The aide said that Tower had not participated in hunting trips.

The twelve members of the House who acknowledged that they were guests at Northrop, Remington, or Rockwell hunting facilities included five who were members of committees dealing with defense or space legislation:

- House Speaker Carl Albert, D-Okla. (Rockwell).
- Silvio O. Conte, R-Mass. (Remington, Rockwell).
- John D. Dingell, D-Mich. (Remington).
- John J. Flynt, Jr. D-Ga, member of the Defense Appropriations Subcommittee. (Rockwell).
- William H. Harsha, R-Ohio (Rockwell).
- Joseph E. Karth, D-Minn. (Rockwell).
- Robert L. Leggett, D-Calif., member of the Armed Services Committee (Northrop).
- Dawson Mathis, D-Ga. (Rockwell).
- Bill Nichols, D-Ala., member of the Armed Services Committee (Northrop).
- Henry S. Reuss, D-Wis., member of the Joint Defense Production Committee (Remington).
- Olin E. Teague, D-Texas, chairman of the Committee on Science and Technology (Rockwell).
- Ray Roberts, D-Texas, who reportedly visited the Remington Arms lodge, neither confirmed nor denied that he was a guest.

Gulf Oil Contributions

The Gulf Oil political contributions scandal that broke in December 1975 implicated dozens of members. But the bulk of public attention focused on charges that Senate Minority Leader Hugh Scott, R-Pa., had received up to $100,000 in illegal campaign contributions from Gulf Oil lobbyist Claude Wild between 1960 and 1973.

According to Senate sources, Scott told the Select Committee on Standards and Conduct that he had received $45,000 from Wild but gave the money to other senators for their political campaigns.

The Senate committee spent ten months trying to figure out what to do about the Scott case before calling him in for questioning. Then, on September 15, the committee voted 5-1 in closed session not to investigate the matter.

Several other Republican senators were questioned by the special prosecutors' office or by a federal grand jury in connection with the Gulf Oil matter. Among them were Strom Thurmond, S.C., Robert P. Griffin, Mich., Charles H. Percy, Ill., and Clifford P. Hansen, Wyo.

Sen. Robert Dole, Kan., then the Republican vice presidential candidate, also appeared before the grand jury but he denied ever having received any money from Gulf Oil or from Scott.

Rep. James R. Jones, D-Okla., pleaded guilty January 29, 1976, to a misdemeanor charge that he failed to report a cash campaign contribution from Gulf Oil in 1972. He was fined $200 on March 16.

"Koreagate"

On October 24, 1976, the *Washington Post* broke the story that the Justice Department was probing "the most sweeping allegations of congressional corruption ever investigated by the federal government."

The *Post* said that South Korean agents dispensed between $500,000 and $1 million a year in cash and gifts to members of Congress to help maintain "a favorable legislative climate" for South Korea. Tongsun Park, a South Korean businessman operating in Washington, was named as the principal dispenser of favors.

Follow-up reports said an influence-buying plan had been hatched in the Blue House, the South Korean equivalent of the White House, in late 1970 or early 1971 by President Park Chung Hee, Tongsun Park, high Korean Central Intelligence Agency (KCIA) officials, and Pak Bo Hi, later a chief aide to Korean evangelist Sun Myung Moon.

President Park reportedly was concerned about a Nixon administration plan to withdraw about a third of the U.S. troops in Korea. Growing opposition in the United States to the war in Vietnam also raised fears in Korea that a pullout would lessen American ability to protect it against an invasion from North Korea like the one that precipitated the Korean War in 1950. Continued U.S. congressional support therefore became a high priority of the Park regime.

The House ethics committee began a slow-moving investigation of the involvement of representatives in the South Korean scheme in January 1977. The Senate Ethics Committee conducted its own investigation of senators' reported roles.

Soon after the initial *Post* story, Tongsun Park fled the country. Indicted by the U.S. government September 6, 1977, Park stayed in Korea while his government and the U.S. Justice Department carried out lengthy negotiations. Finally he agreed to testify before the House ethics committee if granted immunity from prosecution.

The indictment charged Park with thirty-six counts of conspiracy to defraud the United States, bribery, mail fraud, failure to register as a foreign agent, and making illegal political contributions. Former representative Richard T. Hanna, D-Calif., was named as an unindicted coconspirator, as were former KCIA directors Kim Hyung Wook and Lee Hu Rak.

The indictment charged that Park and Hanna, around 1967, concocted a scheme to collect large commissions from sales of U.S. rice to South Korea and to use some of that money to buy friends for Korea in Congress. The KCIA directors were alleged to have cooperated in the scheme. Park, a lavish party-giver in Washington, reportedly received more than $9 million in commissions on rice sales from 1969 to 1976.

Hanna had retired from Congress in 1974 after serving six terms. As a sponsor of the Asian Development Bank, he had made numerous trips to Asia and to Korea. He was later indicted and in March 1978 pleaded guilty to one count of conspiracy to defraud the government. He admitted that he had agreed to use his office to help Tongsun Park and had received $200,000 for his efforts between 1969 and 1975. He began serving a thirty-month prison term in May 1978 but was released in mid-1979.

Before holding hearings, both ethics committees asked House and Senate members to report any contacts they had with South Korean government representatives and any gifts or political contributions received from Tongsun Park or others.

Park's testimony before the House ethics committee began February 28, 1978, and ran for more than a week. While he named members to whom he had given contributions, he denied being a representative of the South Korean government or conspiring to buy influence in Congress. He did, however, describe the help he had received from Rep. Otto E. Passman, D-La., in retaining his lucrative commissions on sales of rice to South Korea. As chairman of the House Appropriations subcommittee that dealt with rice and other Food for Peace commodity sales abroad, Passman had been in a good position to help his rice-growing constituents as well as Park. (Passman was defeated for reelection in the 1976 congressional primary, indicted in 1978 for bribery and conspiracy to defraud the U.S. government, but acquitted of all charges the next year.)

During his testimony, Park said that most of his payments went to three men who had since left the House—Passman, who Park testified received cash and gifts of between $367,000 and $407,000; Hanna, who allegedly received $262,000; and Cornelius Gallagher, D-N.J., who Park said got $211,000. (Hanna admitted receiving $200,000.)

Four sitting representatives became the objects of disciplinary hearings by the House ethics committee. They were three California Democrats, John J. McFall, Edward R. Roybal, and Charles H. Wilson, and New Jersey Democrat Edward J. Patten. The committee's report said McFall had converted a $3,000 campaign contribution from Park to his personal use, Roybal had done the same with a $1,000 contribution and then lied about it

under oath, Wilson had denied receiving money from Park despite the latter's testimony that he gave Wilson $1,000 as a wedding gift, and Patten had forwarded a contribution he received from Park as a personal contribution to a New Jersey political organization.

The committee cleared Patten and recommended reprimands for McFall and Wilson and censure of Roybal for deliberately lying under oath. The probe ended in October 1978 when the House voted to reprimand all three Californians, its mildest form of punishment. *(See Chapter 3.)*

Former representative Nick Galifianakis, D-N.C., was indicted April 10, 1979, by a Washington, D.C., federal grand jury for perjury during his 1978 testimony before the House ethics committee in which Galifianakis denied receiving $10,000 in a cash campaign contribution from Tongsun Park. The charges were dismissed August 3, 1979, after a U.S. district court judge ruled that the alleged perjury actually had taken place during the taking of an unauthorized deposition by Rep. Millicent Fenwick, R-N.J., and an ethics committee attorney.

The Senate Ethics Committee concluded its Korean investigation in October 1978 with a report that recommended no disciplinary action against any incumbent or former senator.

INDIVIDUALS PROSECUTED

Since 1969 there have been at least three cases of senators or representatives being investigated for accepting bribes or prohibited gifts from companies with an interest in legislation. Criminal prosecutions were initiated in two of the cases and one resulted in a no-contest plea.

Brewster

Sen. Daniel B. Brewster, D-Md., was indicted in 1969 for accepting a bribe from a mail-order house to influence his vote on postal rate legislation. A federal court dismissed the charges the following October 9, but on June 29, 1972, the Supreme Court ordered Brewster to stand trial. He was convicted November 17, 1972, of accepting an unlawful gratuity, a lesser charge than bribery. He appealed his two-to-six-year prison sentence and $30,000 fine and was granted a new trial. He pleaded no contest on June 25, 1975, and was fined $10,000.

Garmatz

Rep. Edward A. Garmatz, D-Md., was indicted August 1, 1977, on bribery and conspiracy charges of accepting up to $15,000 from shipping companies in return for help on legislation that benefited them. Garmatz had headed the House Merchant Marine and Fisheries Committee from 1966 until he left Congress in 1973. On January 9, 1978, the Justice Department abandoned the case against him, acknowledging that a key witness had lied to a grand jury and forged documents.

Daniel

The House ethics committee in 1986 found that William Clarence "Dan" Daniel, D-Va., had wrongly accepted numerous free plane rides from a defense contractor and had billed the government as though he had made some of the trips by car. But the panel recommended no punishment.

In a 343-page report released February 10, 1986, the ethics committee reported that Daniel, a member of the Armed Services Committee, had accepted at least sixty-eight and perhaps more than two hundred free trips on a jet owned by Beech Aircraft Corp., a defense contractor. The panel

concluded that Daniel had broken rules prohibiting gifts totaling $100 or more from sources with an interest in legislation, barring use of private funds to augment office allowances, and requiring that members report gifts totaling $250 or more a year. All three rules were based on the 1978 Ethics in Government Act.

Daniel told the committee that he was aware of the ethics law and House rules but had not realized that the thresholds were aggregate amounts, not individual amounts, for gifts received in a year.

The panel also had discovered during its nearly five-month investigation that, after nineteen of the flights on which he was a passenger, Daniel had submitted vouchers seeking reimbursement for auto mileage. Daniel testified that long drives aggravated injuries he had suffered in a 1982 auto accident and that he mistakenly thought he was entitled to repayment when his wife or aides drove his car between Washington, D.C., and his congressional district, even if he was not in the car.

The committee concluded that Daniel had misunderstood federal laws and House rules and decided no sanctions were necessary because he had subsequently complied by repaying Beech Aircraft and the government and by updating his annual financial disclosure statements.

The panel said it was satisfied by Daniel's testimony that he had not violated federal criminal statutes against submitting false claims and embezzling from the government. The committee also found no improper relationship between the nine-term lawmaker and the defense contractor. It did express "concern regarding at least an appearance of impropriety."

Daniel easily won reelection to the House in 1986, but he died January 23, 1988, before completing the term.

CHAPTER 6

Money:

Root of Most Congressional Evils

If Congress could somehow remove money from its dual life as an institution and as a collection of mortal human beings, most of its ethics problems would be solved.

Just as in society as a whole, money is far and away the biggest corrupter of the politicians who manage to gain election to the Senate and House. It takes money to get there and stay there, and the constant pressure to obtain campaign contributions is one of the chief reasons why some members accept tainted funds.

Other factors are financial distress or just plain greed. Whatever the reason, some members have resorted to payroll kickbacks, tax evasion, illegal gratuities, and all manner of other illicit means to get money and keep more of it for themselves than the law allows.

Since World War II there have been some sixty criminal prosecutions of members of Congress, almost all of them having to do with money and many resulting in convictions. Some of the bribery or other offenses have been connected to illegal lobbying schemes, as in the "Koreagate" scandal of the late 1970s. Other offenders have been caught in law enforcers' efforts to expose lawmakers' corruptibilty, as in the 1980 "Abscam" affair. Still

others have arisen from morals indiscretions.

In this book an effort has been made to separate the various types of ethics violations into separate chapters. Those largely related to the influencing of legislation are in Chapter 5. Other types of money-related cases, criminal and non-criminal, are in this chapter (Chapter 6). Those having less to do with money than with sex or alcohol abuse are in Chapter 7. The Senate's one-of-a-kind "Keating Five" scandal is covered in Chapter 10.

Inevitably there is some overlap. Some of the major cases resulted in censure or other disciplinary action against the perpetrator, and those are discussed in more detail in the chapter dealing with the kind of discipline that was meted out. For example, the House's 1976 reprimand of Robert L. F. Sikes, D-Fla., for financial misconduct is found in Chapter 3, Censure/Reprimand: A Public Scolding.

Flood

Rep. Daniel J. Flood, D-Pa., chairman of the Appropriations subcommittee that controlled federal health, education, and welfare spending, was

Rep. Daniel J. Flood, D-Pa., one of the House's most colorful characters, was indicted in 1978 on thirteen criminal charges, including bribery and perjury. He resigned his seat in 1980.

indicted on thirteen criminal charges in 1978. Nevertheless, he was reelected in the November elections that year.

Flood, a mustachioed former actor and one of the House's most colorful characters, was charged with lying to a grand jury about payoffs allegedly made to him and a former aide, Stephen Elko. He was also, along with Elko, indicted for bribery.

The indictment alleged that Flood received payments—ranging from $5,000 to $27,000—from several individuals in exchange for his help in getting them grants or other forms of federal aid or approval. One of the bribery counts also alleged that Flood was promised $100,000 for another favor for a Pennsylvania home builder.

Elko and a business associate had been found guilty in 1977 of accepting bribes in exchange for helping several private vocational schools get federal aid. Testimony alleged that persistent pressure from Flood's congressional office caused the U.S. Office of Education to grant temporary accreditation to the business schools. Flood was charged with perjury in his grand jury testimony in the Elko case.

In 1978 a New York rabbi pleaded guilty to bribing Flood to obtain his help in getting federal grants for a summer program the rabbi operated.

A mistrial was declared February 3, 1979, shortly after Flood's trial began. In very poor health and facing a second trial plus a House ethics investigation, Flood resigned in January 1980. On February 26 he pleaded guilty to a single misdemeanor charge and was placed on probation.

Flood was also linked with charges brought in 1978 against Rep. Joshua Eilberg, D-Pa., for illegally helping Hahnemann Medical College and Hospital in Philadelphia to obtain a $14.5 million federal construction grant. Eilberg was defeated for reelection after being indicted and he pleaded guilty in February 1979. *("Members of Congress and the Practice of Law," box, p. 152.)*

Elko testified that he recommended Eilberg's law firm to the hospital and that Flood was to receive $50,000 from the firm for arranging an appropriation for the grant.

Brooke

The Senate Ethics Committee ended a ten-month investigation of former senator Edward W. Brooke, R-Mass., in March 1979 by concluding there was "credible evidence" of wrongdoing on his part but that the violations did not warrant punishment. Brooke had failed to win reelection to a third term in 1978, partly because of the unfavorable publicity from the probe.

The committee investigated allegations that Brooke had not disclosed $49,000 in interest-free loans from a Massachusetts liquor distributor. Senate rules required reporting of liabilities over $2,500 owed to anyone other than a relative. As a result of the allegations, Brooke's bitter 1977 divorce trial was reopened and Massachusetts officials launched investigations into other aspects of his finances. As attorney-general, Brooke had been the state's highest law enforcement officer before winning election to the Senate in 1966—the only black to serve there since 1881.

Brooke's troubles began when the *Boston Globe* noted discrepancies between the senator's financial disclosure report, filed in May 1978, and sworn testimony he gave a year earlier in his divorce proceedings. Brooke and his wife, Remigia, had been granted a divorce in December 1977, but it was not to take effect until June 15, 1978.

In his court statement, Brooke said he had received the $49,000 over a ten-year period from A. Raymond Tye, a Massachusetts liquor distributor. But the money he had said he owed Tye was not listed in the financial disclosure report Brooke filed with the Senate.

The *Globe* May 26, 1978, reported that Brooke initially said he still owed Tye the $49,000. However, Brooke later told the paper that he had received only $2,000 in loans from Tye. The other $47,000, he said, was money from an insurance settlement he administered on behalf of his mother-in-law, who died in 1977.

In a press conference May 27 Brooke admitted he had made "a misstatement" in the court deposition. But he left unclear whether the $47,000—which was part of a settlement his mother-in-law received after she was severely injured in a car accident—was a loan.

In a statement after the investigation ended, Brooke sharply criticized the committee. Except for the single "misstatement" that he had acknowledged and apologized for, he said, the committee had found nothing "more serious than poor recordkeeping."

"ABSCAM," 1980

An FBI undercover operation known as Abscam in 1980 implicated seven members of Congress in criminal wrongdoing. The "sting" used agents posing as wealthy Arabs to offer bribes to the legislators. By May 1981 juries had convicted the seven—six House members and one senator—for their role in the affair, and by March 11, 1982, none of the seven was still in Congress.

The House members were Democrats John W. Jenrette, Jr., S.C., Raymond F. Lederer, Pa., John M. Murphy, N.Y., Michael J. "Ozzie" Myers, Pa., and Frank Thompson, Jr., N.J., and Republican Richard Kelly, Fla. Another House Democrat, John P. Murtha, Pa., was named an unindicted coconspirator and testified for the government in the trial of Murphy and Thompson. The senator was Harrison A. Williams, Jr., D-N.J.

In summary, Abscam led to the following congressional actions with respect to the convicted seven:

- Myers was expelled from the House of Representatives on October 2, 1980, only the fourth representative ever expelled and the first since the Civil War. *(See Chapter 3.)*
- Three others—Jenrette, Lederer, and Williams—resigned from Congress to avoid almost certain expulsion.
- Kelly, Murphy, and Thompson were defeated by their constituents before being convicted in court.
- The unindicted conspirator, Murtha, was cleared by the House ethics committee over the objections of the committee counsel.

Two elements made Abscam far more than a routine corruption case. One was the FBI's use of videotapes to record the meetings of phony sheiks, members of Congress, and others—a development that allowed the public to see one representative stuffing money into bulging pockets. The other

AP/Wide World Photos

Rep. John W. Jenrette, Jr., shown here with his wife Rita, resigned from the House in 1980 following his conviction on bribery and conspiracy charges in the Abscam affair.

unusual element was the prominence of three of those convicted—senior committee chairmen, two of whom (Thompson and Williams) were generally considered leaders within their party.

The Scam

According to published accounts and subsequent court evidence, an undisclosed number of members of Congress had been approached by intermediaries who offered to introduce them to persons acting on behalf of wealthy Arabs interested in making investments in their districts. The stand-ins were actually undercover FBI agents. Some of the members were asked if they could use their Capitol Hill positions to help the Arabs obtain U.S. residency.

Others were asked to use their influence in government to obtain federal grants and gambling licenses or to arrange real estate deals.

Five of the accused—Williams, Kelly, Lederer, Myers, and Thompson—were videotaped accepting cash or stock. Jenrette was tape-recorded saying he had been given the cash by an associate. Murphy allegedly told an associate to accept the cash. The defendants' claim that the government had entrapped them won support in some legal and congressional circles, and leaks to the press were generally condemned.

Although Attorney General Benjamin Civiletti asked congressional committees to hold up their investigations until the criminal trials were completed, both the Senate Select Ethics Committee and the House Committee on Standards of Official Conduct began probes of their own.

In the end, the House committee waited until Myers, Jenrette, and Lederer had been convicted in court before taking final action. Using court evidence as the basis for its probe, the panel recommended that Myers be expelled, and the full House agreed.

Jenrette resigned from the House just as the Standards Committee was ready to hand down a recommendation for his expulsion. Lederer resigned in 1981 after the committee recommended his expulsion. Because Kelly, Murphy, and Thompson were defeated for reelection, no congressional disciplinary action against them was taken.

The Senate committee unanimously recommended in August 1981 that Williams be expelled. After numerous delays the Senate debated the recommendation for five days in March 1982 before Williams submitted his resignation.

Rep. Michael J. "Ozzie" Myers, D-Pa., was expelled from the House in 1980 as a result of his role in the Abscam affair. He was the fourth representative in history to be expelled.

The Court Cases

Myers and three codefendants were convicted August 30, 1980, of bribery, conspiracy, and interstate travel to aid racketeering. The codefendants were Camden, New Jersey, mayor Angelo J. Errichetti, Philadelphia attorney Howard L. Criden, and Philadelphia city councilman Louis C. Johanson, a partner in Criden's law firm.

The jurors saw videotapes of Myers accepting an envelope with $50,000 in cash from an agent. The government charged that Myers took the money in return for promises to introduce a private immigration bill to help the agent's supposed Arab employer gain permanent U.S. residence. Myers then boasted of his familiarity with Philadelphia government officials and members of the Mafia and agreed to accept an additional $85,000.

On the stand, Myers acknowledged that he had accepted money from the undercover agents. He maintained that he was not bribed, however, because he had never intended to do anything in return for the money.

Following a five-week trial, Jenrette was convicted October 7, 1980, on two counts of bribery and a single count of conspiracy. Convicted with him was a business associate, John R. Stowe. During the trial, government prosecutors charged that Jenrette and Stowe had accepted $50,000 in cash from an undercover FBI agent. Prosecutors described the payment as the first installment of a $100,000 bribe to be paid the two men in return for a promise from Jenrette to introduce a private immigration bill on behalf of the agent's supposed Arab employer.

"I've got larceny in my blood," jurors saw Jenrette say during a videotaped meeting with the agent.

Jenrette was defeated in the November 1980

election. In December the ethics committee recommended that the House discipline him and on December 10 he resigned just before the committee was to vote on his expulsion. Jenrette began serving a two-year prison term April 4, 1985, at a federal prison camp in Atlanta, Georgia.

Murphy and Thompson on December 3, 1980, became the third and fourth members of Congress to be convicted for their involvement in Abscam. After their indictments both men were required by House rules to yield their committee chairmanships until the criminal charges were resolved. Murphy was chairman of the House Merchant Marine and Fisheries Committee and its Merchant Marine Subcommittee. Thompson chaired the House Administration Committee, the Education and Labor Committee Subcommittee on Labor-Management Relations, and the Joint Committee on Printing.

According to the indictment, Philadelphia lawyer Criden introduced Thompson to the undercover agents at an October 1979 meeting in Washington. At that meeting Thompson agreed to use his official position to help a group of Arab businessmen—the agents' supposed employers—on "an immigration matter," the indictment alleged. At a second meeting, Thompson and Criden were given $50,000, the indictment said, which they shared with "others."

The indictment said Thompson then agreed to introduce the agents to other members of Congress willing to take bribes. He subsequently met with Murphy, the indictment said, after which Murphy and Criden met with two FBI agents in a hotel near New York's Kennedy International Airport, where they were given $50,000 in return for Murphy's promise of help on the immigration matter. The cash was shared among Murphy, Thompson, Criden, and "others," the indictment said.

Thompson then introduced Criden to Murtha, the indictment said. In a subsequent meeting with the FBI agents, Criden was given an additional $50,000 payment, which he shared with Thompson and Murphy, according to the indictment. The indictment said Murtha agreed to use his official position to help the Arab businessmen gain United States residency, but he did not share in the cash payments.

The indictment further alleged that Murphy agreed to find investment opportunities in shipping companies for the agents' supposed employers and to use his position as chairman of the Merchant Marine Committee to advance those companies' interests. The indictment said that Murphy and an unnamed associate intended to benefit both directly and indirectly from the investments.

Thompson also sought investments from the Arab businessmen, the indictment said. It added that benefits from the investments were to accrue to Thompson as well as to unnamed former law partners.

During the trial, Thompson took the stand to deny he had ever received any bribe money. Murtha, who was not indicted in the case, testified, however, that Thompson had approached him on the House floor during 1979 to tell him he could share with Thompson and Murphy $50,000 in "walking around" money in return for meeting with the undercover agents. Murtha subsequently met with the agents but accepted no cash from them.

Murphy did not testify in his own defense.

Both Thompson and Murphy were convicted by a Brooklyn jury of conspiracy and acceptance of unlawful gratuity. Thompson also was convicted of bribery but Murphy was exonerated of that charge. The convictions came a month after the two lost their reelection bids.

Kelly, the only Republican caught by Abscam, was convicted January 26, 1981, of bribery and conspiracy. He had been defeated for reelection in the September 9, 1980, Florida primary.

The July 15 indictment alleged that Kelly accepted $25,000 in cash from an FBI undercover agent in return for agreeing to use his influence to help people emigrate to the United States. The indictment alleged further that Kelly was later to have received $75,000 as part of the conspiracy.

When Kelly's name surfaced in February news accounts of the Abscam probe, he admitted to reporters that he took $25,000 in FBI money. But Kelly said it was part of his own investigation of "shady characters."

During the trial, Kelly was seen on videotape at a Washington home rented by the FBI stuffing money into his pockets and asking before he left whether the money made visible bulges in his clothing. On November 4, 1985, Kelly began serving six to eighteen months at the minimum security prison at Eglin Air Force Base, Florida.

Lederer was convicted January 9, 1981, in a Brooklyn federal district court, of bribery, conspiracy, accepting an illegal gratuity, and interstate travel to aid racketeering. His indictment, handed down May 28, 1980, charged that Lederer in September 1979 accepted a $50,000 bribe in a hotel room near Kennedy Airport in New York from an undercover FBI agent who said he represented Arab businessmen. Lederer promised to introduce private bills to give the Arabs permanent U.S. residency, the indictment said. Lederer shared the $50,000 payment with Errichetti, Criden, and Johanson (convicted with Myers), the indictment charged.

As the only Abscam figure reelected to the House in 1980, Lederer faced disciplinary action by the new Congress. Supported by the Philadelphia Democratic organization, he had easily won his primary election over six opponents April 22 and was reelected in November with 55 percent of the vote.

On April 28, 1981, the Standards Committee recommended that Lederer be expelled from the House. The following day he announced that he would resign from the House May 5.

The last two of the seven members of Congress

AP/Wide World Photos

Harrison A. Williams, Jr., D-N.J., resigned from the Senate in 1982 as his colleagues debated expelling him. Williams had been convicted on criminal charges in the Abscam scandal.

convicted in the 1980 "Abscam" scandal began serving prison terms in 1985 after exhausting all legal appeals. Both were convicted of bribery and conspiracy.

Senator Williams

Williams was convicted May 1, 1981, of all nine counts brought against him. They included bribery, conspiracy, accepting outside compensation for the performance of official duties, and aid to a racketeering enterprise. He was only the fourth senator convicted of criminal wrongdoing while in office. *(Box, p. 19)*

Standing seventh in seniority among Senate Democrats, Williams was chairman of the Senate Labor and Human Resources Committee until Republicans gained control of the Senate in 1981. He also was ranking member of the Banking

Committee, former chairman of its Securities Subcommittee, and a member of the Rules and Administration Committee.

Like the other Abscam defendants, he was convicted of promising to introduce a private immigration bill for what turned out to be a phony sheik (actually an FBI agent in disguise). Unlike the others he was not charged with accepting a large cash payment but with accepting shares in a titanium mine in return for a promise to help the enterprise get government contracts. Prosecutors said the stock certificates omitted Williams's name to conceal his interest in the mine. The stock was in the name of a close associate who was an unindicted coconspirator in the case. The scam concerned a scheme to secure a $100 million loan for the mine and processing facility in Piney River, Virginia, from the supposed sheik.

Denying the charges, Williams said he only intended to help friends who owned the mine to obtain a loan from a wealthy Arab. Williams also acknowledged that he had boasted of his influence with high government officials "to an uncomfortable degree" in the presence of the bogus Arab and that he had accepted stock in the mine. But he said he believed the stock certificates to be worthless.

The Senate Ethics Committee, after reviewing the evidence in the court case and hearing Williams present his defense again, voted unanimously August 24, 1981, to recommend that the Senate expel him. That would have been the sixteenth expulsion from the Senate and the first since the Civil War. *(Senate expulsion table, Appendix, p. 168)*

After numerous delays the Senate began debating the recommendation March 3, 1982. Noting Williams's claim that the government tried "to manufacture crime out of nothing," Ethics Vice Chairman Howell Heflin, D-Ala., a former judge, argued that the evidence upheld the case against Williams regardless of the government's conduct.

"At any point in this drawn out, sordid affair," Heflin said, "Senator Williams could have said, 'Wait a minute. What you're proposing is wrong. That is not what I had in mind. I can't be involved in this.' But he didn't. He stayed; he discussed; he agreed; he promised; he pledged—to abuse his office, his public trust, for which now he must be expelled."

The Democratic Whip, Alan Cranston, D-Calif., worked on Williams's behalf to reduce the punishment to a censure motion. But when closer friends of Williams reluctantly endorsed expulsion, it became clear that Cranston's motion would fail and that well over the required two-thirds of the Senate was ready to vote to expel Williams. On March 11, 1982, he resigned from the Senate.

WEDTECH, 1988

Two Democratic House members from New York resigned from Congress after being convicted in connection with a late-1980s scandal involving the Wedtech Corp., a South Bronx concern that began as a machine shop and grew into a multimillion-dollar defense contractor that drew praise from President Ronald Reagan. One of the convictions was overturned.

Wedtech's primary source of business was a federal program that set aside contracts, without bids, for minority-owned companies. It briefly came to symbolize the possibilities of free enterprise in the impoverished South Bronx. But Wedtech was at the center of a wide-ranging scandal by the time it went out of business.

Newspaper reports said that Sen. Alphonse D'Amato, R-N.Y., also had helped Wedtech in return for illegal campaign contributions, but no criminal action was brought against D'Amato. He was rebuked by the Ethics Committee on other matters in 1991.

Stan Barouh   Sue Klemens

Reps. Mario Biaggi (left) and Robert Garcia, both New York Democrats, resigned from Congress after being convicted in connection with a scandal involving the Wedtech Corp., a South Bronx defense contractor. Garcia's conviction was later overturned.

Biaggi

Facing near certain expulsion from the House, Mario Biaggi, D-N.Y., resigned from Congress four days after his August 4, 1988, conviction on felony charges in connection with bribes allegedly paid by Wedtech to obtain the no-bid contracts. It was Biaggi's second conviction in less than a year.

He had been convicted in September 1987 on charges related to his acceptance of Florida vacations after using his influence to help a Brooklyn ship-repair company. Having been found guilty of accepting an illegal gratuity, and of interstate travel and obstruction of justice in connection with that charge, Biaggi was fined $500,000 and sentenced to thirty months in prison but was freed pending appeal.

A preliminary report by the House ethics committee staff in November 1987 concluded that Biaggi's offenses violated House rules as well as the laws governing financial disclosure, travel, and accep-

tance of gifts and brought "discredit upon the House of Representatives." The ethics panel recommended Biaggi's expulsion, but floor action on the resolution, which had been filed February 18, 1988, was put off while Biaggi stood trial in the Wedtech case. The trial resulted in his conviction of racketeering, conspiracy, extortion, and accepting bribes. He was sentenced to eight years in prison, to run concurrently with the previous thirty-month sentence.

Garcia

On November 21, 1988, Rep. Robert Garcia became the second Bronx Democrat to face federal influence-peddling charges in the Wedtech case. The charges included conspiracy, two counts of receipt of bribes, two counts of extortion, and two counts of receipt of gratuities. The seven-count indictment came less than two weeks after voters endorsed Garcia for a sixth full term, giving him 92 percent of the vote.

Under House Democratic Caucus rules, Garcia had to step down from the chairmanship of the House Banking Subcommittee on International Development, Finance, Trade, and Monetary Policy for the remainder of the 100th Congress. Since the Congress had adjourned, there was little impact on the committee, and the House ethics committee could not consider action against Garcia.

A federal jury in New York took six days to find Garcia and his wife, Jane Lee Garcia, guilty October 20, 1989, of two counts of extortion and one count of conspiracy. They were accused of taking more than $170,000 in payments and interest-free loans, plus a diamond necklace, from the defunct Wedtech. Both Garcias were acquitted of four counts of bribery and receipt of illegal gratuities.

Garcia, who had become chairman of another Banking subcommittee, Policy Research and Insurance, in the 101st Congress, stepped down in 1989 to devote full time to an appeal of his conviction. He resigned January 7, 1990, twelve days before he was sentenced to three years in prison for extortion.

A federal appeals court overturned the Garcias' convictions on June 29, 1990. The appellate court said their actions fell short of extortion. "Garcia never even hinted that he was prepared to use his power to harm Wedtech," a three-judge panel of the U.S. Court of Appeals for the 2nd Circuit wrote. "In making the payments, the company was motivated by desire, not fear."

The Garcias sought to block a new trial, but on December 3 U.S. District Judge Leonard Sand refused to rule out that possibility. The Garcias argued that a new trial would violate the Double Jeopardy Clause of the Constitution since they would be tried twice for the same offense. Sand ruled, though, that the Constitution did not bar the retrial of a defendant who obtained a reversal of a conviction on appeal.

CRIMINAL PROSECUTIONS, 1941-80

Following is a summary in chronological order of pre-1980 criminal prosecutions of senators and representatives on charges relating to financial misconduct. Prosecutions that relate more to lobbying or sex scandals are covered in those chapters.

Senate

Edward R. Gurney, R-Fla. Indicted April 6, 1974, by a Florida grand jury on a misdemeanor charge of violating a state campaign finance law. Indictment dismissed May 17, 1974, but on July 10 a federal grand jury indicted Gurney and six other defendants for conspiracy, perjury, and soliciting bribes in the form of campaign contributions from Florida builders with business pending before the Department of Housing and Urban Development. Acquitted August 6, 1975, on the bribe-soliciting charge, but jury failed to reach a verdict on the other charges of perjury and conspiracy to create a political slush fund. Acquitted October 27, 1976, of lying to a federal grand jury, the seventh and final charge brought against him since 1974.

House

James M. Curley, D-Mass. Indicted September 16, 1943, by a federal grand jury, with five others, on charge of using mails to defraud by accepting retainers on false claims of ability to obtain war contracts; November 1, 1943, indictment voided by U.S. District Court, Washington, D.C., on grounds grand jury was illegally summoned; January 3, 1944, indicted on same charge; January 18, 1946, convicted; February 18, 1946, sentenced to six to eighteen months in prison and fined $1,000; January 13, 1947, U.S. Court of Appeals, D.C. Circuit, upheld conviction; June 2, 1947, U.S. Supreme Court upheld conviction; June 26, 1947, began serving sentence; November 26, 1947, President

Harry S. Truman commuted remainder of sentence.

Andrew J. May, D-Ky. Indicted January 23, 1947, with three other men for conspiracy to defraud U.S. government and for accepting money to influence the War Department and other agencies to give contracts to a wartime munitions combine (May was one of its directors); July 3, 1947, convicted of conspiracy and bribery; November 14, 1949, Supreme Court refused to review conviction; December 5, 1949, entered prison; September 18, 1950, paroled after serving nine months of an eight-to-twenty-four-month sentence; December 24, 1950, pardoned by President Truman.

J. Parnell Thomas, R-N.J. Indicted November 8, 1948, for conspiracy to defraud the government through padding his congressional payroll and taking kickbacks from his staff; November 30, 1949, pleaded no contest; December 9, 1949, sentenced to six to eighteen months in prison and fined $10,000; September 10, 1950, paroled after serving eight and a half months in prison.

Walter E. Brehm, R-Ohio. Indicted December 20, 1950, for accepting campaign contributions from two of his congressional office employees; April 30, 1951, convicted on charges involving one employee; June 11, 1951, sentenced to five to fifteen months in prison (sentence suspended) and fined $5,000.

Theodore Leonard Irving, D-Mo. Indicted June 8, 1951, for violation of Corrupt Practices Act and the Taft-Hartley Act for misusing funds of the labor union he headed for his 1948 House campaign; December 28, 1951, acquitted.

John L. McMillan, D-S.C. Indicted January 14, 1953, for violating law barring members of Congress from contracting with the government (he leased oil and gas lands in Utah from Department of Interior); May 16, 1953, acquitted.

Ernest K. Bramblett, R-Calif. Indicted June 17, 1953, for making false statements in connection with payroll padding and kickbacks from congressional employees; February 9, 1954, convicted; April 14, 1954, sentence stayed pending Supreme Court review; April 4, 1955, Supreme Court upheld conviction; June 15, 1955, sentenced to four to twelve months in prison (sentence suspended) and fined $5,000.

Thomas J. Lane, D-Mass. Indicted March 5, 1956, for federal income tax evasion in 1949-51; April 30, 1956, pleaded guilty and sentenced to four months in prison and fined $10,000.

William J. Green, Jr., D-Pa. Indicted December 14, 1956, with six others, for conspiracy to defraud the government by accepting money and bond business for his insurance firm from contractors in return for influencing decisions on the construction in 1951-54 of a $33 million Army Signal Corps depot in Tobyhanna, Pennsylvania; February 27, 1959, acquitted.

Adam Clayton Powell, Jr., D-N.Y. Indicted May 8, 1958, for federal income tax evasion; April 5 and 7, 1960, federal judge dismissed two of three counts and trial on third count declared mistrial April 22, 1960, because of hung jury; May 23, 1960, judge refused to dismiss indictment; April 13, 1961, cased dismissed at request of U.S. attorney.

Thomas F. Johnson, D-Md. Indicted October 16, 1962, with Frank W. Boykin, D-Ala., and two other defendants, for conflict of interest and conspiracy to defraud the government by trying to influence Justice Department action on indictments in a Maryland savings and loan association scandal; Johnson was accused of receiving more than $20,000 for his part in the conspiracy, which included a House speech defending savings and loan institutions; June 13, 1963, convicted; September 16, 1964, Fourth Circuit Court of Appeals set aside conviction on grounds that the House speech was protected by the speech or debate clause of the Constitution, and ordered new trial for Johnson on conflict of interest charges; February 24, 1966, Supreme Court upheld rulings; January 26, 1968, convicted of conflict of interest;

January 30, 1968, sentenced to six months in prison.

Frank W. Boykin, D-Ala. Indicted October 16, 1962, with Rep. Thomas F. Johnson, D-Md., on charges of conflict of interest and conspiracy to defraud the government; June 13, 1963, convicted; October 7, 1963, Boykin placed on probation for six months and fined $40,000; December 17, 1965, pardoned by President Lyndon B. Johnson.

Hugh J. Addonizio, D-N.J. Indicted December 18, 1969, on charges of extortion, conspiracy, and income tax evasion; convicted July 22, 1970, on sixty-four counts for conspiring to extort $235,000 from contractors doing business with the city of Newark, New Jersey, while he was mayor; September 22, 1970, sentenced to ten years in prison and fined $25,000; October 4, 1979, United States Parole Commission abandoned two-year fight to return him to jail following Addonizio's April 1977 release from prison on a court order after having served five years.

John V. Dowdy, D-Texas. Indicted March 31, 1970, for bribery, conspiracy, and perjury in connection with receipt of payment from a Maryland home improvements company accused of defrauding its customers; December 30, 1971, convicted; February 23, 1972, sentenced to eighteen months in prison and fined $25,000; March 13, 1973, Fourth Circuit Court of Appeals reversed conspiracy and bribery convictions on constitutional grounds, but left standing perjury conviction; October 9, 1973, Supreme Court upheld ruling; January 28, 1974, entered prison to serve a six-month term.

Martin B. McKneally, R-N.Y. Indicted December 16, 1970, for failure to file federal income tax returns for 1964-67; October 18, 1971, pleaded guilty to charge that he filed no income tax in 1965 and government dropped other charges; December 20, 1971, sentenced to one year in prison (sentence suspended), placed on one-year probation, and fined $5,000.

Cornelius Gallagher, D-N.J. Indicted April 7, 1972, for federal income tax evasion in 1966-67, perjury, and conspiracy to hide kickbacks for helping two conspirators to evade taxes in 1966-68; December 21, 1972, pleaded guilty to tax evasion charge involving his income; June 15, 1973, sentenced to two years in prison and fined $10,000; November 22, 1974, released from jail eight months before end of two-year sentence.

J. Irving Whalley, R-Pa. Indicted July 5, 1973, for mail fraud for using mail to deposit salary kickbacks he required from congressional staff and obstruction of justice for threatening an employee to prevent her from giving information to the Federal Bureau of Investigation; July 31, 1973, pleaded guilty; October 15, 1973, sentenced to three years in prison (sentence suspended) and fined $11,000.

Bertram L. Podell, D-N.Y. Indicted July 12, 1973, for conspiracy, bribery, perjury, and conflict of interest for receipt of payment to appear before federal agencies to help Florida Atlantic Airlines to obtain approval of a Bahamian route; October 1, 1974, Podell ended nine-day trial by pleading guilty to the conspiracy and conflict of interest charges; January 9, 1975, sentenced to six months in prison and fined $5,000; November 3, 1975, Supreme Court refused to review the case.

Frank J. Brasco, D-N.Y. Indicted October 23, 1973, for conspiracy to receive bribes from a reputed Mafia figure who sought truck leasing contracts from the Post Office and loans to buy trucks; July 19, 1974, convicted; October 22, 1974, sentenced to five years in prison (all but three months suspended) and fined $10,000; June 26, 1975, began three-month sentence; October 6, 1975, Supreme Court upheld conviction.

Angelo D. Roncallo, R-N.Y. Indicted February 21, 1974, for extortion of political contribution from an incinerator contractor at the time Roncallo was comptroller of Nassau County, Long Island; May 18, 1974, acquitted.

Andrew J. Hinshaw, R-Calif. Indicted twice on May 6, 1975—first for soliciting a bribe involving a 1972 campaign contribution, for two counts of bribery involving Tandy Corp., and for embezzlement and for misappropriation of public funds during time he served as assessor of Orange County, California, and second for conspiracy, grand theft, and embezzlement in connection with the use of employees for his 1972 House campaign; October 10, 1975, judge dismissed from the first indictment embezzlement and misappropriation of public funds charges but sustained bribery charges; January 26, 1976, convicted of bribery charges and acquitted of charge of soliciting a bribe; February 24, 1976, sentenced to a one-to-fourteen-year prison term, appeals exhausted January 10, 1977, by U.S. Supreme Court; trial on second indictment began in the fall of 1976; convicted December 3, 1976, of misappropriation of public funds and petty theft; paroled June 5, 1978, from a California prison after serving seven months.

Wendell Wyatt, R-Ore. Pleaded guilty June 11, 1975, to misdemeanor charge of violating federal campaign spending laws by failing to report expenditures from a secret cash fund he controlled while heading President Richard Nixon's reelection campaign in Oregon in 1972; July 18, 1975, fined $750.

Henry J. Helstoski, D-N.J. Indicted June 2, 1976, for bribery, conspiracy, obstructing justice, and perjury for his role in a scheme to solicit and accept payment for the introduction of private immigration bills; September 21, 1979, had seven bribery-related counts of the twelve-count indictment against him dismissed following June 18 U.S. Supreme Court decision barring federal prosecutors from using any evidence of Helstoski's past legislative actions in prosecuting him; announced he would seek dismissal of remaining counts against him.

James F. Hastings, R-N.Y. Indicted September 21, 1976, for operating an alleged kickback scheme with members of his congressional staff; convicted December 17, 1976, on twenty-eight felony counts;

paroled June 5, 1978, from federal prison in Florida after serving fourteen months of a twenty-month to five-year term.

Frank M. Clark, D-Pa. Indicted September 5, 1978, on thirteen counts of mail fraud, perjury, and income tax evasion; June 12, 1979, pleaded guilty, sentenced to two years in prison (followed by five years' probation) and fined $11,000.

Daniel J. Flood, D-Pa. Indicted September 5, 1978, on three charges of lying to a grand jury about payoffs made to him and a former aide. *(Details, Flood case, p. 61)*

Joshua Eilberg, D-Pa. Indicted October 24, 1978, by a federal grand jury for illegally receiving compensation to help a Philadelphia hospital get $14.5 million federal grant; February 24, 1979, pleaded guilty, sentenced to five years of probation and fined $20,000.

1980s AND 1990s: BUMPER CROP OF CASES

The 1980s and early 1990s produced an unprecedented number of money-related congressional ethics cases in addition to the Abscam and Wedtech scandals. A few resulted in convictions on criminal charges, but most were investigated by the Senate and House ethics committees. A chronological summary follows.

Richmond

Rep. Fred W. Richmond, D-N.Y., pleaded guilty August 25, 1982, to charges of tax evasion, possession of marijuana, and making an illegal payment to a government employee. At the same time, he announced his resignation from the House, and, as part of an unusual plea bargain with federal prosecutors, agreed not to run for office again.

In a written statement Richmond said, "These acts to which I have pled guilty were irresponsible,

Rep. Julian C. Dixon, D-Calif. (center), stepped down as chairman of the House ethics committee in 1991 after leading the panel through a mine field of cases in the 1980s. Most members of Congress avoid serving on the ethics committee.

unnecessary, foolish and wrong."

In return for his guilty plea and resignation, the government agreed not to prosecute him for other actions it had been investigating, including cocaine possession and his arranging for a prison escapee, using an alias, to be put on the House payroll.

The House Committee on Standards of Official Conduct, which had been investigating the allegations against Richmond, dropped its probe when he resigned.

The part of the plea bargain involving Richmond's resignation and promise not to run for re-election was voided November 10, 1982, by U.S. District Judge Jack B. Weinstein as an "unconstitutional interference by the executive with the legislative branch of government" that "conflicted with the fundamental right of the people to elect their representatives."

Richmond was sentenced by Judge Weinstein to a year and a day in federal prison and fined $20,000. He began his prison sentence at the federal prison camp at Allenwood, Pennsylvania, on December 6.

The only felony charge to which he pleaded guilty—tax evasion—involved Richmond's 1980 income, which he admitted in court was understated on his tax return. He did not report funds paid by his company, Walco National Corp., for his New York apartment. This reduced Richmond's tax liability by approximately $50,000.

Richmond had had an earlier brush with the law in 1978, when he was arrested on a morals charge. The charges were dropped after he completed a psychiatric treatment program. *(Richmond case, p. 90)*

Ferraro

The Democratic party's 1984 vice presidential candidate, Rep. Geraldine A. Ferraro, New York, was found by the House ethics committee to have technically violated the 1978 Ethics in Government Act. The committee ruled December 3, 1984, that Ferraro committed the technical violations about ten times in failing to report or reporting incorrectly a number of items on her financial disclosure forms from 1978 through 1983. The committee's vote, reportedly 8-2, was taken in secret.

No action was taken against Ferraro before her term expired January 3, 1985. As Walter F. Mondale's running mate she had not sought reelection. The panel decided the House would not have time to act on the complaint against her while she was still a member.

The forty-six-page report also concluded that Ferraro failed to meet the standards necessary for claiming to exempt her husband's financial interests from her financial disclosure forms. But the panel did not investigate that question.

Ferraro told reporters she felt "completely vindicated" by the ethics committee's report.

Hatfield

Sen. Mark O. Hatfield, R-Ore., was investigated in 1984 by the Senate Ethics Committee staff because of questions arising from his wife's business dealings with a Greek businessman, Basil A. Tsakos. Antoinette Hatfield had received $55,000 from Tsakos in connection with a trans-African pipeline project. Hatfield, chairman of the Senate Appropriations Committee, insisted that the payment had been for legitimate work his wife had done on the project. He later said it had been "a mistake" for his wife to take the money while he was supporting the pipeline in Congress. The Ethics Committee found there was insufficient evidence of wrongdoing against Hatfield to justify a full-scale inquiry.

Hatfield's finances came under scrutiny again in 1991-92 following newspaper reports that the senator neglected to disclose nearly $9,300 in gifts from funds controlled by the president of the University of South Carolina, which had given Hatfield's son a $15,000 scholarship. The school received a $16.3 million federal grant in a bill the Appropriations Committee approved in 1986 while Hatfield was its chairman. The Ethics Committee

and the Justice Department were investigating these and similar allegations that Hatfield had accepted loans, gifts, and other favors from persons or organizations with an interest in legislation.

Weaver

The ethics committee concluded in 1986 that Rep. James Weaver, D-Ore., violated House rules when he borrowed campaign funds to speculate in the commodities market, but it recommended against punishment.

In a unanimous decision, the ethics committee found that Weaver, in borrowing $81,667 from campaign funds in 1981-84 for commodity market trades, had violated a House rule against using campaign funds for anything other than "bona fide campaign purposes." His reports on commodity trading, listed only in broad summaries, violated a second rule requiring details of each transaction to be reported on annual financial statements that members were required by law to file.

Weaver variously described the $81,667 in borrowings either as repayment to him for earlier loans he had made to the campaign or as loans he meant to repay—with interest and, if lucky, profits from his investments.

Because Weaver had reported his borrowings and made partial disclosure of his investments on his campaign and financial-worth reports, the committee ruled out sanctions.

"There was no evidence of an intent to avoid public notice" of the loans, the panel's report said. As for the commodities trading, it added, "disclosure was attempted—albeit inadequately."

The committee's 258-page report, released October 7, 1986, ended an eight-month probe. During that period, Weaver won Oregon's Democratic nomination for the Senate and then abruptly dropped out in August, citing the cloud of the unresolved ethics case. He retired from the House in January 1987 after six terms.

Fiedler

The Los Angeles district attorney dropped political corruption charges against Rep. Bobbi Fiedler, R-Calif., on February 19, 1986, saying that the evidence was "not sufficient" to pursue the case.

Fiedler, who unsuccessfully sought the GOP nomination for the U.S. Senate seat held by Democrat Alan Cranston, had been indicted January 23, along with an aide, on charges of violating an obscure California law by offering a rival candidate money to withdraw from the GOP primary. The statute, passed in 1893, apparently had never been used in criminal proceedings.

Boner

An investigation into allegations against Bill Boner, D-Tenn., was ended when he left the House in 1987 to become mayor of Nashville. The ethics committee December 15 released an inconclusive report on allegations against Boner.

The report left many questions unresolved, the committee said, because the inquiry was incomplete when Boner left Congress and the committee thus lost the power to continue investigating him.

Ethics committee chairman Dixon denied suggestions that the committee deliberately delayed the release of the report until after Boner was elected mayor of Nashville in a September 22 election.

The committee began its inquiry into Boner in February 1986. For a year beginning in April 1986, the investigation was suspended at the request of Justice Department officials. It was resumed after Justice announced it would not seek indictments.

The report offered no definitive conclusion on most charges that Boner broke a variety of House rules. It also included no response from Boner.

The staff report did conclude that Boner violated House rules when he used campaign funds to pay for a side trip he and his wife took from Taiwan to Hong Kong, and when he accepted use of a speedboat from a Nashville company for two years without reporting it as a gift.

The staff did not complete its investigation of charges by a defense contractor, who was a former friend of Boner, that he paid the representative nearly $50,000 in bribes by paying Boner's wife legal fees for work she never did. But the staff report suggested that Boner's dealings with the contractor "could be construed by reasonable persons as influencing the performance of his governmental duties."

St Germain

After a fourteen-month investigation, the ethics panel April 15, 1987, absolved Fernand J. St Germain, D-R.I., of allegations that he grew rich through abuse of his office. The committee did find that the chairman of the Banking, Finance, and Urban Affairs Committee repeatedly violated provisions of the 1977 House ethics code and the 1978 Ethics in Government Act, which required members to disclose their finances annually. But it recommended no punishment. St Germain hailed the report as a total vindication.

The ethics committee report did not dispute the accuracy of 1985 articles in the *Wall Street Journal* that led to the inquiry. The report's 50 pages of text and 1,355 pages of supporting material further documented the newspaper's contention that St Germain, who boasted of his working-class background, had built a multimillion-dollar fortune with what the *Journal* called "lots of investment help from people and institutions that have benefited from his official actions."

Summarizing the various violations, the panel concluded that "the identified improprieties do not rise to such a level warranting further action by this committee." As for the potentially more damaging allegations of abuse of office for personal gain, the panel said those "were not substantiated by clear and convincing evidence."

Earlier in 1987 more than one-fourth of St Germain's Democratic colleagues had voted against his reelection as Banking chairman. He won, 182-70, but lost his House seat in a November 1988 upset.

As Banking Committee chairman, St Germain had played a major role in the regulatory changes that helped to bring about the savings and loan industry collapse as well as the investigation of five senators' involvement in the rescue of one of the S&Ls. *("Keating Five," Chapter 10, p. 117)*

Oakar

Questions about Rep. Mary Rose Oakar's payroll led to allegations of conflict of interest and fraud. After an informal review, the ethics committee June 17, 1987, found that the Ohio Democrat broke House rules and federal laws when she paid a former staff member more than $45,000 in salary for nearly two years after the aide had moved to New York.

Personnel rules formulated by the House Administration Committee on which Oakar sat required House employees to work in Washington or in a member's district. Members certified monthly that their payroll was in compliance. Federal law prohibited false claims against the government, under penalty of up to five years in prison and a $10,000 fine.

Oakar was directed to repay the funds, which she said she had already done. Beyond that, the committee concluded, "no disciplinary action is warranted in this matter." In addition, the committee absolved Oakar of any improprieties related to her purchase of a town house with a second aide, who had been given a $10,000-a-year raise the same month they purchased the property.

Sue Klemens

Banking Committee Chairman Fernand J. St Germain, D-R.I., lost his House seat in a November 1988 upset after an ethics committee investigation of his behavior.

Stallings

In a report issued October 19, 1987, the ethics panel concluded that Rep. Richard Stallings had violated House rules by improperly borrowing campaign funds to buy a car and lend money to an aide. The committee issued a letter rebuking him but called for no other disciplinary action.

While the panel concluded Stallings's loans did not meet the rules criterion of being for use solely by the campaign, it concluded that the violation arose from a misunderstanding—Stallings's incorrect assumption that the loans were governed by a less-restrictive federal law allowing campaign funds to be used for "any legal purpose."

Stallings's problems occurred because he reported the $5,800 in borrowing on his July 1987

Federal Election Commission report. The same report showed that Stallings had repaid part of the loan with interest. The ethics committee accepted Stallings's assertion that he did not intend to avoid public disclosure of the loans.

The issue was politically sensitive for the Idaho Democrat because of his narrow 1984 victory over former Republican member George Hansen, who was convicted that year for failing to report $334,000 in loans and profits from 1978 to 1981. *(Hansen reprimand, p. 42)*

Murphy

Accepting the recommendation of its ethics committee, the House December 18, 1987, voted 324-68 to reprimand Austin J. Murphy, D-Pa., for diverting government resources to his former law firm, for allowing another member to vote for him on the House floor, and for keeping a "no-show" employee on his payroll. *(Murphy reprimand, p. 42)*

Wright

The formal investigation into the finances of Speaker Jim Wright, D-Texas, opened in 1988, topping a heavy agenda of congressional ethics issues. The investigation of Wright, in his second year leading the House, carried over into the next Congress and ultimately led to Wright's resignation in 1989. *(Wright resignation, p. 20)*

Coelho

Democratic Whip Tony Coelho, California, abruptly resigned from the House June 15, 1989, putting an end to questions about his financial dealings. Coelho's resignation was followed by Wright's five days later. *(Coelho resignation, p. 19)*

Sunia

Fofo I.F. Sunia, the Democratic delegate from American Samoa, pleaded guilty on August 3, 1988, to charges of conspiring to defraud the government by keeping on his House payroll "ghost employees" who did no congressional work. The House ethics committee had opened a preliminary investigation of Sunia's payroll practices in October 1987, but Sunia's resignation on September 6, 1988, ended its jurisdiction over him.

Swindall

Rep. Pat Swindall, R-Ga., was indicted October 17, 1988, on charges that he lied about a transaction in which he almost borrowed money that allegedly came from illegal drug profits. Swindall was defeated for reelection the next month.

Rose

The ethics panel concluded in 1988 that Rep. Charlie Rose, N.C., violated House rules by putting campaign funds to personal use and by failing to report certain aspects of his financial affairs. But the panel recommended no punishment.

The committee announced its conclusion March 23, when it sent Rose a formal "letter of reproval" for breaking House rules. But it said it believed formal sanctions were not warranted because of mitigating circumstances.

The Rose investigation was begun in response to a complaint filed in October 1986. In its report, released March 31, the panel concluded that Rose had wrongly borrowed $63,995 from his campaign in eight transactions from 1978 to 1985 and had improperly put up a $75,000 certificate of deposit held by his campaign as collateral for a personal loan.

In both cases, the panel said, Rose violated a

House rule that barred members from converting campaign funds to personal use and required that funds be used solely for "bona fide campaign purposes."

The committee also concluded that Rose violated House rules by failing to include in House financial disclosure reports the loans from his campaign and others from several banks. Although it never spelled out which mitigating circumstances led it to conclude formal punishment of Rose was not warranted, the committee noted that he had voluntarily amended his financial disclosure forms and had repaid the money.

Ford

Almost four years after he was accused of influence buying, Rep. Harold E. Ford still faced the prospect of a second trial after the first ended April 27, 1990, with a deadlocked jury in Memphis. Government prosecutors planned to seek another trial of the Tennessee Democrat.

Neither Ford nor any of his three codefendants testified during seven weeks of arguments. The four were indicted April 24, 1987, on nineteen counts of bank, mail, and tax fraud, based on accusations that they participated in an influence-buying scheme.

The trial had been delayed because of a change in venue from Knoxville to Memphis, Ford's hometown. Prosecutors filed motions to move the second trial away from Memphis.

Ford sought to turn his trial to political advantage among Memphis's blacks, repeatedly accusing federal prosecutors of waging a "personal racial vendetta" against him. Shortly after he was indicted, he told a cheering crowd at Memphis's airport that the federal prosecutor "wants to destroy the black political power in Tennessee."

While under indictment, Ford, first elected to the House in 1974, had to give up his chairmanship of the Ways and Means Subcommittee on Human Resources. He won reelection to his seat in November 1990, but his 65 percent showing was his worst since 1976.

Gingrich

The House ethics committee on March 7, 1990, dropped its investigation of House Republican Whip Newt Gingrich of Georgia after a yearlong review of a torrent of allegations.

Dismissing two formal complaints filed by Rep. Bill Alexander, D-Ark., the panel said in its report, "The committee is of the firm view that no adequate basis exists for initiating a preliminary inquiry. . . .

"The facts alleged in the complaints, even if true, have been generally deemed not to state violations" of House rules or law, said the Committee on Standards of Official Conduct. The panel did, however, scold Gingrich for relatively minor violations: an omission from his financial disclosure form and an aide's misuse of congressional stationery.

But the committee found no impropriety in the central focus of the complaint: a partnership, financed largely by his political backers, set up to promote a 1984 book cowritten by Gingrich.

Interest in the case was high because Gingrich instigated the 1988-89 investigation that led to the resignation of Speaker Jim Wright of Texas. At a news conference March 8, Gingrich dismissed the accusations as a "political smear. . . . I am glad the committee was thorough, and I am happy the charges have been exposed as politically inspired nonsense." He narrowly won reelection the following November.

The controversy surrounding Gingrich's book deal began two days before his election as whip when the *Washington Post* on March 20, 1989, published an article detailing the formation of a partnership to promote Gingrich's book, *A Window of Opportunity*. The partnership, managed by

Congressional Quarterly

The ethics committee found no impropriety in the financing arrangements for a book cowritten by House Republican Whip Newt Gingrich, Ga., shown here with his wife Marianne.

Gingrich's wife, Marianne, raised $105,000 to supplement the publisher's meager promotional budget. The enterprise had twenty-two partners, including fourteen who had also made political contributions to Gingrich.

Alexander filed a complaint with the committee April 11, raising questions about whether the arrangement was a means to circumvent House rules on outside income, acceptance of gifts, and conversion of campaign funds or government resources to personal use. Alexander amended his complaint in July and again in October, when he added a long list of allegations unrelated to the book deal.

Among them, the complaint cited Gingrich's failure to mention on his annual financial disclosure report a mortgage he cosigned with his daughter when she bought a house. The complaint also alleged that Gingrich improperly used official stationery to help recruit cruise participants for a Florida travel agency. An aide sent a letter provid-

ing information about a senior citizens' cruise the agency was sponsoring.

Alexander's initial complaint was reviewed by the ethics committee staff, which concluded that many of the allegations were conjectural and that others were not supported by facts, were based on unusual legal arguments, or were accompanied by no facts that amounted to rule violations. The staff concluded in a June 1989 memo that the reams of paper provided by Alexander did not meet the threshold required for opening a preliminary investigation: that the allegations "merit further inquiry."

The same conclusion was reached by the committee's outside counsel in the case, the Chicago law firm of Phelan, Pope, & John, which also handled the Wright investigation. In October the firm presented the committee with its conclusion that there was no basis for opening a formal investigation.

After further questioning of Gingrich, the committee concurred and voted 11-0 on March 7 to dismiss all of Alexander's allegations. "Representative Alexander's complaint asserts that the partnership was, in fact, a scheme whereby influential friends of the Gingriches sought to funnel to them either gifts, campaign contributions or both," the committee report said. "In the committee's view, there is no support for this proposition."

The committee did conclude, however, that Gingrich should have reported his participation in his daughter's home purchase and it directed him to amend his financial disclosure forms to include the transaction. The panel also concluded that a Gingrich aide violated House rules in sending out the cruise promotion on official stationery under the congressional frank.

Gingrich said he had not known of the mailing and that neither he nor the aide profited from it. But the committee told Gingrich "[you are] remiss in your oversight and administration of your congressional office" and directed him to guard against future abuse of mail and office resources.

Stangeland

The Minnesota Democratic Farmer-Labor party the week of April 2, 1990, filed a complaint with the House ethics committee against Minnesota Republican Rep. Arlan Stangeland over a series of telephone calls Stangeland charged to his House credit card. The committee took no action against Stangeland, who lost his 1990 reelection bid.

In a January story, the *St. Cloud Times* reported that Stangeland made 341 long-distance calls, at a cost of $762, to or from phones of a Virginia woman who Stangeland said was a friend and lobbyist. Although he initially said that some of the calls may have been personal, Stangeland later said that all were made for business reasons. A former staff aide, he said, stole phone records from his office to try to smear him.

Dyson

The House ethics committee on February 2, 1990, dropped an investigation into election and sex discrimination accusations against Roy Dyson, D-Md. A Republican official had filed the complaint just before election day 1988, alleging that Dyson misused official funds for campaign purposes and discriminated against women in hiring.

Dyson's office practices had been thrust into the public eye in mid-1988 when his administrative aide, Tom Pappas, committed suicide after a *Washington Post* article reported on his unorthodox personnel practices. Despite the dismissal of the charges, ethics remained a major issue in Dyson's unsuccessful bid for reelection in November 1990. *(See Chapter 7, p. 90.)*

Fauntroy

The Justice Department, after deciding not to prosecute Del. Walter E. Fauntroy, D-D.C., on allegations of payroll padding, referred the case to the House ethics committee in May 1990. The committee took no action against Fauntroy, who gave up his seat to run unsuccessfully for mayor of Washington.

Fauntroy, the District of Columbia's nonvoting delegate, had been the subject of a fifteen-month federal investigation concerning allegations that he improperly kept Thomas John Savage, son of Illinois Democratic Rep. Gus Savage, on his payroll at the same time the younger Savage was living in Chicago and running for the Illinois legislature. House rules required staff members to work in Washington, D.C., or in the representative's district.

The ethics committee dismissed charges against Gus Savage in 1990 after he apologized to a woman who had complained that he sexually harassed her. *(Savage case, Chapter 7, p. 91)*

R. Michael Jenkins

Sen. Alfonse M. D'Amato, R-N.Y., was rebuked in 1991 by the Senate Ethics Committee for running his office in an "improper and an inappropriate manner."

Flake

The government dropped embezzlement and tax evasion charges against New York Democratic Rep. Floyd H. Flake on April 3, 1991, after a federal judge barred what prosecutors called the "heart" of the government's case concerning financial dealings for a housing project sponsored by a church Flake had headed for fifteen years. The indictment alleged that Flake siphoned off $75,000 in transportation funds from the Allen Senior Citizens Apartments and used $66,000 in other church funds for personal purposes.

After the three-week trial ended, jurors told reporters that they found the government's case weak. Much of it was based on confusing financial

records and testimony from church members sympathetic to the Flakes.

Prosecutors denied allegations by Flake, who is black, that racism and politics may have been behind the charges against him.

As pastor of the Allen African Methodist Episcopal church, Flake had organized efforts to obtain projects to assist local low-income residents. One of his successes was a $10 million federal grant to the church to build the three-hundred-unit seniors' housing project.

D'Amato

The Senate Ethics Committee rebuked Sen. Alphonse M. D'Amato, R-N.Y., on August 2, 1991, for running his office in an "improper and an inappropriate manner." At the same time it closed its nineteen-month investigation into sixteen allegations that D'Amato had been influenced by campaign contributors and favor-seeking family members. The committee said it found no or insufficient evidence to support the charges, which initially had been filed by Mark Green, D'Amato's 1986 Democratic opponent.

The most-publicized allegations suggested that D'Amato had improperly pressured Housing and Urban Development Department officials to finance housing projects that benefited his relatives and political contributors. The *New York Times* reported that D'Amato in March 1984 wrote to HUD in support of a Buffalo housing renovation project whose partners included two of his political backers, Angelo Sedita and Peter Elia. *Newsday* reported that D'Amato, in a July 1986 letter, urged HUD to finance a project at Sackets Harbor in upstate New York represented by his brother Armand's law firm and developed by a construction firm whose executives were political contributors.

D'Amato said that he supported projects that benefited his constituents based "solely on merit and need." He said that HUD documents indicating he had requested funding for certain projects in Puerto Rico were mistaken. His support for the Sackets Harbor project predated the involvement of his political contributors, he said.

D'Amato also was accused of helping Wedtech, the Bronx company at the center of the convictions of two New York House members, Democrats Mario Biaggi and Robert Garcia, in return for $30,000 in illegal campaign contributions, and of being the beneficiary of a system under which Unisys, a defense contractor with offices in New York, told executives to donate thousands of dollars to D'Amato's campaign and then to seek reimbursement. D'Amato said he did not know about either contribution scheme.

The *Wall Street Journal* reported that D'Amato, as chairman of the Senate subcommittee overseeing the securities industry in 1985, dropped his backing for legislation restricting high-risk "junk bonds" after receiving $70,000 in donations from the pioneers of junk-bond financing, Drexel Burnham Lambert Inc. D'Amato said there was no connection between the contributions and his position on the legislation.

The Ethics Committee rebuked D'Amato for allowing his brother to misuse his office in behalf of the Unisys Corp. The senator said that what his brother did was "wrong, absolutely wrong." But he said, "I should have known about it.... I'm responsible."

Concerning the allegations of help for contributors in Puerto Rico, the committee said its investigations were hampered because essential witnesses invoked the Fifth Amendment to avoid testifying.

CHAPTER 7

Danger Zones:

Sex and Alcohol

The temptations of the flesh can be fatal attractions for members of Congress. Despite the obvious dangers, several members have become ensnared in sex scandals that ruined or damaged their careers.

Among the most publicized downfalls were those of House committee chairmen Wilbur D. Mills, D-Ark., in 1974 and Wayne L. Hays, D-Ohio, in 1976. Mills cavorted with a stripper, a lapse he blamed on alcoholism, and Hays allegedly put his mistress on the House payroll.

Other congressional leaders have suffered loss of reputation or higher office after their years on Capitol Hill. The extramarital affairs of presidents John F. Kennedy (with actress Marilyn Monroe, among others) and Lyndon B. Johnson were exposed after they left the Senate. Former senator Gary Hart's affair with model Donna Rice forced him to quit the 1988 presidential race.

Former Senate Armed Services Committee chairman John G. Tower, R-Texas, lost his nomination as secretary of defense in the Bush administration, largely because of his reputation as a "womanizer" and alcohol abuser. It was the first rejection of a cabinet nominee since 1959 and the first ever at the start of a new president's administration.

In her 1991 book *Scandal: The Crisis of Mistrust in American Politics,* Suzanne Garment recounts a couple of notorious congressional episodes from the nineteenth century. In one, Rep. Dan Sickles, D-N.Y., shot and killed Phillip Barton Key, son of the *Star-Spangled Banner* author, for having an affair with his wife. Teresa Sickles's lurid confession made headlines and her husband successfully claimed temporary insanity to win acquittal in the case.

Another "portentous sign of the times" Garment cited is the 1893 breach-of-promise suit by the mistress of Rep. William Breckinridge, D-Ky. Breckinridge lost his reelection campaign after feminist Susan B. Anthony led crowds of women into protesting his sexual behavior.

CASES IN THE 1970s

While they were not exactly rare in the past, sexual escapades involving members of Congress have become even more common since the 1970s, homosexual as well as heterosexual. Reports of illicit drug use also have increased, rivaling the more prevalent cases of alcohol abuse.

Besides Hays, three other House members were involved in 1976 sex scandals: John Young, D-Texas, Joe D. Waggonner, Jr., D-La., and Allan T. Howe, D-Utah. House aide Colleen Gardner charged that Young kept her on the payroll primarily to have sex with him. Waggonner was arrested in Washington on charges of soliciting a police decoy for purposes of prostitution. Howe was convicted July 23, 1976, in Salt Lake City for soliciting two policewomen posing as prostitutes. The House took no action against Young, Waggonner, or Howe.

Another House member, J. Herbert Burke, R-Fla., pleaded guilty and was fined $150 in September 1978 on charges stemming from his arrest the previous May 27 at a nude go-go bar in Dania, Florida. He was charged with intoxication, resisting arrest without violence, and trying to influence a witness to lie about the incident.

Michael J. "Ozzie" Myers, D-Pa., who was later expelled from the House after being convicted in the Abscam investigation, pleaded no contest in April 1979 to a disorderly conduct charge. Myers allegedly had attacked a security guard and a female cashier at an Arlington, Virginia, hotel bar on January 16. He received a suspended six-month jail term.

Kennedy

The assassinations of his brothers John and Robert had thrust Sen. Edward M. Kennedy, D-Mass., into the forefront of the 1972 presidential election. But a third tragedy, the death of a young woman in his car, kept Kennedy out of that race and may have cost him his strong effort in 1980 to wrest the nomination from incumbent Jimmy Carter.

Criticism that he showed poor judgment and even cowardice in leaving the scene of the accident continued to dog Kennedy into the 1990s, despite his reelection to the Senate several times in the interval.

The accident happened in July 1969 when the senator's car plunged off a narrow bridge, drowning Mary Jo Kopechne, 28, a former secretary and campaign worker for Kennedy's brother Robert, a U.S. senator from New York who had been killed the previous year while seeking the Democratic presidential nomination. The car sank, upside down, in a tidal pond on Chappaquiddick Island off the coast of Martha's Vineyard in Massachusetts.

Kennedy was slightly injured in the crash, which police said happened between midnight and 1 a.m. July 19. He was able to escape from the vehicle and swim to safety, but he did not report the accident until nearly nine hours later.

Kennedy pleaded guilty July 25 to leaving the scene of an accident and received a two-month suspended jail sentence—the minimum permitted under the misdemeanor charge. Questions that remained not fully answered after Kopechne's death included:

- Why it took Kennedy between eight and nine hours to report the accident to police.
- The discrepancy between Kennedy's report to police that the accident occurred at about 11:15 p.m. July 18 and a report that his car was seen turning down Dike Road toward the bridge at 12:40 a.m.
- How Kennedy turned from a clearly marked asphalt road leading to the ferry he was attempting to reach and onto an unmarked dirt road leading to a beach.
- Why Kennedy did not approach any of several homes near the accident scene to seek help or report the accident.
- Who gave Kennedy a ride to his hotel after the accident and how they made the crossing since the ferry ceased operation at midnight.
- Why Edgartown Police Chief Dominick J. Arena did not seek to question persons who attended a party where Kennedy and

Rep. Wilbur D. Mills, D-Ark., is led on stage at a Boston burlesque show by stripper Fanne Foxe in 1974. Mills later resigned the chairmanship of the Ways and Means Committee and issued a statement that he was being treated for alcoholism.

Kopechne had been before the accident. The amount of alcohol the senator might have consumed, and his condition to drive after the party, were possible factors in the drowning.

Kennedy, in a dramatic twelve-minute nationwide television appearance the night of July 25, said that his failure to reporting the fatal accident until the following morning was "indefensible." He asked the citizens of Massachusetts to help him decide whether he should resign. On July 30, after an outpouring of favorable telegrams and letters, Kennedy announced he would return to the Senate.

District Attorney Edmund Dinis of southeastern Massachusetts in August asked for a formal inquest and petitioned the courts of Pennsylvania, where Miss Kopechne was buried, for permission

for an autopsy. The autopsy request was denied. At Kennedy's request, the Supreme Judicial Court of Massachusetts October 30 ruled that the inquest would be closed.

The inquest report was made public April 29, 1970, along with a 764-page transcript of the hearings. The presiding judge, James A. Boyle, concluded that Kennedy "appears to have contributed" to Kopechne's death. Noting "inconsistencies and contradictions" in the testimony, Boyle said it appeared that Kennedy and his passenger had not been headed for the ferry to Edgartown and that the senator intentionally turned onto Dike Road. Even the speed of twenty miles an hour claimed by Kennedy would have been too fast for the narrow bridge and "at least be negligent and, possibly, reckless," the judge said.

AP/Wide World Photos   AP/Wide World Photos

Elizabeth Ray, who described herself as being unable to type, file, or answer the phone, was hired by Rep. Wayne Hays, D-Ohio, for a $14,000-a-year secretarial job. Hays, who later admitted he had had a "personal relationship" with Ray, resigned from Congress in 1974.

In a statement Kennedy said he had truthfully answered all questions at the inquest and that he rejected the judge's findings. He said he had two rum drinks during the party but was "absolutely sober" when he left with Kopechne.

Kennedy won reelection to six-year terms in 1970, 1976, 1982, and 1988. His prospects for running again in 1994 were clouded by another incident, one that took place in 1991. *(See 1990s cases, p. 93)*

Mills

Publicity about the relationship between Wilbur Mills, the influential chairman of the House Ways and Means Committee, and Argentine striptease dancer Fanne Foxe began with a bizarre incident the night of October 9, 1974. Police stopped Mills's car along the Potomac River tidal basin at 2 a.m. after noticing that it had been speeding. A woman, later identified as Foxe, jumped from the car and into the water but was rescued by a policeman.

Police reports said Mills's face was scratched and bleeding and that he appeared to be intoxicated.

The incident was expected to harm Mills's chances for reelection the following month from his Arkansas district, but he won comfortably. During the campaign he joked about it with his constituents, warning them not to drink with foreigners.

Mills's congressional relations slowly improved after the election but then were seriously damaged November 30 when he appeared on a Boston burlesque stage with Foxe to praise her dance performance.

In early December the House Democratic Caucus enlarged the Ways and Means Committee from twenty-five to thirty-seven members and stripped it of its control of Democratic committee assignments. It was clear that Mills would have been defeated in the caucus if he tried to retain his chairmanship.

On December 3 Mills entered Bethesda Naval Hospital, reportedly suffering from exhaustion. "He was one of the greatest congressmen of my generation," said Speaker Carl Albert, D-Okla., "but he is a sick man."

Mills later formally resigned his chairmanship and issued a statement that he was being treated for alcoholism. He did not seek reelection in 1976.

Hays

A newspaper story touched off the sex-and-public-payroll scandal involving Ohio's Wayne Hays, the powerful chairman of the Committee on House Administration. The *Washington Post* on May 23, 1976, quoted Elizabeth Ray as saying that in April 1974 Hays gave her a $14,000-a-year job on his committee in exchange for sexual favors. Ray described herself as totally unqualified for an office job: "I can't type. I can't file. I can't even answer the phone."

Hays at first denied the Ray charge but then admitted to the House May 25 that he had had a "personal relationship" with Ray. He denied, however, that he had hired her to be his mistress.

Coming only two years after the Wilbur Mills-Fanne Foxe scandal, the sensational Hays-Ray publicity inspired editorial cartoons showing *Congressional Quarterly* being featured on newsstands as an "adult" publication.

Pressure built up quickly in the House to oust Hays from his leadership positions. On June 3

he relinquished his chairmanship of the Democratic Congressional Campaign Committee. Hays won renomination to his House seat in a close Democratic primary in Ohio's Eighteenth District June 8. Then, bowing to pressure from the House Democratic leadership, Hays resigned as chairman of the House Administration Committee June 18 and on August 13 announced he would not run for reelection to Congress in November. On September 1 Hays resigned. The ethics panel then voted, 12-0, to end its investigation of him.

CASES IN THE 1980s

The name of Vice President Dan Quayle, then a Republican House member from Indiana, was linked to one of the first congressional sex scandals of the 1980s—one involving a female lobbyist who later posed for *Playboy*. Quayle denied any personal relationship with the woman, Paula Parkinson, who was dating another congressman at the time. *(Evans-Parkinson case, Chapter 5, p. 52)*

Even the 1980 Abscam bribery investigation had a sex angle. Rita Jenrette, the wife of one of those convicted, Rep. John W. Jenrette, Jr., D-S.C., told the press that she and her husband had once made love on the Capitol steps. She later posed for *Playboy* and John Jenrette entered an alcoholism program. *(Abscam probe, p. 63)*

The House in the 1980s began to show less tolerance of sexual misbehavior. Three members, including avowed homosexuals Barney Frank and Gerry E. Studds, both Massachusetts Democrats, were reprimanded or censured. Studds was censured in 1983 along with Daniel B. Crane, R-Ill., for having sexual relationships with teenage congressional pages, Studds with a male and Crane with a female. Frank was reprimanded in 1990 for his relationship with a male prostitute. *(Studds, Crane cases, p. 40; Frank case, p. 43)*

Bauman

Rep. Robert E. Bauman, R-Md., pleaded innocent October 3, 1980, to a misdemeanor charge of sexual solicitation and agreed to undergo court-supervised treatment for alcoholism in return for dropping the charge. Bauman was accused of committing oral sodomy on a teenage boy in Washington, D.C.

Bauman was defeated for reelection by Democrat Roy Dyson, whose own House office was later touched by an incident with overtones of homosexuality. A male staff member, Tom Pappas, committed suicide in New York following newspaper disclosure of bizarre demands that Pappas had made of his male subordinates. Dyson lost his 1990 bid for reelection. *(Pappas, Chapter 8, p. 103)*

Hinson

Jon C. Hinson, R-Miss., resigned from the House April 13, 1981, after being arrested in a Capitol Hill men's room February 4 on a misdemeanor charge of attempted sodomy. He received a suspended thirty-day jail sentence and a year's probation after pleading no contest and agreeing to continue medical treatment.

Hinson had disclosed in 1980, while seeking election to a second House term, that he had been arrested in 1976 for committing an indecent act in a homosexual trysting place in Arlington, Virginia. He also disclosed that he had been among the survivors of a 1977 fire at a Washington theater frequented by homosexuals, but he denied being a homosexual.

Richmond

Fred W. Richmond, D-N.Y., resigned from the House in 1982 after pleading guilty to marijuana possession and other charges. In an earlier brush with the law, Richmond pleaded innocent in 1978 to a charge that he solicited homosexual sex for pay. Because he had acknowledged the truth of the morals charge, the plea was a technicality to make him eligible for the District of Columbia's first-offender program. The charges were dropped May 3, 1978, after he completed the program. *(Richmond resignation, p. 73)*

McKinney

Stewart B. McKinney, R-Conn., died May 7, 1987, of complications from acquired immune deficiency syndrome (AIDS). He had served in the House since 1971.

McKinney's doctor said that the representative, who had a history of heart ailments, could have contracted the disease from contaminated blood transfusions received during heart bypass surgery in 1979.

Homosexual acts were a more common means of transmission of the AIDS virus, and the *Washington Post* reported that sources in the Washington, D.C., gay community said McKinney was known to have had homosexual relations.

Konnyu

In August 1987 the *San Jose Mercury-News* reported complaints against Rep. Ernie Konnyu, R-Calif., from two former aides and an E. F. Hutton lobbyist. One aide said Konnyu admonished her to move her name tag so that it did not draw attention to her small "boobs." She was dismissed in June 1987.

The other ex-aide said that Konnyu had told her in a job interview to "stand up and turn around. . . . I want to see what you look like," and said she should wear high heels and frilly blouses. She was fired after she refused his invitations to go out after work.

Witnesses said the Hutton lobbyist publicly scolded Konnyu in a restaurant after he touched

Marty LaVor   R. Michael Jenkins

Jim Bates, D-Calif., (left) and Ernie Konnyu, R-Calif., were accused of sexually harassing female congressional aides. An aide to Konnyu said she was told to wear frilly blouses and high heels. Former aides to Bates complained their boss patted them and made suggestive remarks. Both members lost their House seats.

her knee. Konnyu complained to her boss. He subsequently lost his seat in the 1988 election.

Lukens

Donald E. "Buz" Lukens, confronted with new allegations of sexual misconduct, resigned from Congress in 1990 rather than face ethics sanctions in his final days in the House.

The Ohio Republican, who lost his bid for reelection in a May primary, announced his resignation two days after the House ethics committee on October 22 adopted a resolution disclosing charges that he made "unwanted and unsolicited sexual advances to a congressional employee."

The panel had planned to look into the allegations, which centered on reports that Lukens had fondled and propositioned an elevator operator in the Capitol. Lukens did not comment but said in his resignation letter to Ohio Democratic governor Richard F. Celeste that he was leaving "for the

good of the Congress and the integrity of the institution."

The ethics committee first began investigating Lukens in August 1989, after his conviction in May of that year of contributing to the delinquency of a minor for having sex with a sixteen-year-old girl in Columbus, Ohio. He was sentenced to thirty days in jail and given a $500 fine.

Savage

In a report released February 2, 1990, the House ethics committee concluded that Gus Savage, D-Ill., made improper sexual advances to a young woman while on an official trip to Africa. The committee did not propose disciplinary action because Savage had apologized to the woman in writing.

The committee concluded the inquiry without a formal disciplinary hearing. The panel based its conclusion on interviews with Savage and others on the tour, and on a sworn deposition from the woman, a Peace Corps worker who was not further identified.

In his interview with the committee, Savage denied any impropriety—including the woman's allegations that he kissed her and asked her to spend the night with him. But Savage wrote to the woman November 20, 1989, saying: "I never intended to offend and was not aware that you felt offended at the time."

The committee concluded in its report, approved January 31, that "Rep. Savage did, in fact, make sexual advances to the Peace Corps volunteer." The report concluded that his actions were contrary to the House rule requiring members' behavior to "reflect creditably" on the House. "The committee clearly disapproves of Rep. Savage's conduct," the report said.

Accusations of impropriety by Savage surfaced in the *Washington Post* on July 19, 1989. Savage's problems, though, did not end with the committee's conclusion of its inquiry. His criticism of three colleagues who called for the investigation of him prompted the House on February 7 to consider revising its rules that allowed members to change their floor remarks before they were published in the *Congressional Record*. The proposal to review the rules was approved 373-30 after Savage's remarks were omitted from the *Record's* account of his February 1 speech, in which he contended that he was a victim of racism in politics and the media.

The three members who had asked for the investigation of Savage were Democrats Barney Frank of Massachusetts, Matthew F. McHugh of New York, and Patricia Schroeder of Colorado.

In his floor speech, Savage referred to Frank's admitted relationship with a male prostitute. "Believe it or not," he said, "among these self-appointed guardians of personal morality was one who since has admitted keeping and prostituting a homosexual." Frank's reprimand by the House came later.

Most members of Congress routinely edited their remarks before submitting them for the record, but they typically made minor changes, such as corrections of grammar, rather than wholesale deletions.

Bates

On October 18, 1989, the House ethics committee sent Jim Bates, D-Calif., a "letter of reproval" for sexually harassing women on his staff. Former aides had complained that Bates patted their buttocks, asked for hugs, and made suggestive remarks and gestures.

"Your improper conduct and concurrent violations of relevant standards deserve reproval," the committee said in its letter to Bates. It directed him to apologize formally to the complainants.

"I accept the committee's resolution of it and hope to put it behind me," Bates said. "Times are changing. Members of Congress will be carefully scrutinized on personal and professional behavior."

Adams

Faced with allegations that he sexually assaulted a young woman eighteen months earlier, Sen. Brock Adams, D-Wash., branded the charges as "absolutely false" on September 27, 1988. But he said he had made an "error in judgment" in allowing the woman to spend the night at his home.

The woman, Kari Tupper, then twenty-six, was the daughter of longtime friends of Adams, who had helped her to find jobs on Capitol Hill. She filed a complaint against Adams in July 1987, but the U.S. attorney declined to prosecute after reviewing the findings of a District of Columbia police investigation.

Adams and Tupper agreed that she spent the night at his house on March 27, 1987, while the senator's wife was out of town, but they differed about what happened. He said they met to discuss her job situation and that he let her stay the night because she was not feeling well. "I went to bed, alone," Adams said in a statement. "I did not sexually assault the woman."

Tupper told a friend that she had gone to his house not to discuss employment but to put an end to advances he had been making to her. She alleged that Adams drugged her and that the next thing she remembered was waking up to find Adams fondling her in bed, according to the police report. Two hospitals where Tupper was examined, however, said tests at the time showed no evidence of sexual intercourse or drugging.

Adams said after the case was closed that Tupper demanded $400,000 to avoid a civil suit. But her lawyer, Lawrence Baskir, said it was Adams's attorney who initiated the discussions of a settlement.

Tupper's allegations against Adams prompted a prolonged investigation by a newspaper in his state, the *Seattle Times,* which reported March 1, 1992, that it had found eight other women who said they were sexually harassed or abused by Adams. One said that she had been raped.

None of the women were publicly identified, but the newspaper said all had sworn to the truth of their statements and in most cases were willing to come forward and testify if necessary.

At a news conference with his wife at his side, Adams denounced the story as a fabrication but said he would not seek reelection in November.

CASES IN THE 1990s

The early 1990s brought a new round of sex scandals affecting individual senators, as well as complaints that Congress and especially the Senate were insensitive to women.

Women's groups complained about the treatment received by a witness, Anita F. Hill, during October 1991 Senate Judiciary Committee hear- ings on President Bush's nomination of federal judge Clarence Thomas to the Supreme Court. Several senators tried to discredit the testimony of Hill, a University of Oklahoma law professor, that Thomas sexually harassed her when they worked together at the Department of Education and the Equal Employment Opportunity Commission. Thomas, former EEOC chairman, categorically denied the allegations.

Republican senators and the White House attacked Hill's credibility, portraying her as a deluded, scorned woman. Underneath it all, and despite the fact that both Thomas and Hill were black, were Republican broadsides that Thomas was being attacked out of racism. Thomas himself bitterly categorized the hearings as "a high-tech lynching."

In the end the Senate confirmed Thomas on October 15 by 52-48. As a result of Hill's account and earlier dissatisfaction among Democrats with Thomas's reluctance to explain his judicial philosophy, it was the closest vote for a justice in more than a century.

The televised hearings, the most-watched ever for a Court nomination, aroused fierce nationwide differences of opinion about whether Hill or Thomas was telling the truth. Vendors sold T-shirts and buttons that said simply, "I Believe Her" or "I Believe Him."

One woman who came to Hill's aid was Wanda Baucus, wife of Sen. Max Baucus, D-Mont. She phoned her husband and other senators to help explain Hill's reasons for keeping silent ten years about the alleged harassment. Baucus told the *Washington Post* that she, too, had been harassed—by two senators—and had not gone public about it until then. The first incident happened before she was married and she said she did not report it because, like Hill, she wanted to keep her job. She told her husband about the other advance, which she said came from a senator they considered a friend.

Ken Heinen   AP/Wide World Photos

The sexual affairs of presidential contenders have been called to public attention, in large part, by supermarket tabloids. Former senator Gary Hart's affair with Donna Rice was exposed in 1987...

In early 1992 Democratic presidential candidate Bill Clinton, like Gary Hart five years earlier, was accused of marital infidelity. Former cabaret singer Gennifer Flowers claimed that she had a twelve-year affair with Arkansas Governor Clinton, who once worked in a Senate office. Flowers lost her state job a few days after she appeared on television to play tape recordings purporting to be intimate conversations between her and Clinton.

A major difference in the Hart and Clinton scandals was that Clinton's alleged affair was in the past while Hart's was ongoing. Hart dropped out of the presidential race in 1987 after his relationship with Donna Rice was exposed, while Clinton was staying in the 1992 race at least until after the New Hampshire primary. Clinton's wife, Hillary, supported his efforts to weather the storm of unfavorable publicity.

A relatively new and hitherto largely ignored type of magazine—the lurid supermarket tabloid—played a significant role in bringing both affairs to public attention. After major newspapers disclosed

that Hart and Rice spent a night together at his Washington townhouse, a tabloid published color photos taken earlier of the pair on a yacht called *Monkey Business*. And a similar tabloid broke the Clinton story after reportedly paying Flowers large sums of money for her interviews and exclusive rights to her tapes.

Kennedy Redux

Sen. Edward Kennedy drew publicity in a new sex case in 1991, one that involved his nephew, William Kennedy Smith. A twenty-nine-year-old Florida woman told police she was raped by Smith at the family's Palm Beach compound on March 30. The senator and his son Patrick, a member of the Rhode Island legislature, were also staying at the mansion for the Easter weekend.

The allegations and ensuing televised trial involving the famous political family attracted worldwide attention throughout the rest of the year. One aspect that the media found particularly intriguing was that the fifty-nine-year-old senator reportedly

R. Michael Jenkins   AP/Wide World Photos

. . .and in 1992 Gennifer Flowers broke her story of an alleged twelve-year affair with Arkansas governor Bill Clinton.

awakened his son and nephew at 11 p.m. on Good Friday to go to Au Bar for a beer. There they met the woman who accused Smith of raping her after they returned to the mansion.

The woman said that the senator at one point appeared wearing only a shirt, but Kennedy testified that it was a nightshirt. He and other family members said they heard no screams from outside the mansion where the alleged rape took place.

After hearing days of intensely explicit testimony, the jury acquitted Smith of the charges shortly before Christmas. As in the Thomas-Hill case, the public split deeply on whether the verdict was right or wrong. For some, the same "I Believe Her" or "I Believe Him" buttons from the Thomas hearings were usable. But for those who believed her in one case and him in the other, the buttons had to be more specific.

Most news media withheld the identity of Smith's accuser, and during her testimony her face was concealed electronically by a blue circle. But

afterward she revealed her own identity as Patricia Bowman, and she appeared on television to stand by her story. "I'm not a blue blob," Bowman said.

Kennedy, too, made an effort to compensate for the damage done to his reputation by the rape trial and other unfavorable publicity involving drinking and women. Speaking at Harvard in October 1991, before his nephew had been acquitted, the senator offered a public apology for "the faults in the conduct of my private life." His remarks were perceived as an acknowledgement that personal notoriety had reduced his effectiveness as a lawmaker and Democratic liberal. He pledged renewed commitment to "economic justice, progress and compassion."

As a member of the Judiciary Committee, Kennedy had said little during the Thomas-Hill hearings. The press attributed his unusual reticence to fear that he would draw attention—and ridicule—to unfavorable stories of his own relations with women.

R. Michael Jenkins   AP/Wide World Photos

Beauty queen Tai Collins told *Playboy* magazine she had an affair with Sen. Charles S. Robb, D-Va., when he was governor of Virginia. Robb said Collins had only given him a backrub; Collins posed for *Playboy* as the "woman Senator Charles Robb couldn't resist."

Robb

Old allegations against a member by marriage of another presidential family were revived with new vigor in 1991. And again *Playboy* magazine took advantage of a congressional scandal with a cover story about a woman who was totally uncovered on the inside pages.

The NBC program "Exposé" on April 28 alleged that Sen. Charles S. Robb, D-Va., had a sexual relationship with a former beauty queen and had seen cocaine used at a Virginia Beach party while he was the state's governor. Robb, son-in-law of the late president Lyndon Johnson, denied the reports as he had done in his 1988

Senate campaign.

But this time the allegations were more persistent. Tanquil "Tai" Collins, the former Miss Virginia-U.S.A., insisted she had a love affair with Robb in 1983 when she was twenty and he was forty-four. She told *Playboy* the affair lasted through most of 1984.

Robb conceded to reporters that he had accepted a massage from Collins in a New York hotel room in February 1984, but he denied that they made love.

Collins was featured in the October 1991 *Playboy* with a nine-page photo spread, billed on the cover as "The Woman Senator Charles Robb Couldn't Resist."

CHAPTER 8

Staff and Perks:

"The Last Plantation"

For all the glamor of working on Capitol Hill, congressional aides often face long hours, cramped quarters, and the sometimes whimsical demands of politicians at whose pleasure they serve. Some of the conditions they tolerate would be illegal in private industry, but Congress has exempted itself from many of the worker-protection laws it imposed on other employers.

That imperious treatment of people who work there has led the Hill's being called "the last plantation." In the 1990s, however, Congress deserved the epithet less than it did only a few years ago. More and more members have voluntarily complied with antidiscrimination hiring laws, and both the House and Senate have gradually given employees other protection.

But there were still discrepancies between public and private hiring and firing practices, and probably always would be. Members argued that they should not be regulated like private businesses because Congress's political nature required the freedom to hire politically loyal staffers. Members also feared that executive branch enforcement of such laws would violate the constitutional separation of powers.

One major event in late 1991 nudged both branches into greater realization that old rationales for exposing congressional and other public employees to unethical practices were no longer acceptable. That event was the furor over Anita Hill's assertions that she had been sexually harassed by Supreme Court nominee Clarence Thomas.

In the highly charged atmosphere after Thomas won confirmation, President George Bush signed a civil rights bill similar to one he had previously vetoed. The bill extended some protection against discrimination and workplace harassment to Senate and House employees.

Congress also moved, effective in 1991, to restrict some of the perquisites it had long enjoyed, and sometimes abused, such as honoraria, gifts, outside income, and taking jobs as lobbyists after leaving Congress. The Government Ethics Reform Act of 1989 applied most of the new restrictions to high-ranking staffers as well as to members.

Having a taxpayer-paid staff is itself one of the major perquisites of being a senator or representative. Many members view staff—especially large staff—as a symbol of prestige and importance. Similarly, many staffers feel that the more powerful the member or committee they work for, the more powerful they are.

CONGRESS EXEMPTS ITSELF FROM THE LAW OF GRAVITY AND FLOATS AWAY, RESOLVING THE ETHICAL PROBLEM OF CONGRESS EXEMPTING ITSELF FROM LAWS THAT APPLY TO EVERYBODY ELSE.

Sometimes a staffer abuses that power. And the growth of staff—to more than eleven thousand in 1989, not counting committee staff—has complicated Congress's job of policing the behavior of its employees, as well as its own treatment of them.

QUESTIONABLE HIRING PRACTICES

Many ethical problems concerning staff originate right at the first stage—in the hiring process. Who gets hired, or who gets turned away, determines to a large extent whether the member or committee will end up with an efficient, contented staff, or whether the choice eventually embroils the employer in controversy, disciplinary action, or even criminal proceedings.

Nepotism

One of the oldest sources of public dissatisfaction with congressional hiring practices—one now

largely under control—is nepotism. In the past it was common for members to use their staff allowances to hire spouses and other relatives and, in effect, supplement their own income.

The practice began to diminish on May 20, 1932, when the House quietly approved a resolution providing that "The Clerk of the House of Representatives is hereby authorized and directed to keep open for public inspection the payroll records of the disbursing officer of the House."

Few members on the floor understood the import of the resolution, which was adopted without debate. The next day, however, newspapers disclosed that ninety-seven members of the House devoted their clerk-hire allowance, in whole or in part, to paying persons having the same names as their own. Presumably these persons were relatives. The names were published, and "nepotism in Congress" became a subject of wide public discussion. At that time, however, nepotism was not illegal or even a violation of the standing rules.

Senate payroll information did not become

open until twenty-seven years later. On June 26, 1959, the Senate by voice vote ordered the Senate secretary to make public the name, title, salary, and employer of all the chamber's employees. Six months earlier Scripps-Howard newspapers had published a story by Vance Trimble that contained a lengthy list of relatives he said were employed in 1958 by members of Congress. Trimble had obtained the names by checking out similar names in public House and Senate records. He filed a court suit to gain access to Senate payroll records.

On February 23, 1959, the Associated Press published a list of sixty-five representatives who had persons with "the same or similar family name" on their January payrolls. Three members who were on the list denied that their payroll namesakes were in any way related to them.

One of the most notorious practicers of nepotism was Harlem Democrat Adam Clayton Powell, Jr., whom the House ultimately tried to exclude because of payroll and other abuses. Soon after his marriage in December 1960, Powell employed his Puerto Rican wife, Yvette Marjorie Flores, as a paid member of his congressional office staff. Mrs. Powell remained in Puerto Rico after the birth of a son in 1962, but she continued to draw a $20,578 annual salary as a clerk whose job was to answer mail from Spanish-speaking constituents.

The House in 1964 adopted a resolution aimed specifically at the Powell situation: it forbade members to hire employees who did not work either in the member's home district or in the representative's Washington, D.C., office. (That provision was made permanent in 1976.) Mrs. Powell, however, continued to live in Puerto Rico. Following a select committee investigation of the various charges against Powell, the House on March 1, 1967, refused to seat him. The Supreme Court ruled the House action unconstitutional, however, and Powell returned to Congress in 1969. *(Powell case, Chapter 1, p. 11)*

In 1967 Congress curbed nepotism in federal employment. It prohibited public officials, including members of Congress, from appointing or trying to promote the appointment of relatives within their own agency. The ban covered all officials, including the president, but it did not cover relatives already employed. And it did not prevent an official in one agency or one chamber of Congress from seeking to obtain employment for a relative in another agency or chamber.

The *New Member Orientation Handbook,* prepared for all new members and updated periodically by the Senate Rules Committee and the House Administration Committee, lists twenty-seven classifications of relatives whose employment by representatives and senators is prohibited by law (5 U.S.C. 3110). Certification of an employee's relationship to a member of Congress must be made on payroll authorizations by the employing member or by the committee or subcommittee chairman.

Some congressional spouses, among them Heather Foley, wife of House Speaker Thomas S. Foley, D-Wash., worked on the staff without pay and were not affected by the nepotism rule.

Discrimination

Women and blacks have been at a particular disadvantage in congressional hiring. They tended to be concentrated in low-paying jobs.

A 1990 study of House personal staff by Richard Shapiro and Maria Touya of the Congressional Management Foundation showed that even though there were three female employees for every two male employees, women were somewhat overrepresented in lower-paying jobs and underrepresented in higher-paying jobs. The same study found that black House staff members received 89 percent of the pay of their white counterparts and made up 9.4 percent of the total staff, while Hispanic staff earned 82 percent of the salaries of white staff. These differences in average salary were largely due to difference in positions held by minority staff as compared with white staff.

In enacting the 1991 civil rights law, the Senate voted to apply the provisions and other major antibias acts to Senate employees, allowing them redress through an internal process and a limited right of appeal in federal court. Senators would be personally liable for damages.

The act made House employees, already covered by antidiscrimination laws, eligible for damages due to intentional discrimination. But unlike their Senate counterparts, House employees would have to pursue their claims exclusively through an internal grievance procedure with no judicial review. And House members would not be liable for damages.

Civil rights protections were extended to congressional employees with physical disabilities when Congress passed the 1990 Americans with Disabilities Act. The law prohibits discrimination on the basis of disability in employment and public accommodations and requires public transportation systems, other public services, and telecommunications systems to be accessible to the physically disabled. Unlike the general public, however, congressional employees alleging discrimination may not sue their employer in federal court. Claims of discrimination in the Senate are investigated and adjudicated exclusively by the Ethics Committee or another entity the Senate designates. In the House, complaints are handled by the Office of Fair Employment Practices.

Other Violations

In the late 1980s the hiring practices of Rep. Mary Rose Oakar, D-Ohio, and Del. Walter E. Fauntroy, D-D.C., came under scrutiny. *(Details, Chapter 6, pp. 77, 81)*

The House ethics committee found that Oakar broke House rules and federal laws when she paid a former staff member more than $45,000 in salary for nearly two years after the aide had moved to New York. She was directed to repay the funds.

The Justice Department dropped its investigation of Fauntroy after finding insufficient evidence that he improperly kept the son of another House member on his payroll while the son was living in Chicago.

Other recent investigations have concerned aides' complaints of sex discrimination or sexual harassment. Two such allegations involved former House members Ernie Konnyu, R-Calif., in 1987 and Jim Bates, D-Calif., in 1988. *(Details, Chapter 7, p. 85)*

Poor physical working conditions on Capitol Hill also made the headlines in 1988. Employees of the House "folding room," who stuff envelopes with members' newsletters to constituents, were reported to work in "sweatshop" conditions. Workers complained of being forced to work seventy-hour weeks without overtime pay. A House committee found that folding-room employees worked in a cramped basement room with poor air circulation and that they were exposed to noxious fumes.

Complaint Procedures

Critics of congressional employment practices have argued that past procedures for bringing complaints against members—through the ethics committees—were poorly understood and little used. Aggrieved staffers were more likely to quit their jobs or go to the press with their complaints.

After a rash of such reports in the news media, the House in 1988 established new complaint procedures in House Rule 51, which protects House employees and job applicants against employment discrimination on the basis of race, color, national origin, religion, sex, handicap, or age. Members are allowed, however, to consider political affiliation and to refuse to hire persons from districts or states other than their own.

Robert G. "Bobby" Baker (right) resigned his post as secretary of the Senate in 1963 after influence-peddling charges were raised. Baker is shown here with his attorney, Edward Bennett Williams, before a 1964 Senate investigating committee.

The resolution also set up a special in-house office, the Office of Fair Employment Practices (OFEP), to investigate discrimination complaints and decide what remedy an employee deserves. Employees of the office work under the supervision of the clerk of the House, but they are appointed by the chairman and ranking minority member of the House Administration Committee.

Employees have 180 days to file a formal complaint, and the OFEP must first provide counseling and try to mediate the dispute before holding a formal hearing. OFEP decisions may be reviewed by an eight-member panel, composed of two Democratic and two Republican members of the House Administration Committee, two of the four elected officers of the House (who are appointed by the

Speaker), and two House employees appointed by the minority leader.

When the House passed the 1989 Minimum Wage Act increasing the minimum-wage level, it also extended to its employees (including folding-room employees) the rights and protections provided by the Fair Labor Standards Act of 1938—such as minimum wage, overtime compensation, and pay-equity measures.

The Civil Rights Act of 1991 kept in place the House grievance procedures and it established the Senate OFEP to administer the new grievance system in that chamber. The 180-day complaint filing period and counseling/mediation provision were similar to those for House employees. Either side could ask the Senate Ethics Committee to review the decision or could appeal it in federal court within ninety days.

A precedent for court action in such cases had been set in 1979 in a case settled out of court for an undisclosed sum of money. The suit had been filed in 1974 against former representative Otto E. Passman, D-La., by one-time aide Shirley Davis.

The Supreme Court ruling established the constitutional right of a congressional employee to sue a member of Congress for damages in sex-discrimination cases. However, the subsequent out-of-court settlement left open whether the Constitution's "speech or debate" clause immunizes members from such suits in some circumstances. *(Immunity, Chapter 9, p. 109)*

AIDES' MISUSE OF POWER

Just as members of Congress sometimes bring disgrace on their office, congressional employees have been known to overstep their authority, use their positions for personal gain, or otherwise embarrass the institution they were hired to serve.

Baker

Robert G. "Bobby" Baker began his Capitol Hill career as a teenage page in the Senate. Ambitious and aggressive, Baker rose to the position of secretary to the Senate majority, making himself right-hand man to his mentor, Majority Leader Lyndon B. Johnson, D-Texas, in the late 1950s. When he quit his post under fire a few years later, Baker on paper was worth $2 million, most of it gained, the subsequent court records showed, from combining law practice with influence peddling. The notoriety caused by the Baker case is credited with moving the Senate to create an ethics committee.

Baker resigned his Senate job in 1963 after a civil suit was brought against him, charging that he used his influence to obtain contracts for a vending machine concern in which he had a financial interest. Senate investigations conducted over the next two years concluded that Baker was guilty of "gross improprieties." The investigating committee recommended that the Senate require full financial disclosures by senators and top employees of the Senate.

Baker meanwhile was brought to trial on charges of income tax evasion, theft, and conspiracy to defraud the government. He was found guilty in January 1967; after appeals had been exhausted, he began his prison term four years later. The major charge on which he was found guilty was that he had collected more than $99,000 from a group of California savings and loan executives, ostensibly as campaign contributions, but in reality had kept about $80,000 for himself.

At the trial two of the California executives testified that in 1962 they gave Baker about $66,000 for campaign contributions to seven senators and one House member, Ways and Means Committee Chairman Wilbur D. Mills, D-Ark. Mills and one of the senators, Foreign Relations Committee Chairman J. W. Fulbright, D-Ark., testified that they had received none of the money. Defense counsel stipulated that none of the other six senators had received any of the funds. One of the savings and loan executives testified that Baker told him the California savings and loan associations could improve their standing in Congress with a "very impressive" contribution to certain senators and House members and could "win friends" in Congress at a time when a bill was pending to increase taxes on the associations.

Baker testified that he turned the money over to Sen. Robert S. Kerr, D-Okla., a power on the Senate Finance Committee, for his reelection campaign. Kerr was dead by the time Baker told his story.

Sweig

A congressional scandal that attracted nationwide attention when it was revealed in 1969 involved influence peddling in the office of Speaker John W. McCormack, D-Mass. In the end, one of his top aides, Dr. Martin Sweig, was convicted on July 9, 1970, of perjury, and on January 28, 1972, of misusing the Speaker's office to influence government decisions.

Sweig, who had worked for McCormack twenty-four years and was drawing an annual salary of $36,000 in 1969, was implicated with Nathan M. Voloshen, a New York City lawyer-lobbyist and longtime McCormack friend. On June 17, 1970, Voloshen pleaded guilty to charges of conspiring to use the Speaker's office to influence matters before federal government agencies and to three counts of lying to a federal grand jury about the charges.

Mack

John P. Mack, the top aide to the Speaker of the House, resigned in May 1989 because of a violent crime he committed sixteen years earlier. A little more than a month later, the Speaker himself, Jim Wright, D-Texas, resigned from Congress because of ethical problems of an entirely different nature.

Mack's assault on a woman when he was nineteen was far removed from the financial morass that led to Wright's departure. But many members said their constituents expressed more outrage over Wright's hiring of someone convicted of so heinous a crime than they did over his alleged income violations.

Mack, while managing a discount import store in Virginia in 1973, beat and stabbed a woman and left her for dead. He served twenty-seven months in a county jail and was paroled to a $9,000-a-year filing job in Wright's congressional office. At the time, Wright's daughter was married to Mack's brother.

The *Fort Worth Star-Telegram* in Wright's district published an account of Mack's criminal record in 1987, but it caused little stir. Mack offered to resign but Wright asked him to stay on. A longer account in the *Washington Post* on May 4, 1989, during the ethics investigation of Wright, brought an explosive reaction. The victim, Pamela Small, described the terrifying experience and for the first time allowed her name to be used. The *Post* subsequently published a full page of letters protesting Mack's rise to power.

Wright said that when he hired Mack he did not know the details of his crime. "I was willing to give this young man another chance," he said, "and in the intervening years I have never had occasion to regret it."

Pappas

Tom Pappas, the top assistant to Rep. Roy Dyson, D-Md., leaped to his death May 1, 1988, the day that the *Washington Post* published allegations by former aides that Pappas had made extreme demands on their personal loyalty and time. The story, based on interviews with former Dyson aides, portrayed Pappas as an office power who overshadowed Dyson and who pressured the young men he hired to socialize with him. The charges included claims that Pappas had told one aide not to date for a year, fired another after he refused to stay at a party, and told another that he would have to perform a striptease at an office retreat.

A spokeswoman for Dyson said all of the former aides quoted in the story had been fired and had "a bone to pick." Although the story was laden with suggestions of homosexual activity on the staff, Dyson firmly denied that either he or Pappas was homosexual. Dyson said he thought some of the complaints against Pappas were reported out of context.

LEGISLATIVE WORK VS. POLITICS

As Congress has eliminated or diminished some of the older problems of staff usage such as nepotism or favoritism, political work by staffers has emerged as a larger and more troublesome area of concern. The issue invariably comes up at election time when incumbents are accused of using congressional employees to help in the members' reelection campaigns.

When senators and representatives return home to campaign they take with them the customary entourage of staff aides, who must juggle their political work with their status as government employees paid with federal tax dollars. There is no specific federal law against performing political duties, although the practice is somewhat limited by rules in the House and, to a lesser extent, in the Senate.

In his book *In the Shadow of the Dome: Chronicles of a Capitol Hill Aide,* Mark Bisnow commented on the fine line between legislative work and politics:

> [Congress] by its nature is so intensely political that it becomes a practical impossibility to say in many instances where the discharge of official duties leaves off and aspirations to higher office (or reelection) begin. A congressman and his staff, for example, are not supposed to use office typewriters, photocopy machines, and phone lines to solicit financial contributions for election campaigns, but who is to judge their ulterior motives in taking positions, proposing bills and amendments, writing speeches, or issuing press releases that happen to be of value in both legislative and campaign contexts?

To avoid being criticized for using government-paid staff to work on their campaigns, incumbents use several approaches to make it legitimate or at least appear so.

"Because of what has gone under the bridge in the past, people are more aware and more careful," said one legislative aide who took a 50 percent pay cut in 1978 to help his boss, Sen. Robert P. Griffin, R-Mich., in his unsuccessful effort to win a third term. "My sense is that everybody is overly sensitive and overly paranoid about it."

In some cases, House and Senate staffers go on vacation or temporarily take themselves off the government payroll. Others try to mix their congressional job with election campaign duties and agree to a cut in pay to reflect the reduction in their congressional work. Others remain on the payroll to avoid losing benefits but claim to put in a full day of constituent service at the member's district office before going to campaign headquarters to help their boss in his reelection bid. Nonetheless, former aide Bisnow wrote, staffers "simply doing their ordinary job is a large contribution in itself,"

Supreme Court Ruling

In March 1981 the Supreme Court let stand an appeals court ruling that it was up to Congress to determine whether and under what restraints congressional aides may double as campaign workers. The Court's decision appeared to clear the way for a senator or representative to keep staff aides on the government payroll even when they are working almost exclusively on the member's reelection campaign.

The 1981 appeals court ruling came in a suit brought by former Federal Election Commission attorney Joel D. Joseph in 1977 against Sen. Howard W. Cannon, D-Nev., and Chester B. Sobsey, Cannon's $40,000-a-year administrative assistant. Joseph charged that Sobsey had remained on the Senate payroll from March 1975 through November 1976 while working for Cannon's reelection.

The suit claimed that Cannon's approval of Sobsey's salary payments under those circumstances constituted a fraudulent claim against the government. But the appeals court held that to judge the legality of Cannon's actions would violate the Constitution's separation of powers doctrine. Only the House and Senate can judge such "political questions," the appeals court ruled.

The appeals court based much of its ruling on a conclusion that Congress itself has set no hard-and-fast standard that would have enabled Cannon to determine where to draw the line between Sobsey's official duties and his political chores. Existing rules governing staff campaign work are lenient and subject to differing interpretations. In the past both chambers have been extremely reluctant to police their members' use of staff in political campaigns. Congress never allowed its own staffers to be restricted by the Hatch Act—which prohibits federal government employees from participating in partisan political activities.

House regulations permit staff members, who are prohibited from giving cash to a campaign, to assist a member's reelection effort so long as their assigned congressional duties also are being fulfilled. Those duties are set by each member, as is the amount of vacation time granted. "If they are on their own time, they can do all the politicking they want," said a spokesman for the House Committee on Standards of Official Conduct.

Senate restrictions are even more lax. One House aide, who took himself off the payroll in 1978 to manage a Senate campaign, said: "The Senate rules have big wide holes in them large enough to let just about anybody work in the campaign from the federal staff."

The guiding document on the subject is a Senate Rules Committee report of October 17, 1977, which states that "other than actual handling of campaign funds, the Senate has not imposed any restrictions on the participation of a member of a senator's staff in that senator's reelection campaign." Several weeks after the 1981 appeals court decision in the Cannon case, the Senate Select Ethics Committee proposed incorporating into the Senate ethics code a 1977 ruling by the committee declaring that senators should remove from their congressional payrolls staffers who undertake political work to the detriment of their official Senate duties. But the proposal was never acted on by the full Senate.

Flexibility of Staff Use

Unlike the House, which does not allow personal staff aides to solicit and receive campaign contributions, the Senate provides that three members of each staff may be designated for that purpose. In fact, in the Cannon Supreme Court case the senator argued that he had designated Sobsey as one of the staffers allowed to receive campaign funds.

The use of congressional staff on a campaign offers an enormous advantage to members over their challengers, who must use their own campaign funds to finance staff support. Critics of this practice have proposed that legislative aides' salaries for hours spent politicking be counted against the limits on campaign spending. But it is difficult to differentiate political activities from legislative work that is also usable in an election campaign. Some activities, such as managing a campaign, raising money, and dealing with poll results, are clearly political. But casework, speech writing, and preparation of responses on particular issues fall into a gray area.

Most of those engaged in campaign efforts at high levels are the administrative assistants—usually a member's top congressional aide and the one having the most political as well as legislative experience.

In 1978 Tom E. Coker served as campaign manager for Sen. Maryon P. Allen, D-Ala., in the Alabama Democratic primary—lost by Allen—while continuing to receive his $44,000 annual pay as her administrative assistant. Coker said he did not try to hide his political activity. "I didn't feel there was anything wrong with the amount of time

I was putting in on the campaign," which he estimated at about 40 percent of his working day.

For four years Coker had been a chief political contact in the state for Sen. James B. Allen, D-Ala., working out of a third-floor office in the Capitol building. One source in the state Democratic party said the thirty-eight-year-old Coker was "one of the best political operatives the state has ever seen." When Allen died and his widow, Maryon, took his seat and sought the remaining two years of his term, it was considered natural for Coker to head her effort.

Asked if he had considered going off the government payroll, Coker said, "I didn't think too much about it. I felt the government had gotten more than their just due from me." He said he rarely had taken any time off, except for Sundays.

In Oregon, Republican Sen. Mark O. Hatfield's close friend and adviser, Gerald W. Frank, cut his staff salary from nearly $40,000 to $10,000 at the beginning of 1978 when he began to manage Hatfield's reelection campaign. His salary became the minimum that a Senate employee could earn and still be designated to receive campaign contributions in a Senate office. Because Frank said he spent more than half his time on official Senate business, he believed he should retain his ability to carry out campaign work.

In 1985 the Senate Ethics Committee issued an "interpretive ruling" (No. 402) stating that an unnamed senator's personal secretary could receive pay from the campaign committee for off-hours work she did for the senator's reelection. The secretary had been designated to receive campaign contributions for the senator.

Press secretaries often work on campaigns in the final weeks as media inquiries focus on politics. Joe Shafran, press aide to Rep. Marc L. Marks, R-Pa., was taken off the government payroll in 1978 because, Shafran said, Marks was exercising caution and did not want any criticism from his opponent. "Frankly, if I'd stayed on the payroll, I

get the feeling nobody would have cared," Shafran remarked.

In close races, however, it is not unusual to find a massive shift of personnel from congressional work to the campaign. Because this offers an obvious target for an opponent, staff members in these contests almost always leave the government payroll.

Rep. Abner J. Mikva, an Illinois Democrat, won close elections in 1974 and 1976 and again in 1978. He had one of the most extensive House campaign operations in the country, one that included five campaign headquarters. Mikva began depleting his district office staff during the summer. Four staff persons working in his district, plus the campaign coordinator, were on the campaign payroll. And a legislative aide from his congressional office in Washington would leave Washington at the beginning of the year to work in Mikva's Skokie office and lay the groundwork for the campaign. After winning reelection, Mikva resigned in 1979 to become a federal judge.

In 1986 the House ethics committee investigated complaints that Rep. Mac Sweeney, R-Texas, was threatening to fire staff members who refused to perform campaign activities. The committee said it found no evidence of impropriety and it took no further action.

House Minority Whip Newt Gingrich, R-Ga., was investigated by the House ethics committee in 1989-90 for suggestions that he improperly used his congressional payroll for political purposes. The *Atlanta Business Chronicle* reported in its July 24, 1989, issue that Gingrich had given large, but temporary, year-end pay raises to staff members when they returned to his congressional office after taking leave without government pay to work on his campaign in the 1986 and 1988 elections.

Gingrich denied any wrongdoing and said he was being chastised for a legitimate practice that is widespread on Capitol Hill—members giving their staff year-end bonuses. He said the disclosures were part of a political vendetta against him for his actions in the ethics investigation of Speaker Jim Wright, D-Texas. *(Wright resignation, Chapter 2, p. 20)*

Gingrich said he commonly gave bonuses to his low-paid staffers when his office expense account had money left at the end of the year. House regulations stipulated that "year-end increases should be made only on a permanent basis." Nonetheless, Gingrich said, one-time bonuses were common and at least half of the Georgia delegation provided year-end bonuses.

The most serious allegation was that the bonuses amounted to compensation for campaign work. Gingrich said that other congressional aides who did not work for the campaign also got bonuses. However, a review of 1988 payroll records in the House clerk's office showed that the largest bonuses went to two aides who did work on the campaign. The investigation of Gingrich, which included other charges, was dropped in March 1990.

AIDES AND ETHICS

Like the elected members of Congress, employees of the House and Senate must abide by certain ethics rules. These restrictions deal with honoraria, outside income, gifts, travel, financial disclosure, and postemployment lobbying. Most of the rules were amended when Congress passed the Government Ethics Reform Act of 1989. *(Provisions, Chapter 11, p. 155)*

Honoraria

In the House, effective January 1, 1991, members and staff were prohibited from accepting honoraria. House employees could request, however, that charitable contributions be made in their name in lieu of honoraria for speeches and appearances.

Charitable contributions were limited to $2,000 per speech, appearance, or article, and they could not be made to any organization that benefited the person who spoke or any of his or her relatives. Those who had charitable contributions made on their behalf were barred from getting tax advantages.

In mid-1991 the Senate, in return for a pay raise, also eliminated honoraria for members and staff, although charitable contributions could be made.

Other Outside Income

Senior staff in the House—those employees compensated at or above the GS-16 salary level—were barred from keeping more than 15 percent of the Executive Level II salary ($96,600) in outside earned income; from being paid for working or affiliating with a law or other professional firm (they were allowed to teach for pay if the House Committee on Standards of Official Conduct approved); and from serving on boards of directors. Outside earned income included "wages, salary, fees, and other amounts paid for personal services, as opposed to items such as interest, rents, dividends, and capital gains, which represent a return on investments."

There were no limits on outside earnings for Senate employees.

Gifts

As part of the deal under which the House agreed to a Senate pay raise, Congress in 1991 eased some of the gift rules that it had passed less than two years earlier under the 1989 Ethics Reform Act.

The new rules allowed senators, representatives, and their employees to accept up to $250 worth of gifts annually. Members and staff did not have to count gifts worth $100 or less. The new rules eliminated almost all requirements to disclose the receipt of gifts.

Under the 1989 rules, House members and staff were limited to $200 worth of gifts. Senators and their staff were prohibited from receiving gifts from anyone with a direct interest in legislation totaling more than $100 a year or from anyone else but relatives totaling more than $300 a year. In both chambers, gifts worth $75 did not count.

Travel

House staff could not receive more than thirty days of lodging a year from someone other than a relative. If the hospitality was extended more than four days, the employee had to ensure that it was in fact personal—not corporate-financed or being claimed as a business expense. Private sources could pay travel expenses for no more than four days of domestic travel and seven days for international trips (travel time was excluded for both categories). Travel expenses also could be paid for one accompanying relative. The House Committee on Standards of Official Conduct could waive gift and travel restrictions in "exceptional circumstances."

Private sources could pay travel expenses of Senate staff for no more than three days of domestic travel and seven days for international trips (both limits excluded travel time).

The travel expenses for an accompanying spouse also could be paid.

Financial Disclosure

The 1989 act for the first time brought all three branches of government under the same financial disclosure law, although each branch continued to be responsible for administering requirements for its own employees. The new rules on financial disclosure became effective beginning with reports due in 1991.

The income from any source worth more than $200 had to be reported. Gifts worth less than $75 did not need to be reported.

Employees who had charitable contributions made on their behalf in lieu of honoraria had to disclose the source and amount of the contributions. The charities receiving such contributions were to be disclosed in confidential reports to the House Committee on Standards of Official Conduct. In addition, the source and amount of any honoraria received by the spouse of a reporting individual had to be disclosed.

Also required was disclosure of travel reimbursements, including an itinerary and dates of travel.

Staffers were required to file a "termination report" within thirty days after they left office. The termination report was to contain complete financial disclosure information for the previous year up to the date of departure.

Postemployment Lobbying

Effective January 1, 1991, former House and Senate staff members (those at the GS-17 salary level or above) were barred for one year after leaving employment from lobbying the member, office, or committee for which they had worked.

Leadership staff members were barred from lobbying the members and employees of the leadership for the chamber in which they served.

CHAPTER 9

Hill Immunity:
Shielding Legislators

The principle that lawmakers cannot be penalized in court for their official actions is a fundamental one in democratic institutions. Otherwise a despot could intimidate the legislature by threatening members with arrest any time they pass a law he opposes.

Members of Congress enjoy such immunity under the Constitution, and many members have availed themselves of its protection. Where the claim was legitimate, the shield has worked. But the courts have narrowed its protection in cases where the offense has little or nothing to do with the member's official duties.

The immunity concept was already a well-established principle in England when it was added to the American Constitution in Article I, Section 6, which provides that senators and representatives "shall in all Cases, except Treason, Felony and Breach of the Peace, be privileged from Arrest during their Attendance at the Session of their respective Houses, and in going to and returning from the same; and for any Speech or Debate in either House, they shall not be questioned in any other Place."

But as various court decisions have excluded more and more acts and proceedings from it, the privilege-from-arrest clause has become practically obsolete. As currently interpreted, the clause applies only to arrests in civil suits, such as nonpayment of debts or breach of contract; and most state constitutions or statutes prohibit arrest generally in such actions. Civil arrests were more common when the Constitution was adopted than they are now.

Long v. Ansell (293 U.S. 76) in 1934 and *U.S. v. Cooper* (4 Dall. 341) in 1800 declared that the clause does not apply to service of process in civil or criminal cases; nor does it apply to arrest in any criminal case. Furthermore, *Williamson v. United States* (207 U.S. 425, 446) in 1908 interpreted the phrase "treason, felony and breach of the peace" as excluding all criminal offenses from coverage.

Legislative Acts Protected

Members of modern Congresses are more likely to seek protection behind the speech-or-debate clause than the no-arrest clause. Various court decisions have broadly interpreted the former to include virtually everything a member does in carrying out legislative responsibilities.

The first Supreme Court interpretation of the

Immunity in Washington

As the nation's capital, Washington, D.C., has had more than its share of members of Congress being arrested for offenses such as drunk driving or soliciting prostitutes. And for many years those arrested could be fairly assured that the D.C. police would drop the charges once the member's identity became known.

That has been less true since 1976, when the police chief requested a ruling in a case involving Rep. Joe D. Waggonner, Jr., D-La., who had been arrested for allegedly soliciting a policewoman posing as a prostitute. He was released when police identified him as a member of Congress.

Based on Justice's July 23 ruling, D.C. police said, members "and all other elected and appointed federal, state, and local officials are subject to arrest for the commission of criminal offenses to the same extent and in the same manner as all other citizens." An exception would be continued for most parking violations by private automobiles bearing congressional license plates.

The nonarrest policy, which had been in effect for more than a hundred years, had been based on "a misinterpretation of the meaning" of the privilege-from-arrest clause in Article I, Section 6, of the Constitution, a police spokesman said. The Supreme Court in a 1908 case, *Williamson v. United States* (207 U.S. 425, 446), had excluded most criminal actions from the clause's protection, saying the Founders intended it mainly to prevent political harassment through civil arrest. The more sweeping policy against arrest in Washington was thought to have been an attempt to avoid offending the legislators, who controlled the D.C. police budget.

---

speech-or-debate clause occurred in 1881 in *Kilbourn v. Thompson* (103 U.S. 168). The case is also widely cited for its ruling on the limits of congressional investigations. It involved a contempt-of-Congress citation against Hallet

Kilbourn, manager of a real estate pool, for refusing to answer questions before the House Select Committee on the Real Estate Pool and Jay Cooke Indebtedness. The House ordered Kilbourn jailed for contempt. He won release on a writ of habeus corpus and sued the Speaker, members of the investigating committee, and Sergeant at Arms John G. Thompson for false arrest. The Supreme Court upheld Kilbourn's claim, on the grounds that it had not been a legitimate investigation.

The Court decided the case on the basis of Congress's investigatory powers. But since the defendants had raised speech or debate as a defense, the Court commented that the clause protected not only words spoken in debate, but also written reports, resolutions offered, the act of voting, and all things generally done in a session of the House by one of its members in relation to the business before it.

The Supreme Court on February 24, 1966, held in a 7-0 decision that in prosecuting a former member of Congress the executive branch may not constitutionally inquire into the member's motives for making a speech on the floor, even though the speech was made for a bribe and was part of an unlawful conspiracy.

The holdings in *United States v. Johnson* (383 U.S. 169) left members immune from prosecution for their words and legislative deeds on the floor of Congress, with one exception reserved by the Court—prosecution under a "narrowly drawn" law enacted by Congress itself "to regulate the conduct of its Members." Members of Congress already were immune from libel suits for floor speeches.

Johnson was the first case of its kind. The Court was unable to find among the English or American cases any direct precedent. The Court did discuss cases holding that legislators were protected from private suits for their legislative words and deeds; and it cited approvingly a Supreme Court decision, the force of which appeared to extend the *Johnson* doctrine to state legislators.

The *Johnson* case arose out of the conviction of former representative Thomas F. Johnson, D-Md., on June 13, 1963, by a federal jury in Baltimore. The government charged that Johnson, former representative Frank W. Boykin, D-Ala., and two officers of a Maryland savings and loan company then under indictment, J. Kenneth Edlin and William L. Robinson, entered into a conspiracy whereby Johnson and Boykin would approach the Justice Department to urge a "review" of the indictment and Johnson would make a speech on the floor of the House defending savings and loan institutions. Johnson made the speech June 30, 1960, and it was reprinted by the indicted company and distributed to the public. Johnson and Boykin allegedly received money in the form of "campaign contributions." Johnson's share was more than $20,000.

Johnson was convicted on seven counts of violating the federal conflict-of-interest law and on one count of conspiring to defraud the United States; the others were convicted of the same charges. President Lyndon B. Johnson granted Boykin a full pardon on December 17, 1965.

The Fourth Circuit Court of Appeals September 16, 1964, set aside Thomas Johnson's conspiracy conviction on grounds that it was unconstitutional under the speech-or-debate clause. The court ordered a new trial on the other counts on grounds that evidence taken about Johnson's speech on the conspiracy count "infected" the entire case.

The Supreme Court affirmed the lower court's ruling, thus foreclosing further prosecution on the conspiracy count but permitting retrial on the other counts. In the majority opinion, Justice John Marshall Harlan said the purpose of the speech-or-debate clause was "prophylactic," that it had been adopted by the Constitutional Convention (without discussion or opposition) because of the English experience with efforts of the Crown to intimidate and punish Parliament. The clause was intended to protect the independence and integrity of Congress, the Court said, and to reinforce the separation of powers by preventing an "unfriendly" executive and a "hostile" judiciary appointed by the executive from reaching into congressional activity for evidence of criminality.

The government's theory, rejected by the Court, was that Johnson's criminal act—acceptance of a bribe and entering into a conspiracy—predated his floor speech. Justice Harlan said the indictment particularized the speech as part of the conspiracy charged, and evidence about the speech was taken at trial.

On January 26, 1968, Johnson was convicted for a second time on the conflict-of-interest charges by the U.S. District Court in Baltimore. He was sentenced to six months in prison.

Immunity Protection Narrowed

On June 29, 1972, the Supreme Court in effect narrowed the category of protected actions under the immunity clause. The Court's ruling was issued in a case involving former senator Daniel B. Brewster, D-Md.

A federal grand jury on December 1, 1969, had indicted Brewster; Spiegel Inc., a Chicago mail-order company; and Cyrus T. Anderson, a Spiegel lobbyist, on charges of violating federal bribery laws. The indictment charged that Brewster received $24,500 from Spiegel and Anderson to influence his "action, vote and decision" on postal rate legislation.

The grand jury said the payments were made in five installments between January 10, 1966, and January 31, 1968. Brewster was a member of the Senate Post Office and Civil Service Committee during a 1967 debate on postal rate increases for regular third-class mail. Spiegel was a major user of such rates. Brewster had been defeated for reelection in 1968.

Ten months after Brewster's indictment, a U.S. district court judge dismissed it on the grounds that the senator was immune from prosecution because of the speech-or-debate clause. The government took an appeal directly to the Supreme Court, which issued a decision June 29, 1972, narrowing the category of protected actions under the immunity clause. A six-justice Court majority ruled that "Taking a bribe is, obviously, no part of the legislative process or function." *(United States v. Brewster,* 408 U.S. 501)

Chief Justice Warren E. Burger, writing the opinion, continued: "The illegal conduct is taking or agreeing to take money for a promise to act in a certain way. There is no need for the government to show that [Brewster] fulfilled the alleged illegal bargain ... for it is taking the bribe, not performance of the illicit compact, that is a criminal act." Importantly, the Court upheld the validity of the indictment, making it unnecessary for the government to inquire into legislative acts or their motivations to prove a violation of the bribery statute. Brewster was ordered to stand trial and was convicted November 17, 1972.

The jury found Brewster guilty of a lesser bribery charge, that of accepting an unlawful gratuity. Following the verdict, Spiegel Inc. pleaded guilty. Brewster was sentenced to two to six years in prison and fined $30,000. In August 1974 a federal appeals court reversed the conviction on grounds the jury had not been given proper instructions. A new trial was scheduled for August 1975. But on June 25, 1975, Brewster pleaded no contest to a felony charge of accepting an illegal gratuity while he was a senator.

Protected Acts Specified

On June 29, 1972, the Supreme Court took the unusual step of specifying in some detail certain acts of a legislator that were protected by the immunity clause. The case involved Sen. Mike Gravel, D-Alaska, and his actions in releasing portions of the then-classified Pentagon Papers history of United States' involvement in the Vietnam War.

During the controversy over publication of the Pentagon Papers in 1971 by the *New York Times,* the *Washington Post,* and several other newspapers, Gravel on June 29, 1971, convened a special meeting of the Public Works Subcommittee on Public Buildings, of which he was chairman. With the press and the public in attendance, Gravel read classified documents from the Pentagon Papers into the subcommittee record. Subsequently, the senator arranged for the verbatim publication of the subcommittee record by Beacon Press, the nonprofit publishing arm of the Unitarian-Universalist Association.

In August 1971 a federal grand jury in Boston, investigating the release of the Pentagon Papers, ordered an aide to Gravel, Leonard S. Rodberg, to appear before it. Rodberg had been hired the night Gravel called the session of his subcommittee to read excerpts from the secret documents. Rodberg subsequently helped Gravel to edit the papers and to make arrangements for their publication. The grand jury also subpoenaed several persons associated with Beacon Press who were involved in publication of the papers.

Rodberg moved to quash the subpoena on the grounds he was protected from the questioning by congressional immunity, contending such immunity extended to staff members. Gravel filed a motion to intervene on Rodberg's behalf, claiming Rodberg was acting under the senator's orders, which were immune from judicial inquiry.

The Justice Department, in a brief filed September 8, 1971, said no immunity existed for either Rodberg or Gravel. While not saying so directly, the department's action left open the possibility it might subpoena Gravel himself to testify.

A lower court ruled in October 1971 that the grand jury could not question any witness about

Gravel's conduct at the special meeting or about his preparation for the meeting. The grand jury also was prohibited from questioning Rodberg about his own actions taken at Gravel's direction relating to the meeting.

In January 1972 the court of appeals held that Gravel could be questioned about the subsequent publication of the subcommittee record by Beacon Press but not about the subcommittee meeting itself. The same immunities extended to Gravel were also to be applied to Rodberg, the court ruled. But third parties, the court ruled, could be questioned about any of their own actions regarding the publication and the ad hoc committee session.

In a 5-4 decision on June 29, 1972, the Supreme Court specifically enumerated the activities of Gravel and Rodberg that were protected by the immunity clause. *(Gravel v. United States,* 408 U.S. 606)

The Court said no witness could be questioned concerning (1) the conduct of Gravel or his aides at the meeting of the Public Works Subcommittee on Public Buildings and Grounds on June 29, 1971, (2) the motives and purposes behind the conduct of Gravel or his aides at the June 29 meeting, (3) communications between Gravel and his aides during the terms of their employment and related to the June 29 meeting or any other legislative act of the senator, (4) any act, in itself not criminal, performed by the senator or by his aides in the course of their employment in preparation for the subcommittee meeting, except as it proved relevant to investigating possible third-party crime.

The ruling held that Gravel's constitutional immunity did not shield him or his aides from grand jury questioning regarding their activities not directly related to their legislative responsibilities. "While the Speech or Debate Clause recognizes speech, voting and other legislative acts as exempt from liability that might attach," the Court stated, "it does not privilege either senator or aide to violate an otherwise valid criminal law in

Steve Karafyllakis

Following Sen. Mike Gravel's disclosure of the classified Pentagon Papers in 1972, the Supreme Court enumerated the acts of a legislator that were protected by the immunity clause.

preparing for or implementing legislative acts."

The Court concluded that the immunity of Gravel's aide was identical to that of his employer and defined the latter's as immunity from "prosecutions that directly impinge upon or threaten the legislative process." The Court majority concurred with the lower court ruling that the negotiations leading to unofficial publication of the committee record were outside the protection of the speech-or-debate clause; further, however, it also held that both Gravel and Rodberg were vulnerable to grand jury questioning and possible liability regarding their roles in the Pentagon Papers publication.

Legislative Protection Restated

The Supreme Court on October 9, 1973, upheld an appellate court ruling that had reversed five of eight conspiracy, bribery, and perjury convictions against former representative John Dowdy, D-Texas, on grounds that they violated the immunity clause.

A federal grand jury in Baltimore indicted Dowdy on March 31, 1970. The indictment alleged that he had accepted a $25,000 bribe at the Atlanta airport on September 22, 1965, to intervene in a federal and District of Columbia investigation of the Monarch Construction Company of Silver Spring, Maryland.

Dowdy was convicted on December 30, 1971, in U.S. District Court in Baltimore of crossing a state line to receive a bribe, conspiracy to obstruct justice, conspiracy to violate conflict of interest statutes, and five counts of perjury. He was sentenced to eighteen months in prison and fined $25,000.

On March 13, 1973, the Fourth Circuit Court of Appeals reversed five of the eight convictions and reduced Dowdy's sentence to six months in prison and a $3,000 fine. Convictions on three counts of perjury were sustained. *(Dowdy v. United States, 479 F.2d 213)*

The court held that Dowdy's immunity had been violated at the trial by "an examination of the defendant's actions as a congressman, who was chairman of a subcommittee investigating a complaint, in gathering information in preparation for a possible subcommittee investigatory hearing."

Although the alleged criminal act—bribery—was the same in both the Brewster and Dowdy cases, the major difference, which resulted in one prosecution's being upheld and the other's being reversed, was the source of the evidence. In Brewster's case there was enough evidence outside of Brewster's legislative activities to permit the case to go forward. In Dowdy's case so much of the evidence was based on Dowdy's legislative activities that the court reversed five of the eight convictions.

On October 9, 1973, the Supreme Court upheld the ruling of the lower court. *(Dowdy v. United States,* 414 U.S. 866) After losing a bid to stay out of prison for health reasons, Dowdy began his term January 28, 1974.

1979 Rulings

In June 1979 the Supreme Court released two decisions concerning congressional immunity.

In *United States v. Helstoski,* the Court forbade federal prosecutors to use any evidence of past legislative actions in prosecuting former representative Henry Helstoski, D-N.J. He had been indicted in 1976 on charges he accepted money in return for introducing private bills allowing certain aliens to remain in the United States. As a result of the decision the prosecutors dropped seven bribery-related counts against Helstoski and sought reindictment of him on remaining obstruction of justice counts. The district judge, however, dismissed these counts also, ruling they were "tainted" by Helstoski's legislative actions.

In *Hutchinson v. Proxmire,* the Court held that congressional immunity did not protect Sen. William Proxmire, D-Wis., from being sued for libel by a scientist who charged that he had been injured by Proxmire's remarks ridiculing his research. The allegedly libelous remarks were made on the Senate floor in 1975 and then published in a press release and newsletter. The Court ruled that only the remarks on the floor were protected by the speech or debate clause.

Proxmire had been sued by Dr. Ronald Hutchinson, a researcher at the Kalamazoo State Hospital, after the Wisconsin Democrat gave the National Aeronautics and Space Administration and the Office of Naval Research his satiric "Golden Fleece Award." The two federal agencies had awarded Hutchinson $500,000 for research into how monkeys exhibit aggression. Proxmire garnered considerable publicity by periodically giving Golden Fleece Awards to spotlight what he considered outstanding cases of government waste.

In a 1975 Senate speech Proxmire said that Hutchinson had "made a monkey out of the American taxpayer." He also referred to the Golden Fleece Award in a newsletter, in a press release, and on a television interview program. His legislative assistant, Morton Schwartz, telephoned the agencies funding Hutchinson's research, and they subsequently cut off the grants. Repetition of Proxmire's Senate remarks outside the Capitol were ruled to be beyond the reach of his immunity.

Proxmire made an out-of-court settlement with Hutchinson, announcing the settlement in a March 24, 1980, speech on the Senate floor. Although he did not say so in the speech, the senator agreed to pay the scientist $10,000 in return for ending further litigation. Proxmire used the floor speech to "clarify" his 1975 Golden Fleece statements, which had led to the suit in the first place.

Although Hutchinson paid his own legal fees in the lengthy suit, the Senate picked up the $124,351 tab for Proxmire's defense.

CHAPTER 10

The "Keating Five":
A Special Case

One of the most divisive ethics cases in the history of the Senate came to a dramatic but uncertain close in late 1991, leaving the matter only slightly less muddled than when it began more than two years earlier.

Ninety-five senators somberly gathered to watch California Democrat Alan Cranston get scolded for his conduct in the so-called Keating Five case—and ended up getting scolded by the defendant. Cranston apologized for making the Senate look bad and then implied that some of his colleagues looked worse. He expressed sorrow that some people thought he acted improperly but said he had not. He accepted the Ethics Committee's reprimand but rejected its basis.

"My behavior did not violate established norms," he told his colleagues. "Here, but for the grace of God, stand you."

Members looking for retribution were left unsatisfied because the Ethics Committee had entered into an unprecedented plea bargain with the ailing seventy-seven-year-old liberal stalwart. Senators were required to watch Cranston be reprimanded as they sat silently at their desks on the floor, but they were not to judge his behavior by voting, leaving his defiant retort unchallenged by the full Senate.

"The committee whitewashed him, and he tarred us," said Malcolm Wallop of Wyoming. A handful of similarly minded Republicans, who considered trying to force a vote by the full Senate to censure Cranston, were somewhat appeased by the blistering rebuttal that Ethics Vice Chairman Warren B. Rudman, R-N.H., gave to Cranston's defense.

Members looking for lessons likely also were unsatisfied because, in the end, the Senate's ethics watchdogs announced they they could not define improper conduct, but, as with pornography, they know it when they see it.

"Not all standards offer the opportunity to arrive at easy judgments through the mechanical application of a fixed formula," said Ethics Chairman Howell Heflin, D-Ala., who told members that Supreme Court Justice Potter Stewart's oft-borrowed pornography standard applied to their behavior.

That may have been troubling to many senators because the case raised a fundamental question: When does the relationship between members' two most time-consuming tasks—helping constituents and raising money—become improper and unethical?

R. Michael Jenkins

The Keating Five hearings were conducted under the glare of television lights in this Senate hearing room. Eight long tables were reserved for the press.

The Ethics Committee was sure Cranston went too far in his dealings with thrift operator Charles H. Keating, Jr., branding the senator's conduct "improper and repugnant." But many considered the case such a close call that the panel invented a new form of punishment halfway between a committee rebuke and a full Senate censure. The matter was taken to the floor November 20, and, without asking for a vote on the matter, Ethics leaders told the assembled Senate that the committee had reprimanded Cranston for "an impermissible pattern of conduct in which fundraising and official activities were substantially linked."

It was the Senate's first use of the word *reprimand* in place of *censure,* and it was the first time that the Ethics Committee had acted for the full Senate in dispensing a disciplinary action. *(Cranston reprimand, Chapter 3, p. 44)*

A federal grand jury indicted Keating and other former officers of Lincoln's parent company December 12 on securities fraud and racketeering charges. A California jury already had convicted Keating on similar state charges.

DECISION: END OF AN ORDEAL

The reprimand completed the Ethics Committee's sweeping investigation of possible wrongdoing by senators in behalf of Keating's California-based thrift, Lincoln Savings and Loan Association, which failed in 1989 at a $2 billion cost to the taxpayers. Lincoln's failure became a symbol of one of the largest financial debacles ever to hit the nation, the near collapse of the savings and loan industry.

Besides Cranston, the senators investigated were Democrats Dennis DeConcini of Arizona, John Glenn of Ohio, and Donald W. Riegle, Jr., of Michigan, and Republican John McCain of Arizona. All five denied wrongdoing, saying their efforts for Keating were no more than any member of Congress would do to help a constituent having problems with a federal agency. They denied that they helped Keating in return for campaign contributions and maintained that their actions did not influence the decisions of government regulators with regard to Lincoln.

The hearings began November 15, 1990, and ended January 16, 1991. Like previous hearings into the Watergate, Koreagate, and Abscam scandals, the inquiry gave the public an opportunity to look deeply into the inner workings of politics—in this instance, the possible connection between campaign contributions and government favoritism.

After more than thirty-three hours of closed-door deliberations spread over six weeks, the Ethics Committee announced its findings on February 27, 1991. It decided to proceed against Senator Cranston, finding evidence that some of his official actions were "substantially linked" with his fund raising.

The other four senators were criticized in written statements for poor judgment, with DeConcini and Riegle also chided for giving the appearance of acting improperly. But the panel decided that existing rules did not warrant further action.

Cranston protested that he had been "unfairly singled out." The others generally expressed relief at the end of a long ordeal.

More months passed, however, with no final decision on Cranston's fate. In August committee member Jesse Helms, R-N.C., publicly called for censure in a dramatic way—by unilaterally releasing a lengthy report based largely on a secret report by the committee's aggressive special counsel, Robert S. Bennett. A compromise finally began to take shape in November, partly out of consideration for Cranston's age, his problems with prostate cancer, and his decision to retire after 1992. Helms abstained and the other Ethics Committee members approved the compromise 5-0 the day before it went to the floor.

Central Figure: Keating

Charles Keating grew to be a rich and influential figure in the thrift industry as chairman of American Continental Corp., an Ohio-chartered corporation based in Phoenix, and deeply involved in home construction and land development. In 1984 American Continental purchased Lincoln Savings and Loan Association despite Keating's 1979 brush with the Securities and Exchange Commission (SEC) over insider loans.

Lincoln took aggressive advantage of permissive California state and federal rules to become a high-flying institution that boomed on the strength of relatively risky investments. After 1985 Lincoln became the subject of increasing scrutiny from federal regulators. Keating fought back; following long delays, American Continental [Lincoln] filed for bankruptcy in April 1989 and Lincoln was seized by federal regulators.

Keating was generous with his money, especially to the less privileged: Mother Teresa got $1 million; New York's Covenant House for runaway children and all manner of Arizona charities got assistance. And he dabbled in politics, for a time heading the unsuccessful 1980 presidential bid of former Texas governor John B. Connally, Jr.

In 1989 Keating boasted to reporters of the clout his political contributions had given him with Congress. "One question among the many raised in recent weeks had to do with whether my financial support in any way influenced several political figures to take up my cause," Keating said. "I want to say in the most forceful way I can, I certainly hope so." Keating later said his remark was misinterpreted.

Not every politician Keating approached took up his cause. Sen. Jake Garn, R-Utah, who chaired the Banking Committee through the first half of the 1980s, did not like Keating's attitude and after 1981 would have nothing to to do with him. Sen. Pete Wilson, R-Calif., collected about $16,000 for his campaign from Keating in 1985 but never questioned regulators about Lincoln. In fact, Wilson said he approved of the Federal Home Loan Bank Board's efforts to curb thrift industry abuses. Former governor Bruce Babbitt, D-Ariz., disliked Keating's financial dealings and told Cranston in March 1989 that he considered Keating a "crook."

Keating was convicted December 4, 1991, in Los Angeles on seventeen counts of securities fraud under California law. The Superior Court jury acquitted him on one count. But he faced vastly harsher penalties under federal charges lodged December 12 in Los Angeles. A federal grand jury indicted Keating and four other former American Continental officers on seventy-seven charges that could cost him $17 million in fines and $265 million in forfeited assets. The five defendants faced maximum prison sentences of 475 to 525 years if convicted on all counts.

R. Michael Jenkins

Savings and loan figure Charles H. Keating, Jr., arrives to testify before the House Banking
Committee in 1989.

Lincoln's failure was the subject of six intense days of hearings in 1989 by the House Banking Committee. Its chairman, Henry B. Gonzalez, D-Texas, looked broadly at Keating's business practices and the regulatory failures that allowed Lincoln to collapse so spectacularly. He called the scandal a mini-Watergate.

Keating appeared at those hearings but refused to testify, citing his constitutional protection against self-incrimination. (He later claimed the same privilege when subpoenaed to testify by the Senate Ethics Committee, as did six other American Continental employees.)

Ethics Complaint

The Keating case first came to the attention of the Ethics Committee when Ohio Republicans filed a complaint against Glenn on September 26, 1989.

Common Cause, an independent citizens' group that filed the charges leading to the resignation of House Speaker Jim Wright, D-Texas, in 1989, sent a letter October 13 seeking an investigation of all five senators.

On November 17, 1989, the committee named Bennett as special counsel for the matter. Bennett was handling the committee's investigation into the finances of Sen. Dave Durenberger, R-Minn., which resulted in discipline for Durenberger in July 1990. A preliminary inquiry into the Keating case was announced December 22, 1989. *(Durenberger denouncement, Chapter 3, p. 33)*

The committee was the only one in the Senate divided evenly between the two parties. Chairman Heflin was a former chief justice of the Alabama Supreme Court known for his caution and deliberative pace. Almost as important a player was

Vice Chairman Rudman, a hard-charging former state attorney general. The other members were Democrats David Pryor, Ark., and Terry Sanford, N.C., and Republicans Helms and Trent Lott, Miss. (Pryor left the committee for a time in 1991 after a heart attack, returning after his replacement bowed out because of a conflict.)

The investigation remained out of the public eye for the first part of 1990 as Bennett's staff quietly collected documents and interviewed witnesses, including the senators under investigation.

Contributions under Scrutiny

Although none of the senators was up for reelection in 1990, the publicity accorded the Keating case cast a shadow over their future electoral prospects and spilled over into other races.

On November 8, 1990, shortly before the hearings commenced, Cranston announced he would not run again in 1992 because of health problems. The terms of McCain and Glenn lasted through 1992; DeConcini and Riegle would not be up again until 1994.

There were ominous warning signs, however, in the 1990 elections. Two House members with direct thrift connections lost their re-election bids—Charles "Chip" Pashayan, Jr., R-Calif., who had ties to Keating, and Denny Smith, R-Ore., who was personally involved with another failed thrift.

Public opinion polls conducted on election day 1990 reported that, by margins of 60 percent or higher, voters in Arizona and Michigan believed DeConcini and Riegle should resign or not run again when their terms expired.

Political contributions from the savings and loan industry, whether tied to Keating or not, became controversial.

Common Cause released a study June 29 identifying more than $11.6 million in contributions from S&L interests to members of Congress and political parties in the 1980s. Four of the Keating Five senators—Riegle ($200,900), Cranston ($143,700), DeConcini ($84,200), and McCain ($80,393)—ranked among the top ten senators. (Glenn, with $32,600, was thirtieth.)

Tops among all members was Cranston's Republican colleague from California, Wilson, with $243,334. California politicians were seven of the top ten S&L fund-raisers in the House, led by Republican Bill Lowery, with $85,088. Many of the nation's largest and most profitable thrifts were located in California.

To compile the study, Common Cause sifted through Federal Election Commission (FEC) records of contributors from January 1981 to April 1990. It identified money given by 157 PACs operated by thrifts and their trade associations and by 1,074 individuals affiliated with S&Ls, including family members.

Riegle announced July 19 that he would turn over to the Treasury all campaign contributions he had received since 1983 from political action committees (PACs) and individuals tied to the thrift industry. At the same time, Riegle said that he would no longer accept contributions from PACs or officers of companies whose principal business was under the jurisdiction of the Banking Committee or the Finance Subcommittee on Health, both of which he chaired.

Riegle said the amount in question, up to $120,000, was about 2 percent of his total contributions—"a tiny amount, chicken feed." He cast the decision as a personal effort at campaign finance reform. Riegle was cosponsoring a bill to limit campaign spending.

Preliminary Skirmishes

Bennett was preoccupied with the Durenberger investigation until July 25, when the Senate voted to denounce the Minnesota senator. But Bennett's staff had kept working on the Keating case, and on

September 10 he gave the Ethics Committee a 350-page report and thousands of pages of supporting evidence. It was widely reported that he recommended dismissing the cases of Glenn and McCain and proceeding with charges against the other three, but the committee kept silent about the contents of the report.

After studying the report, the committee took testimony from the five senators in early October. In the middle of October, leaks began to spring that increased the heat on Cranston, DeConcini, and Riegle, and the other senators protested that they should be separated from the case.

Reports by the *New York Times,* the *Washington Post,* and the Associated Press, among other media organizations, indicated that the three senators were more deeply involved with Keating than previously had been disclosed.

McCain took the Senate floor October 22 to ask for Bennett's report to be released and its recommendation to be acted on quickly. "Justice delayed is justice denied," McCain said. Other senators joined his cause. Senate Democratic leaders denounced the leaks and suggested that Republicans wanted to hurry the case, leaving only Democrats under suspicion as the elections approached.

On October 23, the committee voted unanimously to open a fact-finding hearing including all five soon after the November elections. The committee reportedly had split in a vote to follow Bennett's recommendation and dismiss McCain and Glenn. Those two senators objected strongly to the decision.

By receiving a report from Bennett at the outset and by scheduling public hearings without making preliminary judgments, the committee departed from the typical steps taken in other recent ethics cases, which would have led to a public hearing only after official charges were filed. The committee's resolution said that the committee would, barring "extraordinary circumstances," conclude the case by December 31. But the hearings continued beyond that date.

Throughout the Senate hearings, Keating remained a shadow on the hearing-room wall. His broad-ranging legal troubles kept him far from the Hart Senate Office Building, where the hearings took place. Committee members said that no thought was given to forcing Keating to testify by granting limited immunity from prosecution—largely because of the chance that doing so would make it difficult to prosecute him in court. Bennett remarked in his opening statement, "One could ask the question: If Mr. Keating was here, would you believe what he said anyway?"

Cranston announced, a week before the hearings were scheduled to begin, that he had prostate cancer and would be unable to attend the hearings while he was undergoing treatment in California beginning in late November. He announced at the same time that he would not seek another term as Democratic whip and would not run for reelection in 1992.

TESTIMONY: COMPLEX AND RANCOROUS

The hearings opened November 15, 1990, to the glare of television lights in a large wood- and marble-paneled hearing room in the Hart Building. Eight long tables were reserved for the press. Each senator was given his own desk, next to one for his attorney.

In his opening remarks, Chairman Heflin provided an evenhanded talk that gave little insight into his own idea of the standard to which the senators would have to be held. Rudman offered an equally oblique view, noting only that "the committee cannot act on the basis of laws, rules, and standards that some people might like to see."

Pryor and Helms did not address the standards issue. But Lott and Sanford, the committees' two most junior members, each offered detailed views of what might constitute an ethical violation.

Sanford seemed to challenge the tough standards Bennett had laid down for the committee to consider. "In rulemaking and administrative matters, the member may . . . specifically or indirectly ask for favorable action," Sanford said. "The member may . . . complain about the treatment of citizens by investigators or other staff members of the agency." And, he said, "the member may call for reconsideration of a decision."

And, Sanford argued, "if indeed there is an appearance of wrongdoing when in fact no wrongdoing is found, the problem is not that of the individual, but of the institution." It would be unfair, he said, "to impose penalties for this appearance on individual senators."

Lott said he could identify a specific point at which intervention with regulators became improper. "The line is crossed, and the action is improper," he said, "if a senator requests that the regulator break the law, if he demands the regulator take a specific action or if he threatens the regulator with reprisal."

On the second day of the hearings, Cranston's attorney, William W. Taylor III, asked Helms to step aside from the deliberations because of remarks Helms had made in an early November campaign appearance drawing connections between Cranston and Keating. Helms refused, and the committee did not press the point.

Bennett's Opening

Committee special counsel Bennett laid out in broad strokes the case he would make over the next two months. Much of what Bennett cited had long been known. But he offered some new information—including affidavits and memorandums—that suggested the possibility of specific connections between Keating's fund raising and some actions by the senators. *(Bennett profile, p. 124)*

Bennett was in an unusual position. Unlike in the Durenberger case, he was not presenting a set of formal charges. Instead, he had to present all relevant facts and gently suggest to the committee members how they might view them.

"I'm not suggesting that there is wrongdoing at this stage," he told the committee at the start of his presentation. Nevertheless, he repeatedly said the evidence would show actions that could be interpreted by the committee as violations.

Bennett noted that he and his staff interviewed 140 people, took affidavits from 44 of them, and deposed 16 witnesses. That did not count the seven—among them Keating—who refused to testify, citing their constitutional prerogatives.

Bennett said his most important witness would not be a person. "The most important witnesses are the product of the examination of the pieces of paper," he said. "Ernest Hemingway once said that paper doesn't bleed, and what I think he meant by that is that paper isn't subject to the normal human frailty." The paper he would introduce, Bennett said, had special credibility because it "never thought it would be here."

Bennett said the evidence pointed to a strategy by Keating to pressure regulators by seeking assistance from members of Congress. And to do so, Bennett said, Keating engineered "substantial sums for political contributions."

"It is clear," Bennett said, "that Senators Cranston and DeConcini were important players in Mr. Keating's strategy." He added, "I must reluctantly state that there is substantial evidence that Senator Riegle played a much greater role than he now recalls. . . . The evidence shows that Senator Riegle played an important role at the early stages."

Bennett confirmed that he had found little evidence that Glenn or McCain had stepped across the line of propriety. "Was there anything improper about Senator McCain's conduct? The evidence discovered by special counsel suggests not," Bennett told the committee. Later he said that "We know of no evidence linking [political] con-

Special Counsel Bennett: No Shrinking Violet

The Keating Five case was the third that cele-brated investigation Washington lawyer Robert S. Bennett handled for the Senate Ethics Committee.

A partner in the Washington office of the New York law firm of Skadden, Arps, Slate, Meagher, & Flom, Bennett was hired in 1989 to lead the committee's investigation into allegations that Sen. Dave Durenberger, R-Minn., breached ethics rules. That case concluded with the Senate's de-nouncing Durenberger. *(Durenberger, Chapter 3, p. 33)*

Bennett also led the Senate inquiry into the actions of Sen. Harrison A. Williams, Jr., in 1981, growing out of the Abscam scandal, which resulted in Williams's resignation in 1982. *(Williams, Chapter 2, p. 18)*

In the Durenberger case, Bennett's manner—tough, even sarcastic at times—had set some senators on edge. During floor proceedings on July 25, 1990, former prosecutor Dale Bumpers, D-Ark., questioned Bennett's role as finder of both facts and law for the committee. "Is that not the prerogative and the duty of the committee and the U.S. Senate and not the special counsel?" he asked. And Don Nickles, R-Okla., went further: "I did not really see a special counsel; I saw a prosecutor. And it bothered me."

Ethics Committee members defended Bennett on the floor then, and the panel's leaders—Chairman Howell Heflin, D-Ala., and Vice Chairman Warren B. Rudman, R-N.H.—frequently came to his defense during the Keating hearings. Heflin cautioned that Bennett's role "must be carried out impartially." But, he added, "It is inevitable that at times he may appear to be prosecutorial."

That was definitely an opinion shared by others. Some of the senators in the dock despised Bennett, and some committee members complained about the relevance and breadth of evidence he mar-shaled. On the first day of the hearings, David Pryor, D-Ark., questioned Bennett's presentation. "In my opinion, you're beginning to reach personal conclusions," he said, "and also, you are deciding for us what is relevant and not relevant. I think that is our decision to make."

Bennett, known as a lawyer who reveled in a courtroom brawl, was hobbled by the rules of the Keating proceeding. Because the hearing took place before any official charges were filed, he was not supposed to act as a prosecutor but—in the words of committee Chairman Heflin—as an impartial fact-finder "to re-create the past events that are at the center of this controversy, in a manner which is not prejudicial to any party." Bennett was clearly unhappy in that corset of impartiality.

Bennett was accused in the first days of tilting the facts. "The facts tilt," he replied. He was accused of creating a new "appearance standard" against which the senators should be judged. "These are not my standards; these are your standards," he told the committee repeatedly. He was accused throughout the hearings of relying upon hearsay rather than hard evidence of impro-priety. But Heflin and Rudman allowed hearsay to be admitted by all parties. *("Appearance Standard," box, p. 128)*

More than any of the other senators under inquiry, Dennis DeConcini, D-Ariz., himself a former prosecutor, bristled at Bennett's perfor-mance, repeatedly calling him a special prosecutor, not a special counsel. James Hamilton, DeConci-ni's attorney, stung Bennett with affidavits from two former U.S. attorneys accusing him of unfairness.

Bennett fired back: "Sen. DeConcini and his counsel would like me to be a flower girl distribut-ing the flowers at a wedding in equal shares to each senator without regard to the evidence. I will not do that. . . . I think the not-so-subtle threat to this committee is an outrage and you should be of-fended by it."

tributions to any action on the part of Senator Glenn."

Keating began to seek help from members of both chambers in 1984-86, when he and other thrift executives from around the country wanted Congress to stop the Federal Home Loan Bank Board from putting in force a regulation limiting direct ownership by thrifts of real estate and other assets.

More than two hundred House members co-sponsored legislation in 1985 to delay the direct investment rule, and numerous senators denounced it. But efforts to nullify the rule went nowhere. Bennett said he looked for but could not find any evidence to suggest that the five senators lobbied on the rule as a result of Keating's contributions.

Where Bennett Saw Problems

The key events of the investigation were two meetings held in April 1987. In the first, on April 2, four of the senators (but not Riegle) met privately in DeConcini's office with Edwin J. Gray, then chairman of the Federal Home Loan Bank Board, which was responsible for regulating the thrift industry. Gray contended that the senators pressured him to withdraw the direct investment rule, which would rein in Lincoln's ability to pursue its high-flying investment strategy. In his opening, Bennett homed in on an unusual aspect of the first meeting: that Gray was told to bring no aides with him. "While in fairness to the senator, Senator DeConcini, he denies that it was his instruction, the overwhelming evidence suggests that the no-aides instruction came from Senator DeConcini's office.... Under all of the circumstances, including the articulated purpose of the meeting, it is at best strange that there was a purposeful effort made to exclude staff."

Detailed notes of the second meeting taken by one of the regulators seemed to be unusually accurate, Bennett said, and they indicated that

DeConcini seemed to be negotiating for Lincoln.

Bennett made clear that he viewed Cranston's efforts in Keating's behalf to be the most questionable. He received the most money from Keating, he allowed his fund raisers to serve as an important link with Keating, he remained active in helping Keating after others had stopped, and he seemed the most ideologically incompatible with Keating.

"The evidence will show," Bennett said, "that on approximately four separate occasions Senator Cranston accepted or solicited several hundred thousand dollars from Mr. Keating for Senator Cranston's voting registration groups and that each of these four occasions was linked by time and circumstance to a request by Mr. Keating for assistance with the bank board."

Those events, from early 1987 to early 1989, were documented by extensive memorandums from Cranston's fund raiser, Joy Jacobson, Bennett said.

"One is forced to ask, didn't the thought ever occur to Senator Cranston—and I suppose I can say this—he's known as a liberal Democrat—why would Mr. Keating, the antipornographer, the well-known Republican—why would he be giving hundreds and hundreds of thousands of dollars" to Cranston's pet political causes, Bennett asked.

Bennett's Standards

Establishing the facts of the case was substantially easier than deciding at what point a senator's conduct crossed ethical boundaries.

The senators maintained to a man that they had been intervening in behalf of their constituents (depositors, American Continental and Lincoln employees, and so forth), and that they had questioned regulators only to ascertain whether an important economic entity was being treated fairly.

Bennett spent much of his opening statement, delivered November 15 and 16, laying out the standards by which he thought a senator should be judged. Bennett said there was no doubt that intervention was proper, but he set several "objective" standards for when such intervention might be appropriate. These were:

- A senator should not take contributions from an individual he or she knows or should know is attempting to procure the senator's services to intervene in a specific matter pending before a federal agency.
- A senator should not take unusual or aggressive action with regard to a specific matter before a federal agency on behalf of a contributor when he or she knows or has reason to know the contributor has sought to procure the senator's services.
- A senator should not conduct fund-raising efforts or engage in office practices that lead contributors to conclude that they can buy access to the senator.
- A senator should not engage in conduct that would appear to be improper to a reasonable, nonpartisan, fully informed person.

Of those standards, the fourth or "appearance standard" was the most controversial. Bennett argued that a senator could be disciplined for violating that standard even if his or her specific actions did not, in themselves, directly violate a Senate rule. (*"Appearance standard," box, p. 128*)

Senators' Presentations

After Bennett finished his overview of the case, the senators responded in person—some claiming that Bennett's presentation exonerated them, others protesting that Bennett gave a one-sided case that ignored exculpatory evidence and drew too-neat connections between Keating's fund-raising efforts and their actions. Four of the senators gave their statements on November 16, immediately after Bennett had finished his; DeConcini waited until the hearing resumed on November 19 after a weekend break.

For Riegle, it was his first detailed comment on the Keating affair, and he held forth for an hour, focusing particularly on Bennett's suspicion that Keating's fund raising might have influenced the senator's actions.

"I would never dishonor my family name or the public trust for any reason or purpose. You couldn't make me do it," Riegle said. "The idea that I would do it for a campaign fund raiser is sheer nonsense."

Glenn emphasized that he had received no contributions from Keating since a year before the 1987 meetings and that he stopped helping Lincoln after learning of its legal troubles. He went on to defend the practice of questioning regulators about their actions. "I believe that a crucial part of my job as a U.S. senator is to ensure that federal regulators and bureaucrats are treating people fairly and carrying out their regulatory activities responsibly," he said.

McCain said he, too, ended his involvement with Lincoln once he heard the federal regulators' side of the story on April 9, 1987. He acknowledged that he and Keating had been friends when he was in the House, taking his family on several vacations at Keating's private resort in the Bahamas, but he insisted he had exerted no improper pressure for Keating.

"When he came to see me in March of 1987 and asked me to do something I thought was improper, I said no," McCain told the committee. "When he asked me to get Ed Gray off his back, I said no. When he asked me to negotiate for him, I said no. The only thing I said I could do was to inquire whether American Continental Corp. and Lincoln Savings were being treated fairly."

Cranston made his only appearance during the hearings a dramatic one November 16 as he displayed a long list of aides, including some in every senator's office, who were designated under Senate rules to accept campaign donations. "It is absurd to suggest that fund raising and substantive issues are separated in Senate offices by some kind of wall," Cranston said. "The notion that it violates Senate rules and established ethical standards if the fund raiser participated in a meeting in which substantive issues were discussed is sheer hypocrisy.... I submit that if you decide that it's improper to take a lawful and proper action at any time in behalf of someone who has contributed legally and properly, then every senator, including every member of this committee, had better run for cover—because every senator has done it; every senator must do it."

Cranston, known as a master fund raiser among Democrats, said that laws and rules governing campaign finance should be reformed. "But they haven't been changed yet," he concluded. "Until they are, the Senate and every senator and candidate will be in dire jeopardy."

DeConcini made his rebuttal November 19, after a weekend's recess. He was particularly aggressive toward the special counsel's tactics, accusing Bennett of behaving like a prosecutor bent on improving his courtroom record. "Bennett says that the facts tilt," DeConcini said. "No, the facts don't tilt. He tilts them, and why does he do that? ... He wants the victory. He wants to nail somebody."

DeConcini insisted that Keating's complaints of harassment by federal regulators seemed to have merit in 1987. Moreover, he said, he did not always do Keating's bidding. When Keating asked him to push through a sale of Lincoln in early 1989, the senator said, "I said no.... I did not push for the approval of that sale." DeConcini acknowledged, however, that he asked regulators about the sale and asked them to give it close consideration.

Witnesses Begin

The first witnesses were aides to the senators. They sought to differentiate the actions of their bosses from those of the other senators, with much testimony focusing on who had taken the initiative in setting up the first meeting with bank board Chairman Gray.

Gwendolyn van Paasschen, McCain's legislative assistant, appeared November 19-20 and testified that she called an independent auditor to check out Keating's claims of unfair treatment by regulators, and that she was convinced they had merit. But, she said, she had an uneasy feeling about Keating and warned McCain not to do too much for him.

Van Paasschen said it was her recollection that Riegle had initiated the meeting, even though he did not attend, and that DeConcini had kept staff away. She also said she heard DeConcini tell McCain in March 1987 that he "wanted to get the regulators off of Mr. Keating's back."

Laurie Sedlmayr, an aide to DeConcini, testified November 26 that she believed the April 2 meeting had been the "brainchild" of Riegle. But under cross-examination by Riegle attorney Thomas C. Green, she said that she had no facts to support her belief.

McCain's attorney, John M. Dowd, endeavored to show that McCain had nothing to do with a letter written by Sedlmayr and signed by DeConcini, inviting Riegle to the April 9 meeting. The letter said the invitation was from DeConcini and McCain; Sedlmayr said that had been her belief, but she had mistakenly forgotten to send a copy to McCain's office.

Sedlmayr also testified that she advised DeConcini to avoid helping Keating. "She let me know she didn't think it was a good idea," DeConcini said November 26.

The Meeting with Gray

For the equivalent of three days in the week of November 26, the panel heard from the best-known accuser of the Keating senators, Edwin Gray. The meeting that four of the senators—all but Riegle—attended with the nation's top savings

The "Appearance Standard:"
Is Conduct Wrong Merely Because It Looks Bad?

Can a senator's conduct be improper merely because it looks bad? In the Keating Five case, Special Counsel Robert S. Bennett urged the Senate Ethics Committee to conclude that, even absent a finding of actual improper conduct, members could be disciplined just for looking as though they behaved improperly—for violating what he called the "appearance standard."

"Legislators who appear to reasonable persons to do wrong actually do wrong by eroding the trust between citizens and their representatives," Bennett told the panel. He argued that longstanding traditions, Senate and House precedents, previous Ethics Committee pronouncements, and common sense supported his position.

Such a finding would be precedent setting. Although Bennett cited several past ethics cases in which appearances came into play, he offered no example of a lawmaker having been punished merely because behavior looked improper.

The senators investigated for their ties to savings and loan executive Charles H. Keating, Jr.—Alan Cranston, D-Calif.; Dennis DeConcini, D-Ariz.; John Glenn, D-Ohio; John McCain, R-Ariz.; and Donald W. Riegle, Jr., D-Mich.—maintained that their actions were in accord with accepted standards and that it should not matter how they could be interpreted by others.

Said Cranston: "We must do what we think is right, not just what appears to be right."

What Is "Improper Conduct?"

Senate rules prohibited members from engaging in "improper conduct which may reflect upon the Senate"—the catchall phrase in S Res 338, the 1964 resolution that created the Ethics Committee.

Bennett did not build his whole case around the appearance standard; he argued that some of the senators' fund-raising activities and actions to help Keating were clear examples of improper conduct. But if the committee decided that none of the senators' actions by themselves violated Senate rules, Bennett said, it still could hold some of them them accountable.

The circumstances, as reflected in many media reports, indeed could look bad. Ethics Committee Chairman Howell Heflin, D-Ala., said that many voters thought the senators were bribed with huge political contributions to come to Keating's aid during his bitter fight with thrift regulators.

Bennett's Standard

Bennett presented his conclusion about the appearance standard in a lengthy legal brief analyzing the history of government ethics. He formulated the suggested standard this way: "A senator should not engage in conduct which would appear to be improper to a reasonable, nonpartisan, fully informed person."

Bennett's first principle was not contested: Senators were required to follow not just written rules and laws; they also had to adhere to certain unwritten standards of conduct. He cited numerous precedents going back to the late 1700s to show that senators could be punished, even expelled, for violating unwritten standards. When the Select Committee on Standards and Conduct first proposed a code of conduct in 1968, it stated in a

and loan regulator on April 2, 1987, was in many ways the beginning of the case against them.

Gray had testified at length before the House Banking Committee a year earlier that the four senators present at the meeting had acted improp-

erly. Gray had been upset by the session and had complained to his aides about it immediately afterward. Gray testified that he had first publicly mentioned the meeting when a reporter called him in May 1989.

report that "the Senate must not only be free of improper influence but must also be . . . free from the appearance of impropriety."

In 1964 the committee's report on its investigation of a top Senate employee (Bobby Baker, who was found to have used his office to promote outside business interests) said that "officials have an obligation . . . to refrain not only from actual wrongdoing but from conduct leaving the appearance of wrongdoing."

In its 1978 report on the Korean influence scandal, the Ethics Committee said "a key element" of previous conduct-related Senate resolutions "is that a senator must avoid the appearance of impropriety, as well as impropriety itself." *(Baker case, p. 102; Korean influence buying, p. 58)*

Durenberger, House Cases

Bennett said that the standard had been invoked most recently in the 1989-90 case against Dave Durenberger, R-Minn. Before the Senate unanimously voted to denounce Durenberger for unethical financial dealings, Warren B. Rudman, R-N.H., vice chairman of the Ethics Committee, said his colleague "failed his obligation of protecting both the appearance and reality of propriety." *(Durenberger case, p. 33)*

Bennett cited three House cases as well: Robert L. F. Sikes, D-Fla., in 1976; Raymond F. Lederer, D-Pa., in 1981; and Mario Biaggi, D-N.Y., in 1988. *(Sikes, p. 41; Lederer, p. 63; Biaggi, p. 69)*

Bennett's precedents involved more than just appearances, however. The committee found that Durenberger violated rules on speech fees, financial disclosure, gifts, and campaign contributions. Lederer and Biaggi were charged with violating criminal bribery statutes, while Sikes was found to

have violated House disclosure requirements.

Senators' Arguments

The Keating senators urged the committee to focus on whether their behavior itself violated any rules, laws, or standards of conduct. DeConcini's attorney, James Hamilton, contended that the standard set in S Res 338—prohibiting "improper conduct which may reflect upon the Senate"—was a "twofold test."

Its appearance standard, he said, could not be imposed independently. First, the conduct in question must be found to be improper, then it must be shown to reflect badly on the Senate.

William W. Taylor III, Cranston's attorney, said that any appearance problems that did arise should be left to the voters: "That is a matter for which the American electorate is uniquely equipped to decide."

Committee Decision

In the end, no precedent was set concerning the appearance standard. The committee based its actions on actual improprieties, not on appearances. On February 27, 1991, it rebuked DeConcini, Glenn, McCain, and Riegle for poor judgment, and it criticized DeConcini and Riegle for creating improper appearances. But it said none of these cases rose to a level that warranted stronger discipline.

When the committee reprimanded Cranston ten months later, on November 20, it made no mention of appearances. Rather, it said that Cranston "engaged in an impermissible pattern of conduct in which fundraising and official activities were substantially linked. . . . " It said further that his conduct was "improper and repugnant."

He told the committee that he was improperly pressured at the meeting to withdraw a bank board regulation adopted February 27, 1987, limiting certain thrift investments in real estate and other enterprises that was being strongly opposed by

Lincoln. And he alleged that DeConcini offered him a "quid pro quo" that Lincoln would change some of its controversial practices if the rule was abandoned. While Riegle did not attend the meeting, Gray testified that the senator had told him to "expect a call" to set it up. Attorneys for the senators homed in on the former regulator, challenging his suitability for the job of bank board chairman, his memory of dates and other facts, and, most of all, his broad assertions that the senators had acted improperly.

Some members of the Ethics panel had trouble with Gray's assertions. Lott acknowledged "shaking my head in disgust" at some statements, and Sanford said to Gray: "I think probably your explanation of all of this as being politicians chasing money is perhaps not quite accurate."

Gray conceded that he had been the one to suggest that the senators hold a second meeting, on April 9, with the regulators who were in charge of the Lincoln case. He said he had been shocked that Riegle had attended that meeting. But he told Green that he had no recollection of meeting with Riegle on April 21, 1987, less than two weeks later, to ask for help in getting a job on Wall Street. His term as bank board chairman was about to expire.

Meeting with Regulators

All five senators attended the meeting a week later in DeConcini's office with examiners from the San Francisco Federal Home Loan Bank and the Washington office of the bank board. Two of the regulators who attended the April 9, 1987, meeting testified at the hearings: William Black, then deputy director of the Federal Savings and Loan Insurance Corporation (FSLIC), and Michael Patriarca, head of the San Francisco regional office.

A memorandum summarizing notes that Black took during the meeting was submitted by Bennett as a reliable account of what went on. "It is a fairly remarkable document," Bennett said. "Everyone who has seen that memo says that this transcript-like memo is accurate in all essential respects."

"A fair reading of that memo," Bennett went on, "reveals clearly that Senator DeConcini was negotiating or trying to strike a deal for Lincoln."

Black, who at the time of the hearings was chief counsel of the western region of the Office of Thrift Supervision (OTS), testified that he and other regulators were improperly pressured by the senators in the controversial meeting. But, he said, he and his colleagues did nothing in response to the meeting.

Black provided the committee with a picture of Lincoln's deep financial problems and the "scam," as he termed it, that the thrift used to stay solvent. He testified that the thrift was basically a Ponzi scheme that used fraudulent accounting of prohibited ownership investments in real estate to generate income that could be paid to the parent corporation, American Continental. When the bank board began in 1986 to crack down on Lincoln's real estate investments, the thrift was put in the position of potential insolvency, Black said.

As had Gray before him, Black drew few distinctions on his own among the senators who met with him on April 9. He noted repeatedly that DeConcini at the meeting had used the word "we" to refer to the senators' concerns about Lincoln and said he assumed DeConcini was speaking for everyone.

Black asserted that, by poisoning the atmosphere involving Lincoln, the actions of the senators may have led to a two-year delay in closing the thrift at tremendous additional cost to the taxpayers. Regulators first formally recommended in May 1987 that Lincoln be closed. It finally happened in April 1989. There was no corroborating evidence for Black's assertion, however, and it seemed not to be accepted by members of the Ethics Committee or even Bennett. None of the regulators present at the April meetings, nor any who came later, testified that they were prevented from doing their jobs because of political pressure from the senators.

Patriarca, the head of the San Francisco regional office of the OTS, confirmed details of Black's memo and agreed with Gray and Black that DeConcini had made the most strenuous efforts in Keating's behalf. He testified that De-Concini had "negotiated" with him for special treatment for Lincoln during the April 9 meeting, which he considered improper. Patriarca described Glenn as "blunt," McCain as "uncomfortable," and Riegle as having conducted a "cross-examination" of the regulators. Cranston made a "cameo appearance," he said. The senators' tone changed markedly, Patriarca said, after the regulators informed them that there would be a criminal referral to the Justice Department because of some of Lincoln's practices.

M. Danny Wall, who succeeded Gray as chairman of the Federal Home Loan Bank Board in July 1987, testified December 4 that he had been approached by both DeConcini and Cranston in Lincoln's behalf and that neither had done anything wrong. Wall, former staff director of the Senate Banking Committee, took sharp issue with Black's testimony that political pressure had led to a delay in closing Lincoln.

Cranston Fund Raising

The committee focused in the week of December 3 largely on the possibility of a connection between Cranston's fund raising and his concern for Lincoln.

In his opening remarks, Bennett had used Cranston's candor against him, particularly his admission that campaign contributions result in favored treatment. Bennett cited Cranston's sworn deposition: "A person who makes a contribution has a better chance to get access than someone who does not."

Memorandums to Cranston from a key aide, Joy Jacobson, released by the committee December 3, showed the possibility that Keating expected help in return for his financial contributions.

Jacobson was chief fund raiser for Cranston's 1986 reelection campaign. She testified that after 1986 she worked regularly out of Cranston's ma-

jority whip office to raise money for a variety of voter-registration and get-out-the-vote drives and for the Democratic Senatorial Campaign Committee. In those efforts, she said, she helped to collect hundreds of thousands of dollars from Lincoln and American Continental.

Jacobson's strongest testimony was contained in a series of memos to Cranston in 1987 and 1988. A January 2, 1987, summary of her fund-raising plans noted that, because the Democrats again had a majority in the Senate, "there are a number of individuals who have been very helpful to you who have cases or legislative matters pending with our office who will rightfully expect some kind of resolution." Among them she listed Keating, who, she said, "is continuing to have problems with the Bank Board and Ed Gray."

In a September 6, 1987, memo, Jacobson noted that Keating should be pleased with the appointment of Wall to succeed Gray at the bank board. Noting that Cranston had an upcoming September 24 meeting with Keating, Jacobson said he should ask for $250,000 for one of the voter-registration committees Cranston supported.

And in a memo January 18, 1988, she noted that Cranston and Keating had recently had dinner and reminded him that Keating wanted him to call Wall about Lincoln's continuing troubles with the bank board. Less than a month later, Keating gave $500,000 to two of Cranston's voter drives during a trip to Keating's headquarters in Phoenix. Jacobson testified under questioning by Cranston's attorney, Taylor, that the senator never said he was taking action because of the money. But she conceded to Bennett that "in retrospect" there was probably a link in Keating's mind.

As evidence of Cranston's continuing help for Keating and the degree to which Keating apparently counted on the California Democrat, Bennett cited an urgent message to the senator from Keating in April 1989. The message asked for Cranston's help to persuade Wall to approve the sale of Lincoln to a group of employees and other investors. Such a sale would have preserved some or all of Keating's investment in the thrift. "The consequences of not doing the above are a political disaster for anybody and everybody connected with Lincoln's past," Keating wrote.

Defending Cranston

Testimony December 11 from another Cranston aide, Carolyn Jordan, appeared to provide some cover for her boss. She testified that although she regularly inquired about Lincoln with regulators, she had no knowledge that Keating had contributed large sums to Cranston or to his various political causes. Although Jordan said she had no knowledge of Keating's contributions at the time she and Cranston were meeting with Lincoln officials, she conceded that Cranston fund raiser Jacobson was also sometimes present.

Jordan testified that on her own, or with the cooperation of others in Cranston's office—but without Cranston's knowledge—she regularly inserted into the *Congressional Record* statements that passed for comments seemingly made during floor debates by Cranston himself.

On one such occasion in 1987 she inserted comments contradicting a floor statement by Banking Committee Chairman William Proxmire, D-Wis., on a subject of direct interest to Lincoln. The thrift later cited those comments, attributed to Cranston, as "legislative history" in a lawsuit against federal regulators. Jordan testified that Lincoln officials had not asked for the action. "It may have inadvertently assisted them, but it was certainly not the purpose of the statement," she said.

DeConcini Fights Back

Of the five senators, DeConcini tried hardest to mount a vigorous defense—largely by calling a phalanx of character witnesses. He called Sen. Daniel K. Inouye, D-Hawaii, and Arizona's governor, Democrat Rose Mofford, to testify for him.

Inouye had experience in dealing with politically sensitive inquiries: He served on the Senate Watergate Committee investigating the Nixon administration in 1973; in 1987 he was chairman of the Senate special committee probing the Iran-contra affair.

Linking DeConcini's actions to the normal duties of a senator, Inouye reminded the Ethics Committee members that they all went to bat for constituents who had battles with government agencies. "I think Sen. DeConcini's conduct was spotless," Inouye said. By implication, the same was true of the rest. If what DeConcini did was improper, "I think all of us at one time or another have done that," he said. "I believe that what is on trial here are not the five colleagues of mine but the United States Senate."

On December 10, DeConcini called former U.S. customs commissioner William Von Raab and three Arizona residents: the head of a drug rehabilitation center, a sheriff, and a disabled World War II veteran, all of whom had sought and received assistance from DeConcini. DeConcini also introduced statements and affidavits from three colleagues and one former senator, all attesting to his character and taking issue with the contention that his actions in the Lincoln case were out of the ordinary. The statements and affidavits were provided by Ernest F. Hollings, D-S.C.; Paul Simon, D-Ill.; Strom Thurmond, R-S.C.; and former senator Robert Morgan, D-N.C.

Von Raab testified that during the eight years he ran the Customs Service, beginning in 1981, DeConcini intervened with him repeatedly, particularly in behalf of importers when the senator believed the agency had overreacted. He said that DeConcini was "always firm, resolute, but always

R. Michael Jenkins

The five senators, shown here with their lawyers, denied that they had used improper influence to help savings and loan head Charles H. Keating, Jr.

fair." And he said DeConcini's behavior was no different from that of any other member of Congress.

DeConcini's aggressive defense backfired somewhat on December 10, when former American Continental tax accountant David Stevens testified that DeConcini had tried to use him to discredit McCain. Stevens had written to the Ethics Committee in October, saying that he believed McCain had never intended to repay American Continental for travel provided members of McCain's family in 1984-86.

Failing to receive a response from the Ethics Committee, Stevens wrote to DeConcini and sent him a copy of the original letter. Stevens testified that DeConcini then called him and asked him to sign an affidavit for use in the hearings. He testified that DeConcini also asked if he could release the letter to the news media. The letter was leaked to several newspapers in late November. Under examination by McCain attorney Dowd, Stevens retracted his assertion that McCain had not intended to reimburse American Continental for the trips.

The issue of DeConcini's request to release the Stevens letter to the media raised a sore point because numerous documents in the case had been leaked and Lincoln had previously complained that federal regulators leaked damaging information about the institution. Committee member Pryor had gone so far in his opening remarks at the hearings to say that staff caught leaking information should be fired, senators who were caught expelled, and lawyers who were caught disbarred.

DeConcini's office asserted that the letter from Stevens was not Ethics Committee property. But Stevens's appearance was plainly damaging to DeConcini.

Surprise Witness: Keating Lobbyist

The hearings got a surprise in December when the committee announced that it would make a grant of immunity from future criminal prosecution to obtain the testimony of a new witness.

James J. Grogan was vice president and chief counsel of Lincoln, corporate counsel for American Continental, and Keating's point man on Capitol Hill. When Keating went to visit a member, Grogan usually went along; when members visited American Continental's Phoenix headquarters, Grogan went too. He talked to all five senators about Lincoln's problems with regulators, and he delivered some of the $1.5 million in contributions made by Keating and his associates to the senators' campaigns and political causes.

Grogan had previously cited constitutional protections against self-incrimination in declining to testify. He faced no criminal charges at the time, but a federal grand jury in Los Angeles was looking broadly into the Lincoln affair.

In a carefully worded statement December 5, the committee said that "it cannot fulfill its obligations to these members [the five senators] and to the Senate without obtaining [Grogan's] testimony." To obtain it, the committee had to grant Grogan limited immunity from prosecution—meaning that he could not be prosecuted for what he told the committee and that prosecutors could not use what he told the committee to develop new evidence against him. He would be subject to prosecution for perjury, however, if he lied under oath.

The committee first questioned Grogan in closed sessions and then put him on the stand publicly on December 14-15. Grogan raised serious questions about the depth of Riegle's involvement with Keating, and he made a direct link between legislative actions that Keating sought from Cranston and financial assistance that Cranston sought from Keating.

He testified that in early 1987 he and Riegle had discussed Lincoln's problems with the Federal Home Loan Bank Board, which Keating thought was harassing Lincoln. Grogan testified that Riegle told him he knew the bank board chairman, Gray. "He had done favors for Ed Gray. He thought that he could set up a meeting," Grogan testified. He said Riegle further suggested that Grogan ask DeConcini and McCain to set up the meeting and have them invite Riegle, apparently to provide Riegle with cover.

"It was apparent to me that Senator Riegle knew, as a shrewd politician, that this was a potentially politically explosive situation," Grogan said. As evidence that Riegle had arranged the April 2 meeting, Grogan testified that the senator had mentioned the idea of a meeting to him in early March 1987 when Riegle was visiting Keating and American Continental headquarters in Phoenix. A few days later, Grogan said, Keating told him that Riegle had called and had spoken with Gray.

Other evidence that appeared to corroborate Grogan's testimony was a page from Cranston's calendar for April 2, which noted a meeting in DeConcini's office with Gray, Riegle, and McCain. It did not mention Glenn. Grogan said the other senators were "miffed" because they had expected Riegle to attend the April 2 meeting. Grogan said the first meeting had gone so badly that he was unsure the second meeting would come off. So, he said, he flew to Washington during the interim "to keep the team together."

He also testified that the original purpose of the meetings—as he had promoted them—was to inquire about the status of a long-running examination of Lincoln by the regulators. Keating wanted more, he said. According to notes of the second meeting, talking points for the meetings drafted by Lincoln employees, and memorandums prepared by DeConcini's staff, the subject expanded to a request that the regulators grant "forbearance" to Lincoln on some of its investments that regulators said violated bank board regulations. And the regulators were asked to reappraise Lincoln's real estate holdings that the thrift said were being undervalued.

The "Mutual Aid Society"

Grogan also testified extensively about Cranston's fund raising. He said that within days of meeting Cranston in 1984 at a Democratic party event, he was called by Cranston fund raiser Jacobson, who asked him to help raise money for the senator. At that time, Grogan said, Cranston said to him: "I've been very good to savings and loans. I worked hard for California savings and loans. You all should really support me."

In late 1986, Grogan testified, he asked Jacobson for help in killing a Senate floor amendment that would have hurt Lincoln's business. According to Grogan, Jacobson called him back to report that she had tried just that. In that same conversation, Grogan testified, Jacobson said she had another matter to discuss. Grogan quoted Jacobson as saying, "I want to switch gears, and I want you to know this is totally unrelated."

Grogan testified that Jacobson then asked for help in securing a personal loan for Cranston's reelection campaign. A short time later, Lincoln granted Cranston a personal line of credit for $300,000, though the senator never used it. Grogan recalled that Cranston greeted Keating at a dinner in Los Angeles in January 1988 by saying, "Ah, the mutual aid society."

Grogan said he had few contacts with DeConcini, Glenn, and McCain, despite the fact that he had once worked for Glenn. DeConcini, Grogan testified, had a personal relationship with Keating. He said the two men had repeated contacts to which Grogan was not a party. He said he was not always privy to Keating's thinking. And, he said, on numerous times he misread Keating's intentions.

Ultimately, he said, he and Keating had a falling out over Grogan's handling of bankruptcy proceedings involving American Continental. They had not spoken since June 1990, he said, when Grogan left the company.

Grogan testified that Keating had decided after the April 1987 meetings not to continue to use the senators to pressure the regulators further. Keating believed the meetings were a "horrible disaster," Grogan said. "It was a mistake. It intensified the wrath of San Francisco."

Grogan was a cooperative witness, answering questions directly. He cast his, Keating's, and Lincoln's actions in the most positive light, insisting—as Keating did—that Lincoln was a profitable firm hounded out of business by zealous regulators. Soliciting help from members of Congress to counter those regulators, he said, was only proper.

According to Grogan, there was never a hint that Keating used political contributions as a means to enlist the senators' help. "It never bothered me because I never, either from the senators—any of them—or from Mr. Keating, I never got even a hint that the money was being given in exchange for anything," Grogan said.

As evidence that contributions do not buy influence, Grogan testified that Cranston, DeConcini, and Glenn had not always done Keating's bidding. And he said that when Riegle announced in early 1988 that he was returning more than $75,000 that Keating had raised for him a year earlier, Keating was angry and offended.

Nevertheless, Grogan said he believed contributions helped to open congressional doors. He also acknowledged the appearance of a conflict of interest when members acted in behalf of large contributors. Grogan also contradicted Jordan's recollections of the genesis of the statement she inserted in the *Congressional Record* to offset comments by Senator Proxmire. Grogan said that he had specifically alerted her to problems in the Proxmire statement and had asked her to insert a statement to neutralize it.

Other Witnesses

The committee on December 2 heard another side to the story of why federal regulators moved slowly to close down Lincoln. According to Rosemary Stewart, former head of enforcement at the Federal Home Loan Bank Board and its successor agency, the Office of Thrift Supervision, the delay had nothing to do with the senators.

Stewart had participated in the 1988 decision to remove the San Francisco regulators from their role in supervising Lincoln, a year after they had recommended that the thrift be seized. Stewart said she believed that the San Francisco regulators had a vendetta against the thrift, as Lincoln was charging at the time. And, she said, the San Francisco regulators had not made their case.

"It would have been unprecedented" to have taken control of an institution that had not yet failed, as the San Francisco regulators were urging, Stewart testified.

Stewart was called as a witness by Cranston's attorney, Taylor. Although her testimony was a strong counterpoint to that of the San Francisco regulators, questioning from Ethics Committee Vice Chairman Rudman showed that he was not convinced Stewart had acted in the government's best interests.

The panel heard January 10, 1991, from a Keating lobbyist, Washington lawyer Margery Waxman, who had written to Keating in May 1988 that he had the regulators "right where you want them." Waxman testified that Keating had hired another attorney and that she had used hyperbole to get Keating to notice her letter. She said she had no contacts with the five senators.

Rebuttal: Glenn, McCain

The senators and their attorneys got a chance to make their cases after the committee took a Christmas and New Year's recess. Glenn and McCain took a low-key approach as they made their cases on January 4, 1991, reflecting the fact that little had appeared in the hearings to damage them. During a day of testimony, the committee heard Glenn and McCain argue that they did nothing inappropriate by attending two April 1987 meetings with federal regulators.

Glenn's attorney, Charles F. C. Ruff, urged the committee to judge Glenn "by the sternest ethical standard that you can apply to the conduct of all of your colleagues in the Senate." Even in that light, he said, Glenn emerged unscathed.

Glenn emphasized that he ended virtually all contacts with Keating after the second April 1987 meeting, at which regulators informed the senators that criminal charges might be filed. "I came to the conclusion that Lincoln was in deep trouble," Glenn said.

Glenn's only action after that time was to set up a lunch meeting in January 1988 between Keating and Speaker Wright. In the summer of 1987, Glenn testified, he turned down Keating's offer to raise campaign contributions because of Keating's battles with the regulators.

McCain testified that he broke off his friendship with Keating just before the April meetings, when Keating asked him to negotiate. "I told him that he was trying to do something that was inappropriate," he said. "I would not do it."

Committee Chairman Heflin questioned McCain closely about vacations he took with Keating between 1983 and 1986, while McCain was still a member of the House. McCain reimbursed American Continental for some of the flights at the time they were taken. In 1989, however, American Continental accountants informed McCain that about $13,400 in flights had not been reimbursed. In May and June of that year, McCain paid the company.

The matter was raised before the House ethics committee, which ruled that his repayment ended the matter. The Senate panel had previously concluded that the matter was one for the House to decide, because McCain had been a representative at the time.

McCain, who became somewhat defensive during the questioning, insisted that he would have paid for the flights if American Continental had told him sooner that the payments had not been made.

There was little suggestion that McCain had done anything wrong beyond not checking on the payments. "You owe John McCain something," argued his attorney, Dowd. "You owe him a straight, crisp, clear finding, based on the overwhelming, undisputed evidence in the record that his actions, at all times, were honest and ethical."

At the conclusion of McCain's testimony, committee member Lott said, "I am compelled to say that you have shown repeatedly that you did nothing improper."

Rebuttal: Riegle, DeConcini

The appearances of Riegle on January 7-8 and DeConcini on January 9-10 concluded the major testimony.

Riegle's attorney blamed "whimsical circumstances" for the close scheduling between a March 23, 1987, Keating-sponsored fund raiser that netted $78,250 and the controversial April 9 meeting that Riegle attended. And he denied that Riegle had had any intention of misleading the committee, particularly with reference to setting up the April 2 meeting with Gray.

Riegle took pains to say that more than $10,000 collected for his campaign from American Continental employees days before the trip to Phoenix was unrelated to his discussions with Keating. In fact, Riegle testified, the money was intended to be given as part of a Keating-sponsored fund raiser scheduled for Riegle in Detroit a few weeks later.

Riegle insisted that he had not discussed fund raising during the trip. Rudman zeroed in on Riegle's inability to recall events and conversations. Rudman said he found Riegle's testimony "remarkably inconsistent."

In particular, he seemed incredulous at Riegle's description of the trip to Phoenix, when Riegle met with Keating, toured American Continental Corp., and—according to other testimony—discussed Keating's problems with federal regulators and proposed a meeting with the senators and Gray.

Rudman said he was confused about why Riegle had visited American Continental but told his aides not to deal with issues involving Lincoln. Riegle said he kept his aides out of the issue because the California-based thrift was not a direct constituent. But he said he visited American Continental because the company was investing in Detroit.

Bennett made clear in his cross-examination of Riegle that he did not believe the protests of several of the senators that they were concerned in the meetings not just about Lincoln but about the entire thrift industry. "I don't see . . . in a year and a half of investigation," Bennett said, "a single piece of paper that suggests you or any of the other senators in connection with this matter were concerned or had an issue about a systematic problem that might be affecting the industry."

DeConcini argued in his own defense that a senator could not be punished for the appearance of improper conduct unless there was improper conduct. And his attorney, James Hamilton, argued that DeConcini had not tried to negotiate for Keating, and even if he had, there would be nothing wrong with it.

Hamilton contested Bennett's contention that senators could be punished merely for violating an "appearance standard." But he also argued that adopting such a standard should not condemn DeConcini because he was only doing what many senators did. "Even under special counsel's standard, Senator DeConcini's conduct is wholly proper. . . . No appearance standard can be used to condemn conduct that is commonplace and generally accepted."

The committee voted January 8 not to call Cranston, who was undergoing treatment for prostate cancer in California. Members decided that the record on Cranston was complete enough to make a decision, and the senator did not ask to speak further.

Speaking on Cranston's behalf, his attorney, Taylor, said senators had a duty to act to help constituents—whether or not they were big contributors. "This duty may create an appearance of mutual dependence," he said. But "there is nothing improper, nor is there an appearance that there is anything improper, about that mutuality."

CLOSING VIEWS: BENNETT AND COMMITTEE

Bennett took more than three hours on January 15-16 to sum up his view of the facts and the standards that should apply to the case.

He distinguished carefully among the five and, without actually making recommendations, in essence urged the committee to find that Cranston, DeConcini, and Riegle had acted improperly. He again called upon the committee to find that Glenn and McCain had acted properly at all times. Bennett distinguished them from the others by arguing that their acceptance of contributions was far removed in time from their actions, eliminating any taint from their fund raising.

Bennett argued that DeConcini had gone beyond the bounds of proper behavior to negotiate for Keating with the regulators in 1987, and he noted that DeConcini weighed in with them again in 1989 on the pending sale of Lincoln, despite knowledge that the regulators had referred evidence of possible criminal conduct at Lincoln to the Justice Department.

Bennett argued that Cranston's case provided the closest connections between money and action.

He cited four separate occasions in which Cranston took actions for Keating after soliciting or receiving large amounts of cash for his own campaign or for voter-registration groups with which he was affiliated.

Of Riegle, Bennett also drew a connection between fund raising and action, all of which occurred in a three-month period in 1987. And he made a damning accusation that Riegle had misled the committee, perhaps intentionally, about his role in the Keating affair.

As for the senators' contention that their meetings with and repeated phone calls to regulators were merely "status inquiries" to find out whether the Lincoln case was being handled properly, Bennett was derisive. "If I'm sitting on a park bench, and an eight-hundred-pound gorilla comes along and says, 'Excuse me, I'm just making a status inquiry if there are any seats available,' you say, 'You're damn right, there's a seat available.' And there's a lot of eight-hundred-pound gorillas around this place."

Bennett reiterated his position that the senators' actions had been wrong, and that they should have known how wrong they would appear to the public. "For this body to conclude . . . that there is no appearance standard requires you to disregard what you have written before, what you have said before, what you have decided before."

The comments of Ethics Committee members made it clear that the panel was not going to reach a ruling quickly in the case.

"I would dare say . . . that there are six visions—six visions—of this case and what it means or what it doesn't mean, what is relevant, what is not relevant," Pryor said in his closing comments on January 16.

A few days earlier, Helms referred to the senators as "Keystone Cops" and to Keating as "Daddy Warbucks." He told Riegle, "I don't believe you would have gone out to Phoenix—I don't believe anybody would have been involved

R. Michael Jenkins

Members of the Senate Ethics Committee announce their findings in the Keating Five investigation. Committee Chairman Howell Heflin stands at the microphones.

with Mr. Keating, if he didn't have the ability to give away other people's money."

Helms added that he was unhappy with the way the senators under investigation seemed to feel that there was nothing in the slightest wrong with anything they had done. "If I'm disturbed about one thing—and I'm disturbed about many things—it's that not once have I heard anything remotely resembling a mea culpa about this," he remarked.

Lott, who seemed uncomfortable with the image problems the whole proceeding was creating for the Senate, told reporters on January 8 that he expected the committee to find some significant violations. "I would be amazed if at least one case did not go to the Senate floor" for punishment, he said.

COMPROMISE: NO FLOOR VOTE

Senator Lott's January remark proved to be prescient. One case, Cranston's, did go to the full Senate on November 20—but only as a fait accompli. The six-member Ethics Committee already had settled on Cranston's punishment—a reprimand. The presentation ended the most involved and wrenching ethics episodes in Senate history—but not before it extracted a few more harsh moments of its own.

"The resolution we bring before the Senate today," said Vice Chairman Rudman, "is not a perfect solution; it is, however, for this institution an acceptable result, and it certainly is better than no resolution at all."

A short time before, that outcome had been a

Ethics Committee Findings

Following are excerpts from the text of the Senate Ethics Committee's resolution of reprimand against Alan Cranston, D-Calif., as adopted November 19, 1991:

The committee finds that in connection with his conduct relating to Charles H. Keating Jr. and Lincoln Savings and Loan Association, Sen. Alan Cranston of California engaged in an impermissible pattern of conduct in which fundraising and official activities were substantially linked.... It is further resolved:

1) That Sen. Cranston's impermissible pattern of conduct violated established norms of behavior in the Senate, and was improper conduct that reflects upon the Senate....

2) That Sen. Cranston's conduct was improper and repugnant.

3) In reviewing the evidence available to it, the committee finds that Sen. Cranston: violated no law or specific Senate rule; acted without corrupt intent; and did not receive nor intend to receive personal financial benefit from any of the funds raised through Mr. Keating.

4) Further, the committee finds that extenuating circumstances exist, including the following:

a) That Sen. Cranston is in poor health....

b) That Sen. Cranston has announced his intention not to seek re-election to the Senate.

5) Sen. Cranston's improper conduct deserves the fullest, strongest, and most severe sanction which the committee has the authority to impose.

Therefore, the Senate Select Committee on Ethics, on behalf of and in the name of the Senate, does hereby strongly and severely reprimand Sen. Alan Cranston.

real possibility. The panel had been deadlocked along party lines for weeks. Republican members had been pushing for a move to have the full Senate censure Cranston—a painfully embarrassing punishment in which senators must cast votes in judgment of their colleague. The Democrats wanted the Ethics Committee to exercise its power to rebuke Cranston, as it had done February 27 to the other four Keating Five senators.

A compromise finally began to take shape in November. Republican senator Trent Lott, who earlier had floated a proposal to declare the panel hopelessly stalemated, took a stab at the middle ground: a committee rebuke that the Senate would vote to accept—sort of an indirect censure.

But the Democrats balked. They wanted to avoid a damaging floor fight, and Sen. Harry Reid, D-Nev., who had been secretly acting as Cranston's liaison to the committee for months, told the panel that Cranston would not accept a vote. A final concession by the Republicans sealed the deal: no floor vote, but the committee reprimand would be delivered in person in full view of Cranston's colleagues. The Republicans fought for the harshest possible language. Senate lawyers informed them that the committee could not censure a member, so they settled for what the reprimand resolution called "the fullest, strongest and most severe sanction which the committee has the authority to impose." It said the committee was acting "on behalf of and in the name of the United States Senate" in reprimanding Cranston "strongly and severely."

"We elevated everything to a level just below a Senate censure," said Lott. The resolution included several clauses to soften the blow, including one that made clear that Cranston had "violated no law or specific Senate rule; acted without corrupt intent; and did not receive nor intend to receive personal financial benefit from any of the funds raised through Mr. Keating."

Aiding Cranston's cause was his illness—he had been treated for prostate cancer in 1990 and was still suffering severe side effects—and his plans to retire after 1992. The resolution called those facts "extenuating circumstances." "The thing that finally got the votes was his horrible physical condition," Rudman said in an interview.

The committee approved the compromise 5-0 on November 19. Helms, who had been pressing for censure, abstained.

Impermissible Linkage

Partisan overtones added to the deadlock, but the facts of the Keating Five affair presented the Senate with its most difficult ethics case in recent times because it cut so close to home.

Almost all Washington lawmakers chase political donations, and they all do their jobs in ways that please their supporters. Everyone agrees that in the abstract an implicit quid pro quo exists: Donors give to influence the political process by rewarding or encouraging favorable consideration—be it in the form of access, votes or other favors. Politicians accept their money knowing this full well.

In looking at Cranston's dealings with Keating, the Ethics Committee decided that the implicit veered too close to the explicit. No one episode sealed Cranston's fate; rather, Heflin said, it was "the totality of the circumstances."

Cranston had accepted nearly $1 million, most of it for nonprofit voter-drive groups at a time when Keating was marshaling political clout in a bitter fight with federal regulators over his thrift, Lincoln Savings and Loan.

Large donations were given or solicited close in time to specific official actions by Cranston in Keating's behalf—mostly calls to regulators. Meetings at which contributions were discussed also included talk about Keating's trouble with the regulators. Memos from Cranston's top fund raiser included discussions of both topics.

The committee called that "linkage" and said it breached "established norms of behavior in the Senate and was improper conduct which reflects upon the Senate" in violation of the chamber's longstanding catchall admonition that members must do more than just obey laws and specific rules.

The Ethics panel walked a fine line in attempting to articulate what was wrong with Cranston's conduct. Its leaders insisted they had not relied on the controversial "appearance standard" advocated by Bennett and Helms—that if conduct looks improper, it is improper and can be punished. But they were careful not to disavow it and in fact reaffirmed their rebuke of Senators Riegle and for giving "the appearance of being improper." In saying that Cranston's actions were linked to Keating's donations in more than appearance, the committee insisted that he had not struck a corrupt bargain. If it had found such evidence, Rudman said on the floor, "this committee would recommend expulsion."

Thus, Cranston's behavior was found to fall somewhere between actually being dishonest and merely looking dishonest. Fund raising and official actions were linked, Heflin explained, but not "causally connected."

Rudman offered a clue as to where he thought his colleague's conduct fell in the continuum when he said Keating's $850,000 in contributions to voter groups associated with Cranston were "the major motivation for his actions."

The committee's report offered a little new guidance to senators on how to avoid "linkage." The "cardinal principle," the report said, is to make decisions "without regard to whether the individual has contributed or promised to contribute."

It cautioned members to consider the following: the merits of the constituent's request; how much money the constituent has contributed; whether the type of official action to be taken in behalf of the constituent deviates from the senator's usual conduct; and, finally, "the proximity of money and action." But the report did not say how to evaluate these considerations.

Floor Statements of Cranston, Rudman

Following are excerpts from the Senate floor statements of Alan Cranston, D-Calif., and Ethics Committee Vice Chairman Warren B. Rudman, R-N.H., following the pronouncement November 20, 1991, of the committee's decision to reprimand Cranston:

Cranston

I rise with deep remorse in my heart to accept the reprimand of the committee. I deeply regret the pain all this has caused my family, my friends, my supporters, my constituents. . . .

My intentions were proper in all I did. . . . The committee acknowledges that. But in retrospect, I grant that I should not have solicited and received, even though it was on behalf of others, charitable donations close in time to official actions. . . . Let me make plain, however, that while I accept the ultimate conclusion of the committee, there is documentary and other irrebuttable evidence that contradicts some of the committee's specific findings. . . .

If the committee had called for any action by the full Senate against me, I would have fought it tooth and nail. . . . Let me tell you why I would have done so. First I ask each of you, I ask everyone to note that the committee found and acknowledged the following: that nothing I did violated any law or specific Senate rule; that I acted without corrupt intent; that no evidence was presented to the committee, no evidence, that I ever agreed to help Charles Keating in return for a contribution; that none of the contributions constituted a personal gift to me; and that I did not receive or intend to receive any personal benefit from any of the funds I raised. . . .

Back in the '70s another large corporation, Lockheed, was facing bankruptcy. The livelihoods of many thousands of my constituents and their families were at risk, as was the case with Lincoln. I devoted far more time and effort and made many more phone calls about Lockheed than I ever did

about Lincoln, as I successfully fought to obtain a government-guaranteed loan for Lockheed. . . . Lockheed had supported and raised money for my opponent in the previous election. . . .

I now realize that what I did looked improper. But . . . I differ very, very deeply with the committee statement in the resolution that my conduct "violated established norms of behavior in the Senate. . . ." There are no such established norms of behavior in the Senate. There is no precedent and there is no rule establishing that it is unethical for a senator to engage in legitimate constituent service on behalf of a constituent because it was close in time to a lawful contribution. . . . At least two-thirds of you, my colleagues in the Senate, are involved with charities or foundations. . . . More than a few of these contributors have benefited from actions taken by the senator involved, sometimes close in time to a contribution. Many of the contributions are immense. . . .

Let me turn to the matter of political contributions. . . . It is now more likely than ever to lead to charges of wrongdoing, because the Ethics Committee has enunciated formally a new principle: that it is improper for a senator to engage in legitimate constituent service on behalf of a contributor close in time to a lawful contribution to a senator's campaign or PAC.

Rudman's Response

I must say regretfully that after accepting this committee's recommendation, what I have heard as [sic] a statement I can only describe as arrogant, unrepentant, and a smear on this institution. Everybody does *not* do it. . . .

I have served only eleven years, far less than the occupant of the chair and many others, but I think I know this, that members of this body attempt by word and deed, publicly and privately, to take great care with their personal conduct as it might be perceived by the American people. . . .

A Somber Floor Scene

Key to the final compromise was the desire by all concerned to avoid a full-scale floor fight. For that, the committee needed Cranston to accept its decision. Cranston's bottom line: "If the committee had called for any action by the full Senate against me, I would have fought it tooth and nail."

Perhaps for this reason, the question of whether there would be a floor vote was a tightly held secret. It had become clear by the morning of November 20 that the committee would not ask members to vote, puzzling some. "They're not?" said a surprised Arlen Specter, R-Pa. "So does that constitute an acceptance of the recommendation?"

There was speculation that somebody might try to force a vote, but President Pro Tempore Robert C. Byrd, D-W.Va., quashed that notion when he took the presiding officer's chair shortly after 2 p.m. and said: "The order does not provide for the taking of any votes by the Senate."

The order, however, required everyone to go to the floor. As members filed in, Senate pages dropped the committee's 79-page report on desks, along with a copy of Helms's harsh 247-page dissent. The only members absent for the somber occasion were four Democrats—Bill Bradley, N.J., Kent Conrad, N.D., Bob Kerrey, Neb., and Tom Harkin, Iowa.

Twenty-six aides and lawyers were granted floor privileges, but Byrd sternly warned them: "Only senators will be given the privilege to speak." Byrd's warning seemed aimed at Alan M. Dershowitz, the outspoken criminal defense lawyer (and author of the book *Chutzpah)* whom Cranston persuaded to represent him for free.

Heflin read the panel's resolution and a lengthy statement slowly and deliberately. It was his last act as an Ethics member after twelve years as chairman or vice chairman. He took thirty-five minutes. A couple of members appeared to doze,

some busied themselves with what appeared to be unrelated reading tasks, a few wandered off the floor and back again, but as Heflin finished each page, the chamber filled with a wave of turning pages.

"The path to judgment is easy when a specific law or rule has been violated," he said. "But for those of us who believe in the rule of law, violations of unwritten ethical standards are far more difficult to resolve."

Rudman was next, reading his own lengthy statement much faster. While Heflin's statement had focused on standards, Rudman gave a more detailed accounting of Cranston's conduct. Among the most disturbing incidents, he said, was when Cranston greeted Keating once in 1988 by patting him on the back and saying, "Ah, the mutual aid society." (Cranston said he did not recall the comment.)

Cranston, frail but resolute, began on a contrite note as his colleagues turned their chairs to face him: "I rise with deep remorse in my heart to accept the reprimand of the committee. I deeply regret the pain all this has caused my family, my friends and my supporters," he said. He choked once as he spoke of how proud he was of his work during the past twenty-three years in the Senate, fourteen as whip.

Then came the defense: He rejected many of the committee's findings in a 126-page submission for the record. He attempted to reinterpret the panel's reasoning, saying he was being reprimanded only because "there appeared to be a proximity in time" between donations and actions.

"That is what we're talking about—appearances," he said. "I now realize that what I did looked improper. But I differ, and I differ very, very deeply, with the committee's statement in the resolution that my conduct violated established norms of behavior in the Senate."

He compared the Ethics Committee to a "tyrant king" for deciding ex post facto that any such norms exist. He said he could and had been prepared to produce "example after example of comparable" conduct to show "that my behavior did not violate any established norms." He spoke of contributions as large as $750,000. "You are in jeopardy," he told his colleagues.

During his speech, many members (especially on the Republican side) appeared to grow tense. Some grumbled to each other. Steve Symms, R-Idaho, said he remarked to Wallop, "I heard the same speech twenty years ago when Spiro Agnew resigned."

Rudman grew visibly angry. When Cranston was done, he said in rage that "what I have heard as *[sic]* a statement I can only describe as arrogant, unrepentant, and a smear on this institution. Everybody does *not* do it. . ." *(Excerpts, Cranston and Rudman statements, box, p. 142)*

CHAPTER 11

The Cleanup Begins:

Three Decades of Reform

To put it mildly, Congress was not enjoying good press as the 1992 elections approached. The voters were riled up. It seemed like every time they picked up a newspaper or turned on the television, there was another horror story about Capitol Hill: bad checks, unpaid restaurant tabs, surprise pay raises, sexual harassment, the Keating Five—you name it.

And to top it all off there was the dismal economy, with layoffs, bankruptcies, and homelessness all contrasting sharply with Congress's generous treatment of itself while it, and the president, appeared haplessly unable to make things better for the suffering millions.

It was not a pretty picture, but Congress had no choice but to look at it. It was, after all, an election year. And that meant from Congress's standpoint that something had to be done about the public's throw-the-rascals-out attitude or lots of incumbents would join the unemployed come November.

When that prospect arises, Congress gets busy cleaning up its act, and 1992 was no exception. Beginning the year before, it took a number of steps to reduce its perquisites of office ("perks") and clamp down on abuses—banning honoraria,

closing the "member-friendly" House bank, and even raising the price of haircuts. Taken together, the several penitent actions came to be known unofficially as "The Congressional Contrition Acts of 1991." *(See p. 159.)*

While the wave of breast-beating was intense, it was not particularly unusual. In the previous three decades Congress had undergone several periods of ethics reform awareness, each one usually preceded by congressional or—in the case of Watergate—White House scandals.

CODES OF CONDUCT

For most of its first two centuries of existence, Congress generally was content to keep its internal affairs undisturbed until outside pressures forced it to act. Occasionally the instigation came from the executive branch, through its Justice Department, which from time to time sued a member of Congress, usually for income tax evasion. But mainly, as in the 1990s, the pressure for reform was generated by news stories about congressional excesses.

No formal ethics guidelines existed until 1958,

Government's Code of Ethics

Congress in 1958 approved the following Code of Ethics (H Con Res 175, 85th Congress, 2nd session) for all government employees, including members of Congress.*

Any person in Government service should:

1. Put loyalty to the highest moral principles and to country above loyalty to persons, party, or Government department.

2. Uphold the Constitution, laws, and legal regulations of the United States and of all governments therein and never be a party to their evasion.

3. Give a full day's labor for a full day's pay; giving to the performance of his duties his earnest effort and best thought.

4. Seek to find and employ more efficient and economical ways of getting tasks accomplished.

5. Never discriminate unfairly by the dispensing of special favors or privileges to anyone, whether for remuneration or not; and never accept, for himself or his family, favors or benefits under circumstances which might be construed by reasonable persons as influencing the performance of his governmental duties.

6. Make no private promises of any kind binding upon the duties of office, since a Government employee has no private word which can be binding on public duty.

7. Engage in no business with the Government, either directly or indirectly, which is inconsistent with the conscientious performance of his governmental duties.

8. Never use any information coming to him confidentially in the performance of government duties as a means for making private profit.

9. Expose corruption wherever discovered.

10. Uphold these principles, ever conscious that public office is a public trust.

* The report of the House Committee on Standards of Official Conduct, *In the Matter of a Complaint Against Rep. Robert L. F. Sikes* (H Rept 94-1364, July 23, 1976), stated that "although the Code of Ethics for Government Service was adopted as a concurrent resolution, and as such, may have expired with the adjournment of the 85th Congress, the standards of ethical conduct expressed therein represent continuing traditional standards of ethical conduct to be observed by Members of the House at all times, which were supplemented in 1968 by a specific Code of Official Conduct."

when Congress enacted a code applying throughout the government. The code was part of the reaction to the 1957-58 investigation of Sherman Adams, chief of staff to President Dwight D. Eisenhower. Adams accepted gifts from a businessman, Bernard Goldfine, who it turned out was seeking favorable treatment from federal agencies. In the aftermath Adams resigned.

In 1959 newspaper reports on nepotism and withholding of payroll information prompted the Senate to open its employees' payroll to public scrutiny. Similar information had been available in the House since 1932. *(Nepotism, Chapter 8, p. 98)*

Beginning in 1960, critical stories on congressional junkets led to a series of curbs on travel expense by members. Congress took no effective action, however, to remedy widespread conflict-of-interest problems, such as acceptance of honoraria, members practicing law for extra income, dealings with regulatory agencies, voting on matters in which the member had a personal stake, and relations with lobbyists and campaign contributors.

Congress also established special committees on ethics. To avoid the sort of partisan bickering that surrounded the Senate Rules and Administration Committee's investigation of Bobby Baker, senators in 1964 voted to set up a strictly bipartisan committee to investigate allegations of improper conduct by senators and Senate employees. The

Select Committee on Standards and Conduct had as its first chairman a respected elder, John Stennis, D-Miss. Its first case was the investigation and censure of Thomas Dodd, D-Conn.

The new rules declared that senators should use the power and perquisites the people entrusted to them "only for their benefit and never for the benefit of himself or of a few." The Senate code also:

- Spelled out conditions under which senators could accept money from fund-raising events and the uses to which contributions could be put. In addition to campaign expenses, contributions could be used for travel and printing or broadcasting of reports to constituents. These accounts were popularly known as "slush funds."
- Prohibited all except designated Senate employees from soliciting or distributing campaign funds.
- Required senators and employees above a certain income to file confidential financial disclosure statements annually with the U.S. comptroller general. Contributions received at fund raisers and honoraria of $300 or more were to be made public.

The 1958 code had been hortatory. It had no legal force. Ten years later the House followed the Senate's example and adopted new rules intended to help prevent conflicts of interest in Congress. The new rules in both chambers were largely a response to the internal investigations of Rep. Adam Clayton Powell, Jr., D-N.Y., Senator Dodd, and Robert G. "Bobby" Baker, secretary to the Senate majority. *(Powell, p. 11; Dodd, p. 30; Baker, p. 102)*

The House in 1967, after the Powell case, established a twelve-member bipartisan Committee on Standards of Official Conduct to recommend a code of conduct for representatives and the powers it might need to enforce it. The first chairman was Rep. Melvin Price, D-Ill.

The committee recommended a code of conduct in 1968, along with a requirement for financial disclosure. In adopting these the House also made the committee permanent and gave it investigative and enforcement powers.

The Code of Official Conduct, among other things, declared that a member may "accept no gift of substantial value, directly or indirectly, from any person, organization or corporation having a direct interest in legislation before the Congress" or accept an honorarium for a speech or article "in excess of the usual and customary value for such services."

The House rule on financial disclosure, unlike the Senate's, required that the information be available to the public. The Senate had rejected a similar requirement by a vote of 40-44. Representatives were told to list financial interests of more than $5,000 or income of more than $1,000 from companies doing substantial business with the government or regulated by the government, and their sources of income for services exceeding $5,000 annually.

In 1970 the House broadened the public disclosure requirements to include two new items—the source of each honorarium of $300 or more earned in one year, and the names of creditors to whom $10,000 or more was owed for ninety days or longer without the pledge of specific security.

Post-Watergate Reforms

The 1972-74 Watergate affair, in which the central crime was abuse of power in the White House, also focused attention on influence buying in Congress and throughout the federal government. Other congressional investigations in this period examined a milk lobby's deal with President Richard Nixon and illegal campaign contributions from powerful corporations.

In the post-Watergate period, Congress

strengthened the public disclosure law on election campaign contributions and then turned to its own ethical standards. Meanwhile the Justice Department began to give more attention to "white-collar crime," including alleged misdeeds by individual members of Congress.

Several years after Watergate a foreign government, the Republic of South Korea, was found guilty by congressional investigating committees of spending hundreds of thousands of dollars, often as campaign contributions, to influence Congress.

The result in the 1970s was the most stringent congressional reform movement up to that time. Like most such waves this one was followed by countermovements and some backsliding, but its major achievements remained historic: for the first time the law required members of Congress to disclose the source and amount of major campaign contributions. And they and top officers of the executive and judicial branches were also required to disclose their financial holdings.

Taking Initiative

The creation of ethics committees institutionalized Congress's responsibility to police itself. But it left open the question of how much initiative the committees should take. In their early years the committees tended to wait until criminal proceedings had started before investigating a member. Critics complained that this approach was too tolerant of borderline behavior. They said that the congressional ethics codes spelled out higher standards than mere avoidance of criminal activity. They suggested that members must be answerable to their colleagues for questionable legislative actions that could not be prosecuted in court because of the Constitution's immunity clause.

The committees' procedures, in which they acted as investigator, prosecutor, and jury, also came under criticism. And because of members'

reluctance to serve on the committees, turnover was rapid and their caliber as a whole was not widely respected in Congress.

In both of the committees' major investigations between 1977 and 1982, the executive branch had acted first. One case concerned South Korea's attempted influence buying, which the Justice Department had secretly been examining, and the other was a follow-up to the FBI's Abscam operation to identify corrupt legislators.

For several years the House ethics committee was reluctant to make any public investigation of misconduct. For example, *Life* magazine on August 9, 1968, raised charges of wrongdoing against Rep. Cornelius E. Gallagher, D-N.J., calling him a "tool and collaborator" of a reputed Mafia figure in New Jersey. The committee, after looking into the *Life* allegations, chose not to release any information on its inquiry and it took no action against Gallagher. Chairman Price said "there was no proof of any violation" of the House's code of ethics.

In 1972 Gallagher was indicted for income tax evasion, perjury, and conspiracy to hide kickbacks. He pleaded guilty to the tax charge, was sentenced to two years in prison, and did not seek reelection. In 1978, during the so-called Koreagate hearings, businessman Tongsun Park testified that among his payments to members of Congress in the early 1970s was $211,000 to Gallagher.

In May 1976, eight years after it gained permanent status, the ethics committee undertook its first investigation of a member—Rep. Robert L. F. Sikes, D-Fla. The case resulted in Sikes's being reprimanded for financial misconduct. *(Sikes, Chapter 3, p. 41)*

A number of criminal prosecutions and sex scandals involving members of Congress also helped to create the climate for the committee's new activism, and for both chambers' adoption of additional new ethics codes in 1977. *(1970s scandals, Chapters 5, 6, and 7)*

CODE, PAY RELATIONSHIP

In 1978 Congress passed the Ethics in Government Act to enforce the new codes and apply their financial disclosure requirements to the other two branches of government. Two public commissions had urged Congress to raise its own pay—but only if it adopted effective codes of ethics.

One group was the quadrennial Commission on Executive, Legislative, and Judicial Salaries, chaired in 1976-77 by businessman Peter G. Peterson, a former secretary of commerce. The other was the special Commission on Operations of the Senate, headed by former senator Harold E. Hughes, D-Iowa, which said the Senate had "insufficient safeguards against conflicts of interest." It recommended banning honoraria and requiring full financial disclosure by senators and the chamber's top employees.

The Peterson commission also called for financial disclosure plus additional steps: a limit on the outside income members could earn in addition to their congressional salaries, accountable expense allowances, and public audits of compliance with the conflict-of-interest restrictions. The commission was regarded as having significant influence because it was the originating body for salary increases at the highest levels of government, including Supreme Court justices and cabinet members.

Limits and Disclosure

President Gerald R. Ford, with the concurrence of president-elect Jimmy Carter, approved the Peterson commission recommendations for pay increases and a congressional code of ethics and forwarded them to Congress on January 17, 1977. Under the proposal congressional salaries would rise 28.9 percent, from $44,600 to $57,500. Other officials, including the top grades of the civil service, would get comparable increases.

Congressional leaders moved swiftly to put the twin proposals for Congress on track. Believing the pay raise was needed but keenly aware of public opinion against it, House Speaker Thomas P. O'Neill, Jr., D-Mass., and Senate Majority Leader Robert C. Byrd, D-W.Va., made passage of strong ethics codes a condition for approval of the salary increase. Both leaders said that a limit on outside income was essential to a strong code; O'Neill called the provision "the heart and soul of the entire package" of ethical standards. It became the most bitterly fought section of the code in each house. It did not apply to "unearned" income such as dividends and capital gains.

O'Neill assigned responsibility for drawing up an ethics code to a bipartisan Commission on Administrative Review headed by Rep. David R. Obey, D-Wis., which began work in late 1976. The commission released a proposed code on February 7, 1977, and the House passed it 402-22 on March 2, after heated debate on the outside income issue.

The Senate used the Obey Commission's work as the basis for a Senate code that paralleled the House code in most respects. It passed the Senate April 1 after two weeks of debate and action on sixty-four amendments.

The 86-9 vote in favor of passage by no means reflected the depth of feeling in the Senate against elements of the new code. Gaylord Nelson, D-Wis., floor manager for the bill, said afterward that many senators who voted for it feared the political consequences of a negative vote.

Nevertheless, Nelson said, Senate acceptance of full financial disclosure was a "milestone" because past efforts to force senators to make public their financial operations had been hotly contested.

In both chambers the earned income limit produced the bitterest opposition, but in each case it was approved by lopsided margins. The House vote was 344-79 and the Senate's was 62-35. It continued to be attacked, however, both before and after its January 1, 1979, effective date. In March

1979 the Senate voted 54-44 to defer imposing the limit on senators for four years, to 1983.

Provisions of 1977 Codes

The limit on outside earned income—set at 15 percent of the congressional salary, or $8,625 at the salary level existing in 1977—was directed at conflict-of-interest problems raised by large honoraria given by interest groups and at the continuing but declining practice of members carrying on as private lawyers or insurance agents while supposedly working full time as members of Congress. The source and amount of this income had to be reported.

The codes also abolished office accounts, which put an end to the last remaining device by which members could accept unreported contributions from organizations or individuals and use the funds for virtually any purpose. Members also were faced with new restrictions on their use of the franking privilege to send mail.

And finally, the idea that personal financial activities were nobody's business but the member's own was put to rest. As passed, the codes required members to make public data on their income, gifts received, financial holdings, debts, securities, commodity transactions, and real estate dealings. Spouses had to report much the same information.

Members were not required to report the exact value of their holdings of different kinds but only a range of value—the scale ran from not more than $5,000 to greater than $5 million (later reduced to $250,000 and over). In the 1978 Ethics in Government Act, Congress applied roughly the same disclosure rules to high officials of the executive and judicial branches.

Both codes prohibited members and employees from accepting gifts of $100 or more from lobbyists and foreign nationals and forbade the conversion of testimonial or campaign funds to personal use. They also set a maximum amount a member could accept as an honorarium.

The Senate code contained three significant sections not in the House code. One was a provision to prohibit senators or employees from engaging in a professional practice, such as law, for compensation. Strom Thurmond of South Carolina, the Republican floor manager of the code, had proposed the flat ban in committee, arguing that senators had "no business" practicing other professions. It was modified on the floor to permit senators and employees to practice a profession so long as they were not affiliated with any firm and so long as their work was not carried out during Senate office hours. *(Law practice by members, box, p. 152)*

The Senate code also prohibited former senators from lobbying in the Senate for one year after leaving office and prohibited former staff members for a senator or committee from lobbying their former employer or committee member and staff for one year.

Unlike the House code, the Senate code declared that no member, officer, or employee could refuse to hire an individual, discharge an individual, or discriminate with respect to promotion, pay or terms of employment on the basis of race, color, religion, sex, national origin, age, or state of physical handicap.

1978 Ethics in Government Act

Besides giving legal force to the 1977 codes, the ethics law enacted in October 1978 contained other strong conflict-of-interest provisions covering executive employees who leave the government (known as "revolving-door" restrictions), but it did not apply those constraints to members and employees of the legislative branch.

President Jimmy Carter had given impetus to these new precautions even before he assumed the presidency. He required his appointees to meet guidelines for financial disclosure, divestiture of holdings that could create conflicts between private and government interests, and postgovernment employment restrictions. He asked Congress to enact these requirements into law.

As a direct outgrowth of the Watergate investigations, the Ethics in Government Act established procedures for court appointment of a special prosecutor to substitute for Justice Department prosecutors whenever a high-ranking federal official was accused of criminal action. The Watergate special prosecutor had been appointed under the attorney general's general authority to name special counsel. The new law set forth a step-by-step process for initiating and carrying out such an investigation.

The act set up an office of legal counsel in the Senate to represent that body and its members in court. The House decided not to be covered by this new office.

The act also established the Office of Government Ethics in the Office of Personnel Management, which Carter created in 1978 by splitting the Civil Service Commission in two. The new ethics office would develop rules and regulations on government conflicts of interest and other ethical problems, and it would monitor and investigate compliance with federal ethics laws.

The basic elements of the Ethics in Government Act having been debated in Congress since 1976, a consensus was clear by the time the House debated the Senate-passed bill in September 1978. Carter signed the final version of the legislation on October 26, 1978.

HONORARIA

Congress first limited how much its members could earn from honoraria in the 1974 campaign finance law. For 1975 senators and representatives could receive no more than $15,000 annually for giving speeches and writing articles and were limited to $1,000 for each item.

Under pressure from the Senate, that ceiling was raised in the 1976 amendments to the campaign law to allow members of Congress to receive $2,000 for each individual event and an aggregate amount of $25,000 a year. However, the $25,000 limit was a net figure because members were allowed to deduct certain expenses such as booking agents' fees and travel expenditures.

The 1977 House and Senate ethics codes, with their 15 percent limit on earned income, cut the ceiling on total honoraria to less than $10,000 and the limit on a single honorarium to $1,000. But the Senate subsequently put off its income limit and repealed the $25,000 honorarium ceiling, keeping only the campaign law's $2,000-a-speech maximum. Critics said senators were placing themselves in bond to interest groups willing to pay generous honoraria. Supporters replied that without the opportunity to earn honoraria the Senate would become even more a rich man's club.

The principal purpose of the limits on earned income and honoraria was to reduce potential conflicts of interest. It was recognized that organizations often gave honoraria to members of Congress serving on committees that handled legislation sought by the donor organization. Getting legislators to speak to a conference and mingle with organization representatives could be an effective lobbying technique.

Under the 1977 House and Senate ethics rules a member had to report gifts of transportation, food, lodging, or entertainment aggregating $250 or more from any one source during the preceding calendar year. The rule applied to individuals and groups that did not have a direct interest in legislation.

But the codes specifically barred members and employees from accepting gifts aggregating more than $100 during a calendar year from persons having direct interests in legislation, or from foreign nationals. Both chambers defined persons with direct interests in legislation as lobbyists (even if

Members of Congress and the Practice of Law

Until World War II, to be a member of Congress was to hold a part-time job. Consequently, certain occupations that demand almost full-time attention—running a business or teaching school, for example—sent few representatives to Congress while others, notably the law, sent many. For years more than half of all members of Congress were lawyers, but the percentage has been dropping. In the 101st Congress (1991-93) it was 45.6 percent. Men and women from business and banking accounted for the second-highest category, 35 percent.

Legal Practice and Past Scandals

The combination of two professions—law and congressional office—has led to numerous scandals. Sen. Daniel Webster's retainer from the Bank of the United States is familiar to many. What is not so well known is that Webster's professional relationship with the bank was no secret; he represented the bank in forty-one cases before the Supreme Court.

It was not an unusual arrangement for the time; neither was it universally condoned. John Quincy Adams, for example, as a member of Congress declined to practice before federal courts.

It was not until the 1850s that members were forbidden to represent claimants against the U.S. government. This restriction grew out of a scandal surrounding senator, and later secretary of the Treasury, Thomas Corwin of Ohio. Corwin successfully recovered half a million dollars (an enormous sum for those days) in a mining case; scandal erupted when it was disclosed that both the claimant and silver mine were frauds.

Legal practice played a supporting role in the great railroad robbery known as the Crédit Mobilier scandal of the Grant administration. In that case, as brought out in a congressional hearing, promoters of the Union Pacific Railroad used stock in Crédit Mobilier, a joint stock company they controlled, to bribe members of Congress to keep up federal subsidies to the railroad. *(Crédit Mobilier scandal, p. 7)*

The early 1900s again brought congressional ethics to a low spot in public opinion. Heavily promoted by publisher William Randolph Hearst, a series of articles by David Graham Phillips called *Treason of the Senate* alleged corrupt behavior by twenty-one senators. The series played a major role in promoting direct election of senators. Only one of the twenty-one senators replied publicly to Phillips's charges. He was Sen. Joseph W. Bailey, D-Texas, who had received more than $225,000 in legal fees for several months' services to a Texas oilman. Bailey vehemently defended his practice of law while serving in the Senate:

> I despise those public men who think they must remain poor in order to be considered honest. I am not one of them. If my constituents want a man who is willing to go to the poorhouse in his old age in order to stay in the Senate during his middle age, they will have to find another senator. I intend to make every dollar that I can honestly make without neglecting or interfering with my public duty.

Bar Association Actions

The legal profession moved to discourage congres-

they were not registered lobbyists), businesses, labor unions, and organizations that maintained political action committees.

Subsequent advisory opinions, however, made it clear that a member could accept more than $100 in food, lodging, transportation, and other "necessary expenses" so long as the member "renders personal services sufficient to constitute 'equal consideration' for the expenses provided by the sponsoring organization." As long as the

sional law practice in the late 1960s. The move came after a series of scandals that involved, sometimes indirectly, congressional law practices. Among those cases (discussed elsewhere in this chapter) were those of Rep. Thomas F. Johnson, D-Md., Senate Majority Secretary Bobby Baker, Sen. Thomas J. Dodd, D-Conn., and Rep. Cornelius Gallagher, D-N.J.

The American Bar Association revised its canons in 1969. Its new Code of Professional Responsibility provided that the name of a public official should not be used in the name of a law firm or in the firm's professional notices "during any significant period in which he is not actively and regularly practicing law as a member of the firm." Most state bar associations and state supreme courts adopted the code, thus clearing the way for formal grievance proceedings if violated.

Following an extensive study in 1967-69, of congressional ethics, a special committee of the Association of the Bar of the City of New York made several recommendations on congressmen and the legal profession. The committee recommended that members of Congress voluntarily refrain from any form of law practice, except for first-termers who foresaw little prospect for reelection. The committee also recommended that Congress enact legislation to forbid "double-door" law partnerships (under which the law partner of a member of Congress engages in federal agency practice prohibited by law to the member) and to prohibit members from appearing for compensation in the courts. The longtime chairman of the House Judiciary Committee, Emanuel Celler, D-N.Y., was a practitioner of a double-door partnership

The New York City Bar Association published the committee's report by James C. Kirby under the title *Congress and the Public Trust: Report of the Association of the Bar of the City of New York Special Committee on Congressional Ethics* (New York: Atheneum, 1970). Kirby's report was a major source for the information in this box.

In 1978 Rep. Joshua Eilberg, D-Pa., was indicted on charges he illegally received legal fees for helping a Philadelphia hospital get a federal construction grant. The House Committee on Standards of Official Conduct said he received more than $100,000 from his law firm under circumstances suggesting he was influenced in "the performance of his government duties." Eilberg was defeated for reelection that fall and pleaded guilty to reduced charges in 1979.

Income from Law Practices

In the 1990s lawyers continued to make up a significant segment of Congress, but the practice of law all but disappeared as a source of outside income for members. In 1975 fifty-three representatives reported at least $1,000 in income from a law practice. Eight House members noted that they had withdrawn from practice. Disclosure reports on 1980 income gave approximately the same figures on present and withdrawn legal practice, but the ethics codes' limit on outside earned income appeared to have reduced the twenty practicing lawyers' income considerably.

A Senate rule effective January 1, 1983, barred the practice of law and other professions for compensation, and the Ethics Reform Act of 1989 extended the same prohibition to House members effective in 1991.

---

service performed "is more than perfunctory in nature," the payment was considered an honorarium.

Any travel provided to the member in connection with speechmaking is counted as a reimbursement, not a gift, the codes stated. In other words, according to a House ethics committee aide, if a member goes to "a company's moose hunting lodge for the weekend, that's a gift." If the member "goes to the lodge to make a speech," however, then the member should disclose his food, lodging, and transportation as a reimbursement.

The Senate's action early in 1979, deferring the limit on senators' outside income for four years, to 1983, created bitter resentment among House members. It enabled senators to collect honoraria up to $2,000 for each speech and $25,000 each year, while representatives were limited to earning no more than $9,099 beyond their salaries and $1,000 for each honorarium. (Since the cap on representatives' outside income was pegged at 15 percent of their salaries, subsequent cost-of-living salary raises also pushed up the earnings ceiling.)

Two years later the Senate poured more salt into representatives' wounds. It voted 45-43 on September 24, 1981, to remove entirely the $25,000 ceiling on honoraria. That galvanized the House Rules Committee to approve a resolution raising the earnings limit to 40 percent of representatives' salaries. When brought to a roll-call vote on the House floor, however, the resolution was defeated 147-271 on October 28.

Six weeks later House leaders arranged a quiet flipflop without a recorded vote. The turnabout occurred December 15 with surprising swiftness and little warning. During a lull in House business, John P. Murtha, D-Pa., rose and asked for unanimous consent to approve a resolution increasing the ceiling on House members' outside earnings from 15 percent of their official salary to 30 percent. When no one objected, Murtha returned to his seat. The entire process, which raised the limit to $18,198, took about ten seconds.

Supporters said privately that surprise was necessary because members needed higher pay—either directly or indirectly—but were unwilling to go on record for it for fear of a public outcry. They compounded their public relations problems the next day, however, when both houses increased the congressional tax deduction for Washington, D.C., living expenses.

Both chambers continued to accept honoraria until 1991 when, again to help justify pay raises for themselves, the House and then the Senate banned the practice altogether. *(Honoraria ban, below)*

1989 REVISION: PAY HIKED, LOOPHOLES CLOSED

Congressional pay raises and codes of ethics continued to be intertwined in the 1990s. Whenever Congress voted itself a big pay increase, it usually tried to dampen public opposition by coupling the action with some offsetting reduction in other benefits or tightening the rules of conduct for members.

The most conspicuous "perk" eliminated in this manner was the acceptance of honoraria payments for speeches or articles. Fees for speeches to groups with an interest in legislation had been particularly controversial. In 1989 Congress banned honoraria for House members as part of the new Ethics Reform Act, the most sweeping rewrite of the congressional conduct code in twelve years.

The 1989 act gave Congress a two-tiered pay system, with higher salaries for representatives than for senators. After chafing under the lower pay for more than a year, the Senate in July 1991 also voted to give up honoraria in exchange for a $23,200 raise that put senators' salaries on a par with House members' $125,100 a year.

As part of the deal under which the House agreed to the Senate pay raise, Congress in 1991 eased some of the gift rules that it had passed less than two years earlier. The new rules allowed senators, representatives, and their employees to accept more expensive gifts (worth up to $250) than permitted under the 1989 rules, and an unlimited number of lesser gifts (worth $100 or less). The rules eliminated almost all requirements to disclose the receipt of gifts.

Changes in Ethics Rules

The 1989 Ethics Reform Act, which President George Bush signed into law, incorporated new restrictions on lobbying by government officials, including members of Congress, after they left office. *("Revolving door," box, Chapter 5, p. 54)*

The changes received little debate on the floor, but they addressed several areas that had brought bad publicity to members for years. The measure eliminated a loophole in a 1979 law that had allowed House members who had been in office at the beginning of 1980 to convert campaign funds to personal use once they retired. Members serving in the 103rd Congress (1993-95) would lose their ability to take advantage of the loophole. Senate rules had previously prohibited the practice.

The measure limited expense-paid travel for nongovernmental trips to no more than seven days for trips abroad. The Senate limited domestic trips to three days; the House, four days. Both chambers tightened rules on gifts—limiting senators to $300 worth of gifts a year from any source other than relatives; the cap on gifts to House members was set at $200 a year. House members were barred from accepting fees for professional services, including the practice of law and serving on boards of directors.

But the measure also loosened restrictions in some areas; for instance, it exempted from the annual limit on gifts all meals in Washington. The law also exempted as "nominal" gifts worth less than $75—up from the previous threshold of $35.

Honoraria were not eliminated altogether, but House members could not keep the payments. They had to be returned or channeled to charities.

Major Provisions

Following are major provisions of the law, as signed by President Bush on November 30, 1989:

Pay

House, Other Federal Officials. Provided, in February 1990, a 7.9 percent pay increase to House members, federal judges, and top executive branch officials who did not receive cost-of-living increases for 1989 and 1990.

- Provided a 25 percent increase for House members and other top executive- and judicial-branch officials on January 1, 1991.

Senate. Provided, in February, a 9.9 percent pay increase for senators.

Future Increases. Provided for automatic, annual cost-of-living adjustments (COLAs) for members of Congress and top federal officials of 0.5 percentage point less than the previous year's Economic Cost Index, which measures inflation of private industry salaries. A ceiling on annual COLAs was set at 5 percent.

- Required the House and Senate to take recorded votes on all future congressional pay increases other than annual COLAs.
- Replaced the "quadrennial commission" that met every four years to recommend salary hikes for top federal officials with an eleven-member Citizens' Commission on Public Service and Compensation, to include five people chosen by lot from voter-registration lists, two by the president, two by congressional leaders, and one by the chief justice of the United States.
- Required the commission to meet every four years and report to the president by December 15.
- Specified that the president's pay recommendations, made after receiving the commission's report, would take effect after the next congressional election and only if both the House and the Senate adopted a resolution of approval by recorded vote within sixty days of its submission.

R. Michael Jenkins

The 1989 Ethics Reform Act tightened rules on gifts that could be accepted by members of Congress. Some of the rules were eased in 1991.

Honoraria

House. Froze at 1989 levels the honoraria and other outside income House members could keep in 1990—$26,850 for most.

- Barred House members, staff, and other federal officials from keeping any honoraria beginning January 1, 1991.
- Allowed House members and others subject to the honoraria ban to request that charitable contributions be made in their name in lieu of honoraria for speeches and appearances.
- Limited such charitable contributions to $2,000 per speech or appearance and prohibited them from being made to any organization that benefited the speaker or his or her relatives.
- Barred those who had such charitable contribu-

tions made on their behalf from getting tax advantages—such as deductions or increases in the amount they could shelter in tax-free Keogh accounts—as a result of those donations.

Senate. Reduced the ceiling on honoraria that senators could keep from 40 percent of salary in 1989 to 27 percent in 1990—$26,568 for most.

- Provided that any cost-of-living pay increase after December 31, 1990, be accompanied by an equivalent reduction in the ceiling on honoraria until it reached zero.

Other Outside Income

House. Barred House members and senior staff from keeping more than 15 percent of the Executive Level II salary ($96,600) in outside earned income beginning January 1, 1991.

- Prohibited House members and senior staff from being paid for working or affiliating with a law or other professional firm. They would be allowed to teach for pay if the ethics committee approved.
- Prohibited House members and senior staff from being paid for serving on boards of directors.
- Applied the above limits on outside income also to federal, noncareer employees at the GS-16 salary level or higher.
- Repealed the House ban on honoraria and other limits on outside income if the 25 percent pay raise in 1991 was repealed.
- Clarified House rules exempting copyright royalties from the cap on outside income to specify that exempt royalties must be paid by an established trade publisher, in line with customary contract terms.

Campaign Funds

- Eliminated, by the time the 103rd Congress began in 1993, an exemption in election law that allowed House members elected before 1980 to convert campaign funds to personal use when they retired from Congress.

- Froze what such funds members could convert, if they retired before the end of the 102nd Congress, at no more than what they had on hand when the 1989 ethics law was enacted.

Gifts and Travel

- Authorized the Office of Government Ethics to issue rules for receipt of gifts by all federal employees.

House. Amended rules governing House members and employees to bar receiving gifts from any one person, except relatives, valued at more than the ceiling set by the Foreign Gifts Act—a cap that was set at $200 beginning January 1, 1990, and would be automatically adjusted for inflation every three years.

- Exempted from the annual gift limit the value of meals and drinks, unless they were part of overnight lodging.
- Raised from $35 to $75 the threshold below which gifts would not count toward the annual ceiling.
- Limited the exemption on gifts of "personal hospitality" to bar receiving more than thirty days of lodging a year from someone other than a relative and to require members to ensure that any hospitality extended for more than four days was in fact personal—not corporate-financed or being claimed as a business expense.
- Allowed private sources to pay travel expenses for no more than four days of domestic travel and seven days (excluding travel time) for international trips.
- Allowed travel expenses for one accompanying relative.
- Allowed the Committee on Standards of Offi-

cial Conduct to waive gift and travel restrictions in exceptional circumstances.

Senate. Amended rules governing senators and Senate employees to prohibit their receiving more than $300 a year in gifts from any one source other than relatives and kept the $100 limit on gifts from people with a direct interest in legislation.

- Dropped an exemption allowing unlimited gifts of entertainment.
- Allowed private sources to pay travel expenses for no more than three days of domestic travel and seven days for international trips. Both limits excluded travel time.
- Allowed travel expenses to be paid for one accompanying Senate aide or a spouse.

Ethics Committee

House. Expanded the Committee on Standards of Official Conduct, beginning in the 102nd Congress, from twelve to fourteen members and limited each member to no more than three terms during any five successive Congresses.

- Required the committee to divide its investigative and adjudicative functions by naming a four- or six-member subcommittee to review allegations whenever a preliminary inquiry was opened. The other members would hold disciplinary hearings when the investigative subcommittee found reason to believe that rules were violated and issued a statement of alleged violation.
- Prohibited the committee from making public a statement of alleged violation until the accused could draft a response, and required that the two documents be released simultaneously.
- Required the committee to issue a report on any investigation, regardless of the case's disposition.
- Allowed the committee to investigate only violations alleged to have occurred in the three

most recent Congresses, unless older violations related to more recent ones or unless specifically instructed by the House.

- Allowed members facing ethics sanctions to bring an attorney onto the House floor during consideration of the committee's recommendations.
- Directed the committee to establish an Office on Advice and Education to guide members and employees.

Financial Disclosure

Brought all three branches of government under the same financial disclosure law, although each would continue to be responsible for administering requirements for its own employees.

- Raised from $100 to $200 the threshold below which income from any source need not be disclosed and raised from $35 to $75 the threshold below which gifts need not be reported.
- Required members of Congress and other federal officials who had charitable contributions made on their behalf in lieu of honoraria to disclose the source and amount of such contributions beginning in 1991. The charities receiving such contributions would not have to be publicly reported, but their identities would have to be disclosed in confidential reports to the House Committee on Standards of Official Conduct or other ethics offices.
- Required disclosure of the source and amount of any honoraria spouses of reporting officials earned.
- Required more detailed disclosure of travel reimbursements, including an itinerary and dates of travel.
- Specified that underlying assets of regulated investment companies did not have to be reported if the firm was widely diversified and the reporting official had no control over it.

- Required all federal officials, including members of Congress, to file a final financial disclosure form, known as a "termination report," after they left office.
- Extended the time within which financial disclosure reports must be made available to the public from fifteen days to thirty days after they were filed.
- Doubled from $5,000 to $10,000 the maximum civil penalty for violation of financial disclosure law and established a $200 penalty fee for late filing.

Postemployment Lobbying

- Barred members and officers of Congress from lobbying the legislative branch for a year after they left office.
- Barred former congressional staff members for a year after leaving employment from lobbying the member, office, or committee for which they had worked. Leadership staff members were barred from lobbying the members and employees of the leadership for the chamber in which they served.
- Kept a lifetime ban on all former executive branch employees from lobbying on matters in which they were "personally and substantially involved" while in office and kept a two-year ban on matters that were "under their official responsibility within the year preceding termination of government service." No such prohibitions would be applied to the legislative branch, however.
- Barred former Executive Level I officials throughout the government and Level II officials in the White House for a year after leaving office from lobbying any officials at Levels I through V.
- Imposed a one-year ban on lobbying by former executive employees and military officers at the GS-17 pay level or above at the agency

they had served. Although the civil service pay scale did not apply to congressional staff, any legislative branch employees paid at the GS-17 level or higher would be barred for a year from lobbying the members who employed them or the committees for which they had worked. Former employees would also be barred from "representing, aiding or advising" foreign governments or foreign political parties for a year.

- Barred executive branch employees who were "personally and substantially" involved in trade or treaty negotiations within a year before leaving office from representing or advising people concerned with such negotiations. The ban would last a year.

Miscellaneous Provisions

Conflict of Interest. Barred House employees from participating in contacts with the judiciary or government agencies with respect to nonlegislative matters in which they had a significant financial interest.

- Added civil and misdemeanor penalties to the criminal ones already available that may be imposed on federal employees for violating conflict-of-interest law.

Procurement Law. Postponed for one year implementing procurement-reform laws that barred former federal employees from working on a procurement contract for two years if they played a role in awarding the contract.

Car Rentals. Relaxed rules barring government officials from using officially leased cars for incidental personal use.

Senior Executive Service. Required members of the executive branch's Senior Executive Service to be recertified in that status every three years beginning in 1991, unless they had been employed as a senior executive for at least thirteen years.

"CONTRITION ACTS"

Worried about their political futures, senators and representatives were trying hard as the 1992 elections approached to atone for the behavior that recently had brought Congress scads of unfavorable publicity. The voter-appeasement efforts were so blatant that they were nicknamed "The Congressional Contrition Acts of 1991."

As an example, the Senate decided overwhelmingly that its members should pay for their sins—in cash, from their own pockets: Aggrieved employees in discrimination cases would be able to collect damages directly from individual senators—and to drag them into federal court. The Senate's move was unprecedented in that members cast aside longstanding concerns over the separation of powers and deep-seated fears of politically motivated complaints.

"Our people are so frightened to death about their political futures that they'll do almost anything," said Sen. Warren B. Rudman, R-N.H. He proved it: After failing to kill the court-redress idea on constitutional grounds, Rudman shamed members into accepting personal liabiiity.

Atonement in Congress's other chamber, already manifested in previously curbed perks, included big price hikes at the government-subsidized House Barber Shop. The increases—a haircut doubled to $10—were the first in more than a decade.

Members' continuing embarrassment over their misdeeds—from kiting checks to vilifying witnesses—was producing consequences on a broad array of fronts. They included unusual personal apologies, as two prominent senators issued public mea culpas.

"Congress Hits Bottom"

Congress's reputation had suffered in recent years with the resignations of a House Speaker and

"Rubbergate" Scandal

Although it was small potatoes by comparison, a scandal involving the House's own bank quickly aroused a louder outcry than the multibillion-dollar bank and savings and loan failures that made headline news throughout 1991.

The public outrage erupted after Congress's General Accounting Office reported September 18 that House members had bounced 8,331 checks between July 1989 and June 1990. The "user-friendly" House bank had covered the overdrafts without penalty.

Voters were furious that representatives freely indulged in practices that would cost ordinary citizens hefty fees or even criminal penalties. The overdrafts included 581 checks for $1,000 or more written by 134 members.

"It is unmistakably clear that the American people look at this as an intolerable exercise in arrogance or worse," said Minority Leader Robert H. Michel, R-Ill.

Responding to the criticism, the House voted 390-8 on October 3 to shut down the sergeant at arms's bank and check-cashing service and send its audit records to the Standards of Official Conduct (ethics) Committee for review. The bank was to close no later than December 31.

Earlier the same day it was reported that members owed substantial sums for meals and catering services they had received from House restaurants. The original figure of more than $300,000 owed was reduced to less than $10,000 in early 1992 after the food service company, Service America, apologized for what it said was an unauthorized release of the information. House sources said the larger amount was erroneous because of problems with the computerized billing system.

Speaker Thomas S. Foley, D-Wash., and Minority Whip Newt Gingrich, R-Ga., were among members who acknowledged having written bad checks, once in Foley's case and three times in Gingrich's. Gingrich said the attention should focus on those who routinely abused the system, rather than on those who may have done so inadvertently on a few occasions.

The adverse publicity over "rubber" checks and restaurant deadbeats aggravated widespread dissatisfaction with Congress and fueled rising demands for limitations on the number of terms that members can serve. Several states were considering such legislation for state and local officials, but serious doubts existed about the constitutionality of any law that attempted to restrict service in Congress.

Democratic whip, the Keating Five affair, and several furors over large pay raises. But none of those episodes produced anything like the 1992 fallout.

The House bank's check-kiting scandal in late 1991 started this latest ball rolling. Then came revelations about skipped restaurant bills and a barrage of stories about other congressional perks.

The icing was the uproar over the Senate's handling of Clarence Thomas's Supreme Court nomination, during which his reputation and that of a woman who accused him of sexual harassment were both riddled in a vicious partisan cross-fire.

Congress responded with uncharacteristic speed to these flaps, with both chambers approving potentially far-reaching ethics inquiries and the House closing its bank and curtailing other privileges. But the moves proved inadequate. Individual apologies became fashionable.

Sen. Edward M. Kennedy, D-Mass., expressed remorse that his much-publicized social conduct had inhibited his public effectiveness. Kennedy disappointed many women and liberals by remaining mostly silent during the hearings on Anita F. Hill's charges against Thomas. Sen. Alan K. Simpson, R-Wyo., followed suit with an apology for his attacks on Hill's credibility, promising to be less mean-spirited in the future.

"We have reached the point where a healthy skepticism about public officials has become an unhealthy cynicism with widespread distrust and ridicule of the institution," said Senate Majority Leader George J. Mitchell, D-Maine.

Opinion polls confirmed that view. "Congress Hits Bottom," said a headline in the October 28, 1991, issue of *The Polling Report,* a compilation of survey data.

Senate Employees' Rights

Members felt they needed to do something. Some called the process self-flagellation. The vehicle was an amendment proposed by Sen. Charles E. Grassley, R-Iowa, to the 1991 civil rights bill. Grassley and others had for years advocated subjecting Congress to the same labor and antidiscrimination laws it imposes on private businesses. Congress had exempted itself from coverage because those laws included remedies that involve policing by the executive branch and adjudication by the courts, which House and Senate leaders felt would give those two branches too much leverage over individual members of the legislative branch, thereby violating the Constitution's separation-of-powers doctrine.

After defeating Grassley's proposal in 1990, the Senate decided to codify in law its antidiscrimina-

tion rule and to declare that employees generally are protected by the major civil rights acts—the 1964 law and the 1990 disabilities law, as well as the Rehabilitation Act of 1973 and the Age Discrimination in Employment Act of 1967. But employees got few of the same enforcement and adjudication remedies available to private workers. Instead of being able to take complaints to agencies such as the Equal Employment Opportunity Commission or the federal courts, employees could go only to the Ethics Committee.

Goaded by President George Bush and business lobbyists to go further with the Senate's reform, both sides took action. Grassley and Mitchell devised a compromise that went two crucial steps further than the system in place in the House since 1988. Like the House system, it set up a Fair Employment Practices Office to handle complaints about alleged violations of the four major job-bias laws.

Either side could appeal to the Senate Ethics Committee—a step not provided in the House. The other major concession was allowing any unsatisfied Senate worker an additional appeal—to federal court. To appease members worried about the separation of powers, the appeal would go straight to the U.S. Court of Appeals, bypassing the trial courts.

Final approval came when President Bush signed the amendment into law as part of the civil rights bill. It was a small step, but it went a long way toward erasing Capitol Hill's reputation as being "The Last Plantation."

Appendix

Senate Cases Involving Qualifications for Membership   165

House Cases Involving Qualifications for Membership   166

Cases of Expulsion in the House   167

Cases of Expulsion in the Senate   168

Censure Proceedings in the Senate   169

Censure Proceedings in the House   170

Reprimand Proceedings in the House   172

Party Abbreviations   173

Senate Rule XXXV   174

Senate Rule XXXVII   175

House Rule XLIII   178

Ethics Committee Chairs, 1966-92   179

Senate Cases Involving Qualifications for Membership

Congress	Session	Year	Member-elect	Grounds	Disposition
3rd	1st	1793	Albert Gallatin, D-Pa.	Citizenship	*Excluded*
11th	1st	1809	Stanley Griswold, D-Ohio	Residence	Admitted
28th	1st	1844	John M. Niles, D-Conn.	Sanity	Admitted
31st	Special	1849	James Shields, D-Ill.	Citizenship	*Excluded*
37th	2nd	1861	Benjamin Stark, D-Ore.	Loyalty	Admitted
40th	1st	1867	Phillip F. Thomas, D-Md.	Loyalty	*Excluded*
41st	2nd	1870	Hiram R. Revels, R-Miss.	Citizenship	Admitted
41st	2nd	1870	Adelbert Ames, R-Miss.	Residence	Admitted
59th	2nd	1907	Reed Smoot, R-Utah	Mormonism	Admitted*
69th	2nd	1926	Arthur R. Gould, R-Maine	Character	Admitted
74th	1st	1935	Rush D. Holt, D-W.Va.	Age	Admitted
75th	1st	1937	George L. Berry, D-Tenn.	Character	Admitted
77th	2nd	1942	William Langer, R-N.D.	Character	Admitted*
80th	1st	1947	Theodore G. Bilbo, D-Miss.	Character	Died before Senate acted
88th	2nd	1964	Pierre Salinger, D-Calif.	Residence	Admitted

* The Senate decided that a two-thirds majority, as in expulsion cases, would be required for exclusion. The resolution proposing exclusion did not receive a two-thirds majority.

Source: Senate Committee on Rules and Administration, Subcommittee on Privileges and Elections, *Senate Election, Expulsion, and Censure Cases from 1793 to 1972,* compiled by Richard D. Hupman, 92nd Cong. 1st sess., 1972, S Doc 92-7.

House Cases Involving Qualifications for Membership

Congress	Session	Year	Member-elect	Grounds	Disposition
1st	1st	1789	William L. Smith, Fed-S.C.	Citizenship	Admitted
10th	1st	1807	Philip B. Key, Fed-Md.	Residence	Admitted
10th	1st	1807	William McCreery,—Md.	Residence	Admitted
18th	1st	1823	Gabriel Richard, Ind-Mich. Terr.	Citizenship	Admitted
18th	1st	1823	John Bailey, Ind-Mass.	Residence	*Excluded*
18th	1st	1823	John Forsyth, D-Ga.	Residence	Admitted
27th	1st	1841	David Levy, R-Fla. Terr.	Citizenship	Admitted
36th	1st	1859	John Y. Brown, D-Ky.	Age	Admitted
40th	1st	1867	William H. Hooper, D-Utah Terr.	Mormonism	Admitted
40th	1st	1867	Lawrence S. Trimble, D-Ky.	Loyalty	Admitted
40th	1st	1867	John Y. Brown, D-Ky.	Loyalty	*Excluded*
40th	1st	1867	John D. Young, D-Ky.	Loyalty	*Excluded*
40th	1st	1867	Roderick R. Butler, R-Tenn.	Loyalty	Admitted
40th	1st	1867	John A. Wimpy, Ind-Ga.	Loyalty	*Excluded*
40th	1st	1867	W.D. Simpson, Ind-S.C.	Loyalty	*Excluded*
41st	1st	1869	John M. Rice, D-Ky.	Loyalty	Admitted
41st	2nd	1870	Lewis McKenzie, Unionist-Va.	Loyalty	Admitted
41st	2nd	1870	George W. Booker, Conservative-Va.	Loyalty	Admitted
41st	2nd	1870	Benjamin F. Whittemore, R-S.C.	Malfeasance	*Excluded*
41st	2nd	1870	John C. Conner, D-Texas	Misconduct	Admitted
43rd	1st	1873	George Q. Cannon, R-Utah Terr.	Mormonism	Admitted
43rd	2nd	1874	George Q. Cannon, R-Utah Terr.	Polygamy	Admitted
47th	1st	1881	John S. Barbour, D-Va.	Residence	Admitted
47th	1st	1882	George Q. Cannon, R-Utah Terr.	Polygamy	Seat vacated[1]
50th	1st	1887	James B. White, R-Ind.	Citizenship	Admitted
56th	1st	1899	Robert W. Wilcox, Ind-Hawaii Terr.	Bigamy, treason	Admitted
56th	1st	1900	Brigham H. Roberts, D-Utah	Polygamy	*Excluded*
59th	1st	1905	Anthony Michalek, R-Ill.	Citizenship	Admitted
66th	1st	1919	Victor L. Berger, Socialist-Wis.	Sedition	*Excluded*
66th	2nd	1920	Victor L. Berger, Socialist-Wis.	Sedition	*Excluded*
69th	1st	1926	John W. Langley, R-Ky.	Criminal misconduct	Resigned
70th	1st	1927	James M. Beck, R-Pa.	Residence	Admitted
71st	1st	1929	Ruth B. Owen, D-Fla.	Citizenship	Admitted
90th	1st	1967	Adam C. Powell, Jr., D-N.Y.	Misconduct	*Excluded*[2]
96th	1st	1979	Richard A. Tonry, D-La.	Vote fraud	Resigned

1. Discussions of polygamy and an election contest led to a declaration that the seat was vacant.
2. The Supreme Court June 16, 1969, ruled that the House had improperly excluded Powell.

Sources: Hinds and Cannon, *Precedents of the House of Representatives of the United States,* 11 vols. (1935-41); Joint Committee on Congressional Operations, *Exclusion, Censure, and Expulsion Cases from 1789 to 1973,* 93rd Cong., 1st sess., 1973, committee print.

Cases of Expulsion in the House

Congress	Session	Year	Member	Grounds	Disposition
5th	2nd	1798	Matthew Lyon, Anti-Fed-Vt.	Assault on representative	Not expelled
5th	2nd	1798	Roger Griswold, Fed-Conn.	Assault on representative	Not expelled
5th	3rd	1799	Matthew Lyon, Anti-Fed-Vt.	Sedition	Not expelled
25th	2nd	1838	William J. Graves, Whig-Ky.	Killing of representative in duel	Not expelled
25th	3rd	1839	Alexander Duncan, Whig-Ohio	Offensive publication	Not expelled
34th	1st	1856	Preston S. Brooks, State Rights Dem.-S.C.	Assault on senator	Not expelled
34th	3rd	1857	Orsamus B. Matteson, Whig-N.Y.	Corruption	Not expelled
34th	3rd	1857	William A. Gilbert, Whig-N.Y.	Corruption	Not expelled
34th	3rd	1857	William W. Welch, American-Conn.	Corruption	Not expelled
34th	3rd	1857	Francis S. Edwards, American-N.Y.	Corruption	Not expelled
35th	1st	1858	Orsamus B. Matteson, Whig-N.Y.	Corruption	Not expelled
37th	1st	1861	John B. Clark, D-Mo.	Support of rebellion	*Expelled*
37th	1st	1861	Henry C. Burnett, D-Ky.	Support of rebellion	*Expelled*
37th	1st	1861	John W. Reid, D-Mo.	Support of rebellion	*Expelled*
38th	1st	1864	Alexander Long, D-Ohio	Treasonable utterance	Not expelled*
38th	1st	1864	Benjamin G. Harris, D-Md.	Treasonable utterance	Not expelled*
39th	1st	1866	Lovell H. Rousseau, R-Ky.	Assault on representative	Not expelled*
41st	2nd	1870	Benjamin F. Whittemore, R-S.C.	Corruption	Not expelled*
41st	2nd	1870	Roderick R. Butler, R-Tenn.	Corruption	Not expelled*
42nd	3rd	1873	Oakes Ames, R-Mass.	Corruption	Not expelled*
42nd	3rd	1873	James Brooks, D-N.Y.	Corruption	Not expelled*
43rd	2nd	1875	John Y. Brown, D-Ky.	Insult to representative	Not expelled*
44th	1st	1875	William S. King, R-Minn.	Corruption	Not expelled
44th	1st	1875	John G. Schumaker, D-N.Y.	Corruption	Not expelled
48th	1st	1884	William P. Kellogg, R-La.	Corruption	Not expelled
67th	1st	1921	Thomas L. Blanton, D-Texas	Abuse of leave to print	Not expelled*
96th	1st	1979	Charles C. Diggs, Jr., D-Mich.	Misuse of clerk-hire funds	Not expelled*
96th	2nd	1980	Michael J. "Ozzie" Myers, D-Pa.	Corruption	*Expelled*

* Censured after expulsion move failed or was withdrawn.

Sources: Hinds and Cannon, *Precedents of the House of Representatives of the United States,* 11 vols. (1935-41); Joint Committee on Congressional Operations, *House of Representatives Exclusion, Censure, and Expulsion Cases from 1789 to 1973,* 93rd Cong., 1st sess., 1973, committee print; *Congressional Quarterly Almanac 1980.*

Cases of Expulsion in the Senate

Congress	Session	Year	Member	Grounds	Disposition
5th	2nd	1797	William Blount, Ind.-Tenn.	Anti-Spanish conspiracy	*Expelled*
10th	1st	1808	John Smith, D-Ohio	Disloyalty	Not expelled
35th	1st	1858	Henry M. Rice, D-Minn.	Corruption	Not expelled
37th	1st	1861	James M. Mason, D-Va.	Support of rebellion	*Expelled*
37th	1st	1861	Robert M. T. Hunter, D-Va.	Support of rebellion	*Expelled*
37th	1st	1861	Thomas L. Clingman, D-N.C.	Support of rebellion	*Expelled*
37th	1st	1861	Thomas Bragg, D-N.C.	Support of rebellion	*Expelled*
37th	1st	1861	James Chesnut, Jr., States Rights-S.C.	Support of rebellion	*Expelled*
37th	1st	1861	Alfred O.P. Nicholson, D-Tenn.	Support of rebellion	*Expelled*
37th	1st	1861	William K. Sebastian, D-Ark.	Support of rebellion	*Expelled*[1]
37th	1st	1861	Charles B. Mitchel, D-Ark.	Support of rebellion	*Expelled*
37th	1st	1861	John Hemphill, State Rights D-Texas	Support of rebellion	*Expelled*
37th	1st	1861	Louis T. Wigfall, D-Texas[2]	Support of rebellion	Not expelled
37th	1st	1861	Louis T. Wigfall, D-Texas	Support of rebellion	*Expelled*
37th	1st	1861	John C. Breckinridge, D-Ky.	Support of rebellion	*Expelled*
37th	1st	1861	Lazarus W. Powell, D-Ky.	Support of rebellion	Not expelled
37th	2nd	1862	Trusten Polk, D-Mo.	Support of rebellion	*Expelled*
37th	2nd	1862	Jesse D. Bright, D-Ind.	Support of rebellion	*Expelled*
37th	2nd	1862	Waldo P. Johnson, D-Mo.	Support of rebellion	*Expelled*
37th	2nd	1862	James F. Simmons, Whig-R.I.	Corruption	Not expelled
42nd	3rd	1873	James W. Patterson, R-N.H.	Corruption	Not expelled
53rd	1st	1893	William N. Roach, D-N.D.	Embezzlement	Not expelled
58th	3rd	1905	John H. Mitchell, R-Ore.	Corruption	Not expelled
59th	2nd	1907	Reed Smoot, R-Utah	Mormonism	Not expelled
65th	3rd	1919	Robert M. La Follette, R-Wis.	Disloyalty	Not expelled
73rd	2nd	1934	John H. Overton, D-La.	Corruption	Not expelled
73rd	2nd	1934	Huey P. Long, D-La.	Corruption	Not expelled
77th	2nd	1942	William Langer, R-N.D.	Corruption	Not expelled
97th	2nd	1982	Harrison A. Williams, Jr., D-N.J.	Corruption	Not expelled[3]

1. The Senate reversed its decision on Sebastian's expulsion March 3, 1877. Sebastian had died in 1865 but his children were paid an amount equal to his Senate salary between the time of his expulsion and the date of his death.

2. The Senate took no action on an initial resolution expelling Wigfall because he represented a state that had seceded from the Union; three months later he was expelled for supporting the Confederacy.

3. Facing probable expulsion, Williams resigned March 11, 1982.

Sources: Senate Committee on Rules and Administration, Subcommittee on Privileges and Elections, *Senate Election, Expulsion and Censure Cases from 1793 to 1972,* compiled by Richard D. Hupman, 92nd Cong., 1st sess., 1972, S Doc 92-7; *Congress and the Nation 1981-84,* vol. 7.

Censure Proceedings in the Senate

Congress	Session	Year	Member	Grounds	Disposition
11th	3rd	1811	Timothy Pickering, Fed-Mass.	Breach of confidence	*Censured*
28th	1st	1844	Benjamin Tappan, D-Ohio	Breach of confidence	*Censured*
31st	1st	1850	Thomas H. Benton, D-Mo.	Disorderly conduct	Not censured
31st	1st	1850	Henry S. Foote, Unionist-Miss.	Disorderly conduct	Not censured
57th	1st	1902	John L. McLaurin, D-S.C.	Assault	*Censured*
57th	1st	1902	Benjamin R. Tillman, D-S.C.	Assault	*Censured*
71st	1st	1929	Hiram Bingham, R-Conn.	Bringing Senate into disrepute	*Condemned*[1]
83rd	2nd	1954	Joseph R. McCarthy, R-Wis.	Obstruction of legislative process, insult to senators, etc.	*Condemned*[1]
90th	1st	1967	Thomas J. Dodd, D-Conn.	Financial misconduct	*Censured*
96th	1st	1979	Herman E. Talmadge, D-Ga.	Financial misconduct	*Denounced*[2]
101st	2nd	1990	Dave Durenberger, R-Minn.	Financial misconduct	*Denounced*[2]
102nd	1st	1991	Alan Cranston, D-Calif.	Improper conduct	*Reprimanded*[3]

1. The word *condemned* as used in the Bingham and McCarthy cases is regarded as the same as *censured*.
2. As in the Bingham and McCarthy cases, the word *denounced* as applied to Talmadge and Durenberger is considered virtually synonymous with *censured*.
3. The Ethics Committee reprimanded Cranston on behalf of the full Senate, after determining that it lacked the authority to issue a censure in the same manner. It was the Senate's first use of *reprimand*.

Sources: Senate Committee on Rules and Administration, Subcommittee on Privileges and Elections, *Senate Election, Expulsion and Censure Cases from 1793 to 1972,* compiled by Richard D. Hupman, 92nd Cong., 1st sess., 1972, S Doc 92-7; *Congress and the Nation 1977-80,* vol. 6; *Congressional Quarterly Almanac 1990.*

Censure Proceedings in the House

Congress	Session	Year	Member	Grounds	Disposition
5th	2nd	1798	Matthew Lyon, Anti-Fed-Vt.	Assault on representative	Not censured
5th	2nd	1798	Roger Griswold, Fed-Conn.	Assault on representative	Not censured
22nd	1st	1832	William Stanbery, JD-Ohio	Insult to Speaker	*Censured*
24th	1st	1836	Sherrod Williams, Whig-Ky.	Insult to Speaker	Not censured
25th	2nd	1838	Henry A. Wise, Tyler Dem.-Va.	Service as second in duel	Not censured
25th	3rd	1839	Alexander Duncan, Whig-Ohio	Offensive publication	Not censured
27th	2nd	1842	John Q. Adams, Whig-Mass.	Treasonable petition	Not censured
27th	2nd	1842	Joshua R. Giddings, Whig-Ohio	Offensive paper	*Censured*
34th	2nd	1856	Henry A. Edmundson, D-Va. }	Complicity in assault on senator	Not censured
34th	2nd	1856	Laurence M. Keitt, D-S.C. }		*Censured*
36th	1st	1860	George S. Houston, D-Ala.	Insult to representative	Not censured
38th	1st	1864	Alexander Long, D-Ohio	Treasonable utterance	*Censured*
38th	1st	1864	Benjamin G. Harris, D-Md.	Treasonable utterance	*Censured*
39th	1st	1866	John W. Chanler, D-N.Y.	Insult to House	*Censured*
39th	1st	1866	Lovell H. Rousseau, R-Ky.	Assault on representative	*Censured*
40th	1st	1867	John W. Hunter, Ind-N.Y.	Insult to representative	*Censured*
40th	2nd	1868	Fernando Wood, D-N.Y.	Offensive utterance	*Censured*
40th	3rd	1868	E. D. Holbrook, D-Idaho[1]	Offensive utterance	*Censured*
41st	2nd	1870	Benjamin F. Whittemore, R-S.C.	Corruption	*Censured*
41st	2nd	1870	Roderick R. Butler, R-Tenn.	Corruption	*Censured*
41st	2nd	1870	John T. Deweese, D-N.C.	Corruption	*Censured*
42nd	3rd	1873	Oakes Ames, R-Mass.	Corruption	*Censured*
42nd	3rd	1873	James Brooks, D-N.Y.	Corruption	*Censured*
43rd	2nd	1875	John Y. Brown, D-Ky.	Insult to representative	*Censured*[2]
44th	1st	1876	James G. Blaine, R-Maine	Corruption	Not censured
47th	1st	1882	William D. Kelley, R-Pa.	Offensive utterance	Not censured
47th	1st	1882	John D. White, R-Ky.	Offensive utterance	Not censured
47th	2nd	1883	John Van Voorhis, R-N.Y.	Offensive utterance	Not censured
51st	1st	1890	William D. Bynum, D-Ind.	Offensive utterance	*Censured*
67th	1st	1921	Thomas L. Blanton, D-Texas	Abuse of leave to print	*Censured*

Congress	Session	Year	Member	Grounds	Disposition
95th	2nd	1978	Edward R. Roybal, D-Calif.	Lying to House committee	Not censured[3]
96th	1st	1979	Charles C. Diggs, Jr., D-Mich.	Misuse of clerk-hire funds	Censured
96th	2nd	1980	Charles H. Wilson, D-Calif.	Financial misconduct	Censured
98th	1st	1983	Gerry E. Studds, D-Mass.	Sexual misconduct	Censured
98th	1st	1983	Daniel B. Crane, R-Ill.	Sexual misconduct	Censured
101st	2nd	1990	Barney Frank, D-Mass.	Discrediting House	Not censured[3]

1. Holbrook was a territorial delegate, not a representative.
2. The House later rescinded part of the censure resolution against Brown.
3. Reprimanded after censure resolution failed or was withdrawn.

Sources: Hinds and Cannon, *Precedents of the House of Representatives of the United States,* 11 vols. (1935-41); Joint Committee on Congressional Operations, *House of Representatives Exclusion, Censure, and Expulsion Cases from 1789 to 1973,* 93rd Cong., 1st sess., 1973, committee print; *Congress and the Nation 1977-80, 1981-84, 1985-88,* vols. 5-7; *Congressional Quarterly Almanac 1990.*

Reprimand Proceedings in the House

Congress	Session	Year	Member	Grounds	Disposition
94th	2nd	1976	Robert L. F. Sikes, D-Fla.	Financial misconduct	Reprimanded
95th	2nd	1978	John J. McFall, D-Calif.	Financial misconduct	Reprimanded
95th	2nd	1978	Edward R. Roybal, D-Calif.	Financial misconduct	Reprimanded
95th	2nd	1978	Charles H. Wilson, D-Calif.	Financial misconduct	Reprimanded
98th	2nd	1984	George V. Hansen, R-Idaho	Financial misconduct	Reprimanded
100th	1st	1987	Austin J. Murphy, D-Pa.	Misuse of office	Reprimanded
101st	2nd	1990	Barney Frank, D-Mass.	Discrediting House	Reprimanded

Note: The only significant difference between *censure* and *reprimand* in the House is that censured members must stand before the House as the Speaker reads the censure resolution. This is not required in reprimand cases.

Sources: Congress and the Nation 1973-76, 1977-80, 1981-84, 1985-88, vols. 4-7; *Congressional Quarterly Almanac 1990.*

PARTY ABBREVIATIONS

AD	Anti-Democrat	Jeff.R	Jeffersonian Republican
Ad.D	Adams Democrat	L	Liberal
AF	Anti-Federalist	Lab.	Laborite
AJ	Anti-Jacksonian	L&O	Law & Order
AL	American Laborite	LR	Liberal Republican
ALD	Anti-Lecompton Democrat	N	Nullifier
ALot.	Anti-Lottery Democrat	Nat.	Nationalist
AM	Anti-Monopolist	New Prog.	New Progressive
AMas.	Anti-Mason	Nonpart.	Nonpartisan
AP	American Party	NR	National Republican
C	Conservative	O	Opposition Party
Coal.	Coalitionist	P	Populist
Confed.D	Confederate Democrat	PD	Popular Democrat
Const U	Constitutional Unionist	PR	Progressive Republican
CR	Conservative Republican	Prog.	Progressive
D	Democrat	Prohib.	Prohibitionist
DFL	Democrat Farmer Labor	R	Republican
DR	Democratic Republican	Read	Readjuster
F	Federalist	Sil.R	Silver Republican
FL	Farmer Laborite	Soc.	Socialist
FS	Free-Soiler	SR	State Rights Party
FSD	Free-Soil Democrat	SRD	State Rights Democrat
FSil.	Free-Silver	SRFT	State Rights Free-Trader
G	Greenbacker	U	Unionist
I	Independent	UD	Union Democrat
ID	Independent Democrat	UL	Union Laborite
IP	Independent Populist	UR	Union Republican
IR	Independent Republican	UU	Unconditional Unionist
IRad.	Independent Radical	UW	Union Whig
IW	Independent Whig	W	Whig
J	Jacksonian		

SENATE RULE XXXV

[Revisions in rule XXXV were anticipated in the 102nd Congress to reflect 1991 changes in congressional limits on accepting gifts and disclosing them (HR 2506—PL 102-90). The revisions had not been made as of mid-September 1991. *(See Chapter 11, p. 157)]*

Gifts

1. (a) (1) No Member, officer, or employee of the Senate, or the spouse or dependent thereof, shall knowingly accept, directly or indirectly, any gift or gifts having an aggregate value exceeding $100 during a calendar year directly or indirectly from any person, organization, or corporation having a direct interest in legislation before the Congress or from any foreign national unless, in an unusual case, a waiver is granted by the Select Committee on Ethics.

(2) No Member, officer, or employee of the Senate, or the spouse or dependent thereof, shall knowingly accept, directly or indirectly, any gift or gifts having an aggregate value exceeding $300 during a calendar year from any person, organization, or corporation unless, in an unusual case, a waiver is granted by the Select Committee on Ethics.

(3) In determining the aggregate value of any gift or gifts accepted by an individual during a calendar year from any person, organization, or corporation, there may be deducted the aggregate value of gifts (other than gifts described in subparagraph (c)) given by such individual to such person, organization, or corporation during that calendar year.

(b) For purposes of subparagraph (a), only the following shall be deemed to have a direct interest in legislation before the Congress:

(1) a person, organization, or corporation registered under the federal Regulation of Lobbying Act of 1946, or any successor statute, a person who is an officer or director of such a registered lobbyist, or a person who has been employed or retained by such a registered lobbyist for the purpose of influencing legislation before the Congress; or

(2) a corporation, labor organization, or other organization which maintains a separate segregated fund for political purposes (within the meaning of Section 321 of the Federal Election Campaign Act of 1971 (2 U.S.C. 441b)), a person who is an officer or director of such corporation, labor organization, or other organization, or a person who has been employed or retained by such corporation, labor organization, or other organization for the purpose of influencing legislation before the Congress.

(c) The prohibitions of subparagraph (a) do not apply to gifts—

(1) from relatives;

(2) with a value of less than $75;

(3) of personal hospitality of an individual; or

(4) from an individual who is a foreign national if that individual is not acting, directly or indirectly, on behalf of a foreign corporation, partnership or business enterprise, a foreign trade, cultural, educational or other association, a foreign political party or a foreign government.

2. For purposes of this rule—

(a) the term "gift" means a payment, subscription, advance, forbearance, rendering, or deposit of money, services, or anything of value, including food, lodging, transportation, or entertainment, and reimbursement for other than necessary expenses, unless consideration of equal or greater value is received, but does not include (1) a political contribution otherwise reported as required by law, (2) a loan made in a commercially reasonable manner (including requirements that the loan be repaid and that a reasonable rate of interest be paid), (3) a bequest, inheritance, or other transfer at death, (4) a bona fide award presented in recognition of public service and available to the general public, (5) a reception at which the Member, officer, or employee is to be honored, provided such individual receives no other gifts that exceed the restrictions in this rule, other than a suitable memento, (6) meals or beverages consumed or enjoyed, provided the meals or beverages are not consumed or enjoyed in connection with a gift of overnight lodging, or (7) anything of value given to a spouse or dependent of a reporting individual by the employer of such spouse or dependent in recognition of the service provided by such spouse or dependent;

(b) the term "relative" has the same meaning given to such term in section 107(2) of title I of the Ethics in Government Act of 1978 (Public Law 95-521).

(c) the term 'necessary expenses' means reasonable expenses for food, lodging, or transportation which are incurred by a Member, officer, or employee of the Senate in connnection with services provided to (or participation in an event sponsored by) the organization which provides reimbursement for such expenses or which provides the food, lodging, or transportation directly, however necessary expenses do not include—

(1) the provision of food, lodging, or transportation, or the payment for such expenses, for a continuous period in excess of 3 days (and 2 nights) exclusive of travel time within the United States or 7 days (and 6 nights) exclusive of travel time outside of the United States unless such travel is approved by the Committee on Ethics as necessary for participation in a conference, seminar, meeting or similar matter, and

(2) the provision of food, lodging, or transportation, or the payment for such expenses, for anyone accompanying a member, officer, or employee of the Senate, other than the spouse of a Member, officer, or employee of the Senate or one Senate employee acting as an aide to a Member.

3. If a Member, officer, or employee, after exercising reasonable diligence to obtain the information necessary to comply with this rule, unknowingly accepts a gift described in paragraph 1, such Member, officer, or employee shall, upon learning of the nature of the gift and its source, return the gift or, if it is not possible to return the gift, reimburse the donor for the value of the gift.

4. (a) Notwithstanding the provisions of this rule, a Member, officer, or employee of the Senate may participate in a program, the principal objective of which is educational, sponsored by a foreign government or a foreign educational or charitable organization involving travel to a foreign country paid for by that foreign government or organization if such participation is not in violation of any law and if the Select Committee on Ethics has determined that participation in such program by Members, officers, or employees of the Senate is in the interests of the Senate and the United States.

(b) Any Member who accepts an invitation to participate in any such program shall notify the Select Committee in writing of his acceptance. A Member shall also notify the Select Committee in writing whenever he has permitted any officer or employee whom he supervises (within the meaning of paragraph 11 of rule XXXVII) to participate in any such program. The chairman of the Select Committee shall place in the Congressional Record a list of all individuals participating; the supervisors of such individuals, where applicable; and the nature and itinerary of such program.

(c) No Member, officer, or employee may accept funds in connection with participation in a program permitted under subparagraph (a) if such funds are not used for necessary food, lodging, transportation, and related expenses of the Member, officer, or employee.

SENATE RULE XXXVII

Conflict of Interest

1. A Member, officer, or employee of the Senate shall not receive any compensation, nor shall he

permit any compensation to accrue to his beneficial interest from any source, the receipt or accrual of which would occur by virtue of influence improperly exerted from his position as a Member, officer, or employee.

2. No Member, officer, or employee shall engage in any outside business or professional activity or employment for compensation which is inconsistent or in conflict with the conscientious performance of official duties.

3. No officer or employee shall engage in any outside business or professional activity or employment for compensation unless he has reported in writing when such activity or employment commences and on May 15 of each year thereafter so long as such activity or employment continues, the nature of such activity or employment to his supervisor. The supervisor shall then, in the discharge of his duties, take such action as he considers necessary for the avoidance of conflict of interest or interference with duties to the Senate.

4. No Member, officer, or employee shall knowingly use his official position to introduce or aid the progress or passage of legislation, a principal purpose of which is to further only his pecuniary interest, only the pecuniary interest of his immediate family, or only the pecuniary interest of a limited class of persons or enterprises, when he, or his immediate family, or enterprises controlled by them, are members of the affected class.

5. No Member, officer, or employee of the Senate compensated at a rate in excess of $25,000 per annum and employed for more than ninety days in a calendar year shall (a) affiliate with a firm, partnership, association, or corporation for the purpose of providing professional services for compensation; (b) permit that individual's name to be used by such a firm, partnership, association or corporation; or (c) practice a profession for compensation to any extent during regular office hours of the Senate office in which employed. For the purposes of this paragraph, "professional services" shall include but not be limited to those which involve a fiduciary relationship.

6. No Member, officer, or employee of the Senate compensated at a rate in excess of $25,000 per annum and employed for more than ninety days in a calendar year shall serve as an officer or member of the board of any publicly held or publicly regulated corporation, financial institution, or business entity. The preceding sentence shall not apply to service of a Member, officer, or employee as—

(a) an officer or member of the board of an organization which is exempt from taxation under section 501(c) of the Internal Revenue Code of 1954, if such service is performed without compensation;

(b) an officer or member of the board of an institution or organization which is principally available to Members, officers, or employees of the Senate, or their families, if such service is performed without compensation; or

(c) a member of the board of a corporation, institution, or other business entity, if (1) the Member, officer, or employee had served continuously as a member of the board thereof for at least two years prior to his election or appointment as a Member, officer, or employee of the Senate, (2) the amount of time required to perform such service is minimal, and (3) the Member, officer, or employee is not a member of, or a member of the staff of any Senate committee which has legislative jurisdiction over any agency of the Government charged with regulating the activities of the corporation, institution, or other business entity.

7. An employee on the staff of a committee who is compensated at a rate in excess of $25,000 per annum and employed for more than ninety days in a calendar year shall divest himself of any substantial holdings which may be directly affected by the actions of the committee for which he works, unless the Select Committee, after consultation with the employee's supervisor, grants permission in writing to retain such holdings or the employee makes other arrangements acceptable to the Select Committee and the employee's supervisor to avoid participation in committee actions where there is a conflict of interest, or the appearance thereof.

8. If a Member, upon leaving office, becomes a registered lobbyist under the Federal Regulation of Lobbying Act of 1946 or any successor statute, or is employed or retained by such a registered lobbyist for the purpose of influencing legislation, he shall not lobby Members, officers, or employees of the Senate for a period of one year after leaving office.

9. If an employee on the staff of a Member, upon leaving that position, becomes a registered lobbyist under the Federal Regulation of Lobbying Act of 1946 or any successor statute, or is employed or retained by such a registered lobbyist for the purpose of influencing legislation, such employee may not lobby the Member for whom he worked or that Member's staff for a period of one year after leaving that position. If an employee on the staff of a committee, upon leaving his position, becomes such a registered lobbyist or is employed or retained by such a registered lobbyist for the purpose of influencing legislation, such employee may not lobby the members of the committee for which he worked, or the staff of that committee, for a period of one year after leaving his position.

10. (a) Except as provided by subparagraph (b), any employee of the Senate who is required to file a report pursuant to rule XXXIV shall refrain from participating personally and substantially as an employee of the Senate in any contact with any agency of the executive or judicial branch of Government with respect to non-legislative matters affecting any non-governmental person in which the employee has a significant financial interest.

(b) Subparagraph (a) shall not apply if an employee first advises his supervising authority of his significant financial interest and obtains from his employing authority a written waiver stating that the participation of the employee is necessary. A copy of each such waiver shall be filed with the Select Committe.

11. For purposes of this rule—

(a) "employee of the Senate" includes an employee or individual described in paragraphs 2, 3, and 4(c) of rule XLI;

(b) an individual who is an employee on the staff of a subcommittee of a committee shall be treated as an employee on the staff of such committee; and

(c) the term "lobbying" means any oral or written communication to influence the content or disposition of any issue before Congress, including any pending or future bill, resolution, treaty, nomination, hearing, report, or investigation; but does not include—

(1) a communication (i) made in the form of testimony given before a committee or office of the Congress, or (ii) submitted for inclusion in the public record, public docket, or public file of a hearing; or

(2) a communication by an individual, acting solely on his own behalf, for redress of personal grievances, or to express his personal opinion.

12. For purposes of this rule—

(a) a Senator or the Vice President is the supervisor of his administrative, clerical, or other assistants;

(b) a Senator who is the chairman of a committee is the supervisor of the professional, clerical, or other assistants to the committee except that minority staff members shall be under the supervision of the ranking minority Senator on the committee;

(c) a Senator who is a chairman of a subcommittee which has its own staff and financial authorization is the supervisor of the professional, clerical, or other assistants to the subcommittee except that minority staff members shall be under the supervision of the ranking minority Senator on the subcommittee;

(d) the President pro tempore is the supervisor of the Secretary of the Senate, Sergeant at Arms and Doorkeeper, the Chaplain, the Legislative Counsel, and the employees of the Office of the Legislative Counsel;

(e) the Secretary of the Senate is the supervisor of the employees of his office;

(f) the Sergeant at Arms and Doorkeeper is the supervisor of the employees of his office;

(g) the Majority and Minority Leaders and

the Majority and Minority Whips are the supervisors of the research, clerical, or other assistants assigned to their respective offices;

(h) the Majority Leader is the supervisor of the Secretary for the Majority and the Secretary for the Majority is the supervisor of the employees of his office; and

(i) the Minority Leader is the supervisor of the Secretary for the Minority and the Secretary for the Minority is the supervisor of the employees of his office.

HOUSE RULE XLIII

[Revisions in Rule XLIII were anticipated in the 102nd Congress to reflect 1991 changes in congressional limits on accepting gifts and disclosing them (HR 2506-PL 102-90). The revisions had not been made as of mid-September 1991. *See Chapter 11, p. 157]*

Code of Official Conduct

There is hereby established by and for the House of Representatives the following code of conduct, to be known as the "Code of Official Conduct":

1. A Member, officer, or employee of the House of Representatives shall conduct himself at all times in a manner which shall reflect creditably on the House of Representatives.

2. A Member, officer or employee of the House of Representatives shall adhere to the spirit and the letter of the rules of the House of Representatives and to the rules of duly constituted committees thereof.

3. A Member, officer or employee of the House of Representatives shall receive no compensation nor shall he permit any compensation to accure to his beneficial interest from any source, the receipt of which would occur by virtue of influence improperly exerted from his position in the Congress.

4. A Member, officer or employee of the House of Representatives shall not accept gifts (other than the personal hospitality of an individual or with a fair market value of $75 or less) in any calendar year aggregating more than the minimal value as established by paragraph (5) of section 7342 of title 5, United States Code, directly or indirectly from any person (other than from a relative), except to the extent permitted by written waiver granted in exceptional circumstances by the Committee on Standards of Official Conduct pursuant to clause 4(e)(a)(E) of rule X.

5. A Member, officer or employee of the House of Representatives shall accept no honorarium for a speech, writing for publication, or other similar activity.

6. A Member of the House of Representatives shall keep his campaign funds separate from his personal funds. A Member shall convert no campaign funds to personal use in excess of reimbursement for legitimate and verifiable campaign expenditures and shall expend no funds from his campaign account not attributable to bona fide campaign or political purposes.

7. A Member of the House of Representatives shall treat as campaign contributions all proceeds from testimonial dinners or other fund raising events.

8. A Member or officer of the House of Representatives shall retain no one under his payroll authority who does not perform official duties commensurate with the compensation received in the offices of the employing authority. In the case of committee employees who work under the direct supervision of a Member other than a chairman, the chairman may require that such Member affirm in writing that the employees have complied with the preceding sentence (subject to clause 6 of rule XI) as evidence of the chairman's compliance with this clause and with clause 6 of rule XI.

9. A Member, officer or employee of the House of Representatives shall not discharge or refuse to hire any individual, or otherwise discriminate against any individual with respect to compensation, terms, conditions, or privileges of employment, because of such individual's race, color,

religion, sex (including marital or parental status), handicap, age, or national origin, but may take into consideration the domicile or political affiliation of such individual.

10. A Member of the House of Representatives who has been convicted by a court of record for the commission of a crime for which a sentence of two or more years' imprisonment may be imposed should refrain from participation in the business of each committee of which he is a member and should refrain from voting on any question at a meeting of the House, or of the Committee of the Whole House, unless or until judicial or executive proceedings result in reinstatement of the presumption of his innocence or until he is reelected to the House after the date of such conviction.

11. A Member of the House of Representatives shall not authorize or otherwise allow a non-House individual, group, or organization to use the words "Congress of the United States", "House of Representatives", or "'Official Business'", or any combination of words thereof, on any letterhead or envelope.

12. (a) Except as provided by paragraph (b), any employee of the House of Representatives who is required to file a report pursuant to rule XLIV shall refrain from participating personally and substantially as an employee of the House of Representatives in any contact with any agency of the executive or judicial branch of Government with respect to nonlegislative matters affecting any nongovernmental person in which the employee has a significant financial interest.

(b) Paragraph (a) shall not apply if an employee first advises his employing authority of his significant financial interest and obtains from his employing authority a written waiver stating that the participation of the employee is necessary. A copy of each such waiver shall be filed with the Committee on Standards of Official Conduct.

As used in this Code of Official Conduct of the House of Representatives—(a) the terms "Member" and "Member of the House of Representatives" include the Resident Commissioner from Puerto Rico and each Delegate to the House; and (b) the term "officer or employee of the House of Representatives" means any individual whose compensation is disbursed by the Clerk of the House of Representatives.

For the purposes of clause 4 of this Code of Official Conduct, the term "relative" means, with respect to any Member, officer, or employee of the House of Representatives, an individual who is related as father, mother, son, daughter, brother, sister, uncle, aunt, first cousin, nephew, niece, husband, wife, grandfather, grandmother, grandson, granddaughter, father-in-law, mother-in-law, son-in-law, daughter-in-law, brother-in-law, sister-in-law, stepfather, stepmother, stepson, stepdaughter, stepbrother, stepsister, half brother, half sister, or who is the grandfather or grandmother of the spouse of such Member, officer, or employee, and shall be deemed to include the finace or fiancee of the Member, officer, or employee.

ETHICS COMMITTEE CHAIRS, 1966-92

Senate Committee on Standards and Conduct
John Cornelius Stennis, D-Miss., 1966-75
Howard Walter Cannon, D-Nev., 1975-77
(Committee renamed Select Committee on Ethics in 1977.)

Senate Select Committee on Ethics
Adlai Ewing Stevenson III, D-Ill., 1977-81
Malcolm Wallop, R-Wyo., 1981-83
Theodore F. "Ted" Stevens, R-Alaska, 1983-85
Warren Bruce Rudman, R-N.H., 1985-87
Howell Thomas Heflin, D-Ala., 1987-91
Terry Sanford, D-N.C., 1991—

House Committee on Standards of Official Conduct
Charles Melvin Price, D-Ill., 1969-75
John James Flynt, Jr., D-Ga., 1975-77
Charles Edward Bennett, D-Fla., 1977-81
Louis Stokes, D-Ohio, 1981-85
Julian Carey Dixon, D-Calif., 1985-91
Louis Stokes, D-Ohio, 1991—

SELECTED READINGS

Alexander, De Alva Stanwood. *History and Procedure of the House of Representatives*. New York: Lenox Hill, 1916.

Baker, Richard A. *The Senate of the United States: A Bicentennial History*. Malabar, Fla. Krieger Publishing. 1988.

Beard, Edmund, and Stephen Horn. *Congressional Ethics: The View from the House*. Washington, D.C.: Brookings Institution, 1975.

Currie, James T. *The United States House of Representatives*. Malabar, Fla.: Krieger Publishing, 1988.

Drew, Elizabeth. *Politics and Money: The New Road to Corruption*. New York: Macmillan, 1983.

Garment, Suzanne. *Scandal: The Crisis of Mistrust in American Politics*. New York: Times Books, 1991.

Getz, Robert S. *Congressional Ethics: The Conflict of Interest Issue*. New York: D. Van Nostrand, 1966.

Hamilton, Charles V. *Adam Clayton Powell, Jr.: The Political Biography of an American Dilemma*. New York: Atheneum, 1991.

House Committee on Standards of Official Conduct. *Ethics Manual for Members, Officers, and Employees of the U.S. House of Representatives. 100th Cong., 1st sess., 1987.*

Hupman, Richard D. *Senate Election, Expulsion, and Censure Cases from 1793 to 1972*. S Doc 92-7, 92nd Cong., 1st sess., 1972.

Joint Committee on Congressional Operations. *House of Representatives Exclusion, Censure, and Expulsion Cases from 1789 to 1973*. 93rd Cong., 1st sess., 1973, committee print.

Maskell, Jack. *Expulsion and Censure Actions Taken by the Full Senate Against Members*. Washington, D.C.: Congressional Research Service, 1990.

———. *Reports Concerning Investigations and/or Disciplinary Recommendations from the House Committee on Standards of Official Conduct since Its Inception in 1968*. Washington, D.C.: Congressional Research Service, 1989.

Riddick, Floyd M. *Senate Procedure, Precedents, and Practices*. S Doc 97-2, 97th Cong., 1st sess., 1981.

Sabato, Larry J. *Feeding Frenzy: How Attack Journalism Has Transformed American Politics*. New York: The Free Press, 1991.

Senate Select Committee on Ethics. *In re The Matter of Senator Alan Cranston, Senator Dennis DeConcini, Senator John Glenn, Senator John McCain, Senator Donald Riegle. Prepared Text of the Opening Statement of Special Counsel Robert S. Bennett*. 101st Cong., 2nd sess., 1990, committee print.. *Interpretive Rulings of the Select Committee on Ethics*. S Prt 101-18, 101st Cong., 1st sess., 1989.

Simon, Paul. *The Glass House*. New York: Continuum Publishing, 1984

Stern, Philip M. *The Best Congress Money Can Buy*. New York: Pantheon Books, 1988.

Weeks, Kent M. *Adam Clayton Powell and the Supreme Court*. New York: Dunellen, 1971.

INDEX

Abscam scandal, 3, 15
  chairmanship losses, 48, 49
  court cases, 65-67
  expulsion of Myers, 18, 65
  FBI scam, 64-65
  resignations, 18, 19, 65, 67-68
  sex angle, 89
  summary of, 63-64
Acquired immune deficiency syndrome (AIDS), 90
Adams, Brock, 92-93
Adams, John G., 29
Adams, John Quincy, 16, 21, 37, 152
Adams, Sherman, 146
Added qualifications issue, 11-14
Addonizio, Hugh J., 72
Adenauer, Konrad, 31
Aides and staffers
  complaint procedures for, 100-102
  discrimination against, 99-100
  ethics rules and laws for, 107-108, 158-159
  hiring practices regarding, 98-102
  Keating Five investigation and, 127
  legal protections for, 97, 100, 161
  misuse of power by, 102
  nepotism and, 98-99, 146
  political work by, 104-107
  working conditions, 100
Albert, Carl, 21, 49, 57, 89
Alcohol abuse, 85
  Mills case, 87, 88-89
Alexander, Bill, 79, 80
Allen, James B., 106
Allen, Maryon P., 105, 106
American Bar Association, 153
Americans with Disabilities Act of 1990, 100
Ames, Oakes, 7, 8, 38
Anderson, Cyrus T., 111
Anderson, Jack, 31
Anthony, Susan B., 85
Apologies by congressmen, 160-161
"Appearance standard" issue, 126, 128-129, 137-138, 141
Arena, Dominick J., 86
Armstrong, William L., 1
Army-McCarthy hearings, 28-29

Atlanta Business Chronicle, 106

Babbitt, Bruce, 119
Bailey, Joseph W., 152
Baker, Richard A., 47
Baker, Robert G. "Bobby," 30-31, 101, 102
Bakker, Jim, 2
Bank of Commerce and Credit International (BCCI), 2
Bank of the United States, 51, 152
Barry et al. v. United States ex rel. Cunningham (1929), 11
Baskir, Lawrence, 93
Bates, Jim, 91, 92
Baucus, Wanda, 93
Bauman, Robert E., 90
Beacon Press, 112, 113
Beech Aircraft Corp., 60
Bennett, Robert S.
  "appearance standard" issue, 126, 128-129
  Durenberger case, 33-34, 35
  Keating Five investigation, 119, 120, 122, 123, 124, 125-126, 128-129, 131, 137, 138-139
  profile of, 124
Benton, Thomas H., 26
Benton, William, 27, 28
Berger, Victor L., 13
Biaggi, Mario, 69, 129
Biddle, Nicholas, 51
Bingham, Hiram, 27
Bisnow, Mark, 104
Black, William, 130
Blacks, discrimination against, 99-100
Blaine, James G., 7, 21, 38
Blanton, Thomas L., 26
Blount, William, 17
Boner, Bill, 76
Book publishing scams
  Durenberger case, 34-35
  Gingrich case, 79-80
  Wright case, 22, 23
Boschwitz, Rudy, 36
Boston Globe, 63
Bowman, Patricia, 95
Boykin, Frank W., 71, 72, 111

Boyle, James A., 87
Bramblett, Ernest K., 71
Brasco, Frank J., 72
Breckinridge, John C., 17
Breckinridge, William, 85
Brehm, Walter E., 71
Brewster, Daniel B., 59-60, 111-112
Bribery. *See* Abscam scandal; Financial misconduct
Bright, Jesse D., 17, 18
Brooke, Edward W., 62-63
Brooks, James, 7, 38
Brooks, Preston S., 36
Brown, John Y., 38
Bumpers, Dale, 124
Burger, Warren E., 112
Burke, J. Herbert, 86
Burnett, Henry C., 18
Burton, Joseph R., 10, 19, 50
Burton v. United States (1906), 10
Bush, George, 97, 155, 161
Butler, A. P., 36
Butler, Benjamin, 38
Byrd, Robert C., 143, 149

Califano, Joseph A., Jr., 40
Campaign finance legislation, 53
Campaign funds
  misuse of, 75, 77, 78-79
  personal use of funds after retirement, 155, 156-157
Cannon, Howard W., 57, 104-105
Cannon, Joseph G., 20
Car rental rules, 159
Carroll, Daniel, 6
Carter, Jimmy, 149, 150, 151
Celeste, Richard F., 91
Celler, Emanuel, 12, 13, 153
Censure/reprimand, 1, 15
  alternative words for, 25
  Cranston case, 44-45, 117, 139-144
  difference between censure and reprimand, 41, 45
  Diggs case, 38-39
  Dodd case, 31
  Durenberger case, 33-36
  Frank case, 43-44
  grounds for, 25

Hansen case, 42
history of, 25
in House, 36-44
McCarthy case, 27-30
McFall-Roybal-Wilson case, 41-42
Murphy case, 42-43
proceedings for, 25-26
rescinding of resolutions, 38
resolution of condemnation, example of, 30
in Senate, 26-36, 44-45, 117, 139-144
Sikes case, 41, 48
Studds and Crane cases, 39-41
Talmadge case, 31-33
Wilson case, 39
Chairmanships, offenders' loss of, 47-49
Chappaquiddick incident, 86-88
Check-kiting scandal of 1991-92, 160
Cilley, Jonathan, 37
Civiletti, Benjamin, 64
Civil Service Commission, 56
Civil War expulsion cases, 17-18
Clark, Frank M., 73
Clark, John B., 18
Clay, Henry, 21, 51
Clifford, Clark F., 2
Clinton, Bill, 94, 95
Clinton, Hillary, 94
Coelho, Tony, 19-20, 78
Cohn, Roy M., 27, 29
Coker, Tom E., 105-106
Colfax, Schuyler, 7, 8
Collins, Tanquil "Tai," 96
Commission on Administrative Review, 149
Commission on Executive, Legislative, and Judicial Salaries, 149
Commission on Operations of the Senate, 149
Common Cause, 21, 22, 41, 120, 121
Conflict-of-interest regulations
  laws for aides and staffers, 159
  rules for members, 56
Congress and the Public Trust (Kirby), 153
"Congressional Contrition Acts of 1991," 145, 159
Congressional Control of Administration (Harris), 7
Connally, John B., Jr., 119
Conner, John C., 13
Constitution, U.S.
  disciplining of members provision, 6, 8
  immunity provision, 109

incompatible office provision, 16
qualifications for membership provisions, 5-6
Constitutional Convention of 1787, 5, 6
Conte, Silvio O., 57
Corwin, Thomas, 152
Cossolotto, Matthew, 22
Crane, Daniel B., 39-41, 89
Cranston, Alan, 1
  Keating Five investigation, 118, 119, 121, 123, 125, 126-127, 131-132, 134, 135, 138
  reprimand of, 44-45, 117, 139-144
  retirement decision, 122
  Williams case, 68
Crédit Mobilier scandal, 7-9, 38, 51, 152
Criden, Howard L., 65, 66, 67
Criminal statutes regarding members, 8-9
Curley, James M., 70-71

D'Amato, Alphonse M., 68, 82-83
Daniel, William Clarence "Dan," 60
Dannemeyer, William E., 44
Darden, George "Buddy," 44
Davis, Jefferson, 17
Davis, Shirley, 102
DeConcini, Dennis, Keating Five investigation, 118, 119, 121, 122, 123, 124, 125, 127, 129, 130-131, 132-133, 135, 137, 138
Defense contractors, influence buying by, 55-57
Denial of representation issue, 10-11
Denunciation. *See* Censure/reprimand
Dershowitz, Alan M., 143
Diamond, Gary L., 34
Dietrich, Charles H., 19
Diggs, Charles C., Jr., 38-39, 48, 49-50
Dingell, John D., 57
Dinis, Edmund, 87
Disabled persons, discrimination against, 100
Disciplining of members
  added qualifications issue, 11-14
  chairmanships, offenders' loss of, 47-49
  chamber rules, 9, 36, 50, 56
  constitutional provision on, 6, 8
  court rulings on, 6-7, 8-10
  criminal statutes, 8-9
  denial of representation issue, 10-11
  primary election misconduct and, 10
  separation of powers issue, 11

voting privilege, suspension of, 49-50
  See also Censure/reprimand; Expulsion
Discrimination by members, 99-100
Dixon, Julian C., 2, 43, 74, 76
Dodd, Christopher J., 31
Dodd, Thomas J., 31, 45, 147
Dole, Robert, 36, 58
Dowd, John M., 127, 133, 137
Dowdy, John V., 49, 72, 114
Dowdy v. United States (1973), 114
Drexel Burnham Lambert Inc., 83
Drug abuse, 85
Dueling by members, 37
Durenberger, Dave, 1, 33-36, 124, 129
Dwight, John W., 55
Dyson, Roy, 81, 90, 103

Edlin, J. Kenneth, 111
Edmundson, Henry A., 36
Eilberg, Joshua, 62, 73, 153
Eisenhower, Dwight D., 146
Elia, Peter, 82
Elko, Stephen, 62
Elmore, Franklin H., 37
Employees of Congress. *See* Aides and staffers
Errichetti, Angelo J., 65, 67
Ethics code of Congress, 146
Ethics committees, 1-2, 3
  establishment of, 146-148
  reforms regarding, 157-158
Ethics in Government Act of 1978, 53, 54-55, 149, 150-151
Ethics reform, 145
  codes of conduct, enactment of, 145-147
  "Congressional Contrition Acts of 1991," 145, 159
  ethics committees, establishment of, 146-148
  financial disclosure rules, 147, 148, 149, 158
  gift rules, 56, 107-108, 150, 151-153, 154, 155, 157
  honoraria limits, 151-154, 156
  law practice by members and, 150, 152-153
  1989 reform act, 97, 107, 155-159
  office to develop rules and regulations, 151
  outside income, regulation of, 150, 152-153, 156

pay-ethics relationship, 149-151, 154, 155

personal liability for senators, 159

postemployment lobbying, 150, 155, 158-159

travel expense regulation, 155, 157

Watergate-inspired reforms, 148-149

Ethics Reform Act of 1989, 97, 107, 154-155

provisions of, 155-159

Evans, Tom, 52

Expulsion, 1, 15

Abscam and, 18, 65

Civil War cases, 17-18

court rulings on, 9-10

failed attempts, 18

grounds for, 15-18

history of, 15

incompatible office issue, 16

prior offenses issue, 16

resignation to avoid expulsion, 10, 18, 19-23, 65, 67-68

reversal of, 17

Eyanson, Charles L., 27

Fair Labor Standards Act of 1938, 101

Fauntroy, Walter E., 81, 100

Fazio, Vic, 43

Federal Bureau of Investigation (FBI), Abscam scandal and, 63-68

Federal Corrupt Practices Act of 1910, 10

The Federalist, 13

Federal Regulation of Lobbying Act of 1946, 53

Fenwick, Millicent, 59

Ferraro, Geraldine A., 74-75

Fiedler, Bobbi, 76

Financial disclosure rules

for aides and staffers, 108

for members, 147, 148, 149, 158

Financial misconduct, 61

Brooke case, 62-63

cases of 1980s and 1990s, 73-83

censure/reprimand for, 31-36, 38-39, 41-42

Crédit Mobilier scandal, 7-9, 38, 51, 152

criminal prosecutions (1941-80), 70-73

Flood case, 61-62

resignations due to, 10, 19-23

Wedtech scandal, 49, 68-70

See also Abscam scandal; Influence buying

Flake, Floyd H., 82

Flanders, Ralph E., 27, 29

Flood, Daniel J., 61-62, 73

Flores, Yvette Marjorie, 99

Flowers, Gennifer, 94, 95

Flynt, John J., Jr., 41, 57

Foley, Heather, 99

Foley, Thomas S., 99, 160

Foote, Henry S., 26

Ford, Gerald R., 12, 149

Ford, Harold E., 48, 49, 79

Ford, Henry, 10

Foreign Agents Registration Act of 1938, 53

Fort Worth Star-Telegram, 103

Foxe, Fanne, 87, 88

Frank, Barney, 43-44, 89, 92

Frank, Gerald W., 106

Fulbright, J. W., 102

Galifianakis, Nick, 59

Gallagher, Cornelius E., 59, 72, 148

Garcia, Jane Lee, 70

Garcia, Robert, 48, 49, 69-70

Gardner, Colleen, 86

Garfield, James A., 7, 8, 13-14

Garmatz, Edward A., 60

Garment, Suzanne, 2-3, 85

Garn, Jake, 119

Gesell, Gerhard A., 16

Gift rules

for aides and staffers, 107-108

for members, 56, 150, 151-154, 155, 157

Gillett, Frederick H., 26

Gingrich, Marianne, 80

Gingrich, Newt

check overdrafts, 160

Diggs case, 38-39

charges against, 44, 79-81, 106-107

Frank case, 43, 44

Studds and Crane cases, 40-41

Wright case, 20, 21, 22

Glenn, John,

Keating Five investigation, 118, 119, 120, 121, 122, 123, 125, 126, 131, 136, 138

Gobie, Steve, 43-44

Golden Fleece Awards, 114-115

Goldfine, Bernard, 146

Goldwater, Barry, 57

Gonzalez, Henry B., 120

Government Ethics Reform Act of 1989. *See* Ethics Reform Act of 1989

Grant, Ulysses S., 7

Grassley, Charles E., 161

Gravel, Mike, 112-113

Gravel v. United States (1972), 113

Graves, William J., 37

Gray, Edwin J., 125, 127-130, 134

Green, Mark, 82

Green, Thomas C., 127, 130

Green, William J., Jr., 71

Griffin, Robert P., 58, 104

Grinnell, Josiah B., 37

Griswold, Roger, 36-37

Grogan, James J., 134-135

Gulf Oil Company, 57-58

Gurney, Edward, 19, 70

Haircut prices for members, 159

Hamilton, Alexander, 13

Hamilton, James, 124, 129, 137-138

Hanna, Mark, 51

Hanna, Richard T., 58-59

Hansen, Clifford P., 58

Hansen, George V., 42

Harlan, John Marshall (elder), 10

Harlan, John Marshall (younger), 111

Harris, Joseph, 7

Harsha, William H., 57

Hart, Gary, 2, 85, 94

Hart, George L., Jr., 14

Hastings, James F., 73

Hatch Act, 105

Hatfield, Antoinette, 75

Hatfield, Mark O., 75, 106

Hays, Wayne L., 47-48, 85, 88, 89

Hearst, William Randolph, 152

Heflin, Howell

Durenberger case, 35

Keating Five investigation, 117, 120, 122, 124, 136, 139, 141, 143

Williams case, 50, 68

Helms, Jesse, 119, 121, 123, 138-139, 141

Helstoski, Henry J., 73, 114

Hill, Anita F., 2, 93, 97, 161

Hinshaw, Andrew J., 3, 73

Hinson, Jon C., 90

Hollings, Ernest F., 132

Honoraria, 34, 150

for aides and staffers, 107

limits on, 151-154, 156

House Democratic Caucus, 48

House of Representatives

censure/reprimand cases, 36-44

chairmanships, offenders' loss of, 47-49

check-kiting scandal, 160

complaint procedures for aides, 100-102

conflict-of-interest rules, 56

ethics code, establishment of, 147

expulsion cases, 18

leadership resignations, 19-23

Speakers, controversies concerning, 20-23

voting privilege, suspensions of, 49-50

See also specific members and issues

House Standards of Official Conduct Committee. *See* Ethics committees

Housing and Urban Development Department (HUD), 82-83

Howe, Allan T., 86

Huff, Corinne A., 12

Hughes, Harold E., 149

Hunter, John W., 37

Hutchinson, Ronald, 114-115

Hutchinson v. Proxmire (1979), 114-115

Immunity protection

arrest in Washington, policy against, 110

constitutional provision on, 109

legislative responsibilities and, 109-111

narrowing of, 111-112

1979 rulings on, 114-115

purpose of, 109

specification of protected acts, 112-114

Incompatible office issue, 16

Influence buying, 51

by defense contractors, 55-57

group scandals, 52

history of, 51

honoraria issue, 151-154

immunity protection and, 110-112, 114

investigations of, 55-59

lobbying laws and, 51, 52-55

by oil interests, 57-58

prosecutions resulting from, 59-60

registration of lobbyists and, 53-54

"revolving-door" problem, 54-55, 108, 150, 155, 158-159

sex as offered inducement, 52

See also Keating Five investigation; Korean lobbying scandal

Ingersoll, Ebon C., 14

Inouye, Daniel K., 132

In re Chapman (1897), 9-10

In the Shadow of the Dome (Bisnow), 104

"Ironclad Oath Law" of 1862, 13

Irving, Theodore Leonard, 71

Jackson, Andrew, 51

Jacobson, Joy, 125, 131, 132, 135

James, Esther, 12

Jefferson, Thomas, 9, 20

Jenkins, Ray H., 29

Jenrette, John W., Jr., 19, 63, 64, 65-66, 89

Jenrette, Rita, 64, 89

Johanson, Louis C., 65, 67

Johnson, Lyndon B., 56, 72, 85, 102, 111

Johnson, Thomas F., 71-72, 111

Johnson, Waldo P., 17, 18

Jones, George W., 37

Jones, James R., 58

Jordan, Carolyn, 132, 135

Joseph, Joel D., 104

Karth, Joseph E., 57

Keating, Charles H., Jr., 118, 119-120, 122, 131-132, 134-135

Keating Five investigation, 1, 4

aides' testimony, 127

"appearance standard" issue, 126, 128-129, 137-138, 141

Bennett's role, 124

Black's testimony, 130

character witnesses for senators, 132-133

closing statements, 138-139

complaints of ethics violations, 120

findings of, 140

floor statements following, 142-144

fund-raising issue, 125, 131-132, 135, 141

Gray's testimony, 127-130

Grogan's testimony, 134-135

hearings, 118-119, 122-138

inconclusiveness of results, 117-118

investigating committee members, 120-121

Keating's lobbying, 119-120, 131-132

leaking of information, 133

"linkage" issue, 141

opening statements, 122-123, 125-126

Patriarca's testimony, 130-131

preliminary reports, 121-122

reprimand of Cranston, 44-45, 117, 139-144

S&L political contributions issue, 121

senators' interventions on Keating's behalf, 125, 127-131, 134, 138

senators' presentations, 126-127

senators' rebuttals, 136-138

standards issue, 125-126, 128-129, 137-138, 141

vacations issue, 136-137

Wall's testimony, 131

Keitt, Laurence M., 36

Kelly, Richard, 63, 64, 65, 66-67

Kennedy, Edward M.

apology by, 160-161

Chappaquiddick incident, 86-88

Smith rape case, 2, 94-95

Kennedy, John F., 85

Kennedy, Patrick, 94

Kerr, Robert S., 102

Key, Francis Scott, 16

Key, Phillip Barton, 85

Kilbourn, Hallet, 110

Kilbourn v. Thompson (1881), 7, 110

Kim Hyung Wook, 58

Kirby, James C., 153

Klein, Julius, 31

Knowland, William F., 29

Konnyu, Ernie, 90-91

Kopechne, Mary Jo, 86

Korean Central Intelligence Agency (KCIA), 58

Korean lobbying scandal, 21, 148

censures resulting from, 41-42

details of, 58-59

La Follette, Robert M., 18

Lane, Thomas J., 71

Langer, William, 18

Large, Arlen J., 13

Lattimore, Owen J., 28

Law practice by members, 150, 152-153

Lederer, Raymond F., 19, 63, 64, 65, 67, 129

Lee Hu Rak, 58

Leggett, Robert L., 57

Life magazine, 148

Lincoln Savings and Loan Association. *See* Keating Five investigation

Lobbying misconduct. *See* Influence buying

Long, Huey P., 18

Long, Russell B., 25

Long v. Ansell (1934), 109

Lott, Trent, 121, 123, 130, 137, 139, 140

Lowery, Bill, 121

Lukens, Donald E. "Buz," 91
Lyon, Matthew, 36-37

Macon, Nathaniel, 20
Mack, John P., 103
Madison, James, 6
Mahoney, Michael C., 35
Mallick, George, 22, 23
Marks, Marc L., 106
Maskell, Jack, 45
Mason, George, 6
Mathis, Dawson, 57
Mattingly, Mack, 50
May, Andrew J., 71
McCain, John, Keating Five investiga-
  tion, 118, 119, 121, 122, 123, 126, 127,
  131, 133, 136-137, 138
McCarthy, Joseph R., 25
  censure of, 27, 29, 30
  chairmanships, loss of, 49
  investigations by, 28-29
McCormack, John W., 21, 103
McDermott, James T., 55
McFall, John J., 41-42, 59
McHugh, Matthew F., 92
McKinley, William, 51
McKinney, Stewart B., 90
McKneally, Martin B., 72
McLaurin, John L., 26-27, 45, 50
McMillan, John L., 71
Michel, Robert H., 41, 44, 160
Mikva, Abner J., 106
Mills, Wilbur D., 85, 87, 88-89, 102
Minchew, Daniel, 32-33
Minimum Wage Act of 1989, 101
Mitchell, George J., 161
Mitchell, John H., 19
Mofford, Rose, 132
Monroe, James, 51
Monroe, Marilyn, 85
Moore, Carlos, 22
Morgan, Robert, 132
Morrill, Lot M., 7
Morris, Gouverneur, 6
Morse, Wayne, 30
Moss, Frank E., 57
Mulhall, Col. Martin M., 55
Mundt, Karl E., 29
Murphy, Austin J., 42-43, 78
Murphy, John M., 48, 63, 64, 65, 66
Murtha, John P., 63, 66, 154
Myers, Michael J. "Ozzie"
  Abscam scandal, 63, 64, 65
  disorderly conduct charge, 86

expulsion of, 3, 18, 65

National Association of Manufacturers
  (NAM), 53, 55
Nelson, Gaylord, 149
Nepotism, 98-99, 146
Newberry, Truman H., 10, 19
Newberry v. United States (1921), 10
New Member Orientation Handbook, 99
Newsday, 82
Newsweek, 19
New York City Bar Association, 153
New York Times, 50, 82, 122
New York World, 55
Nichols, Bill, 57
Nickles, Don, 124
Nixon, Richard M., 27, 147
Norris, George W., 27
Northrop Corporation, 55-56, 57

Oakar, Mary Rose, 77, 100
Obey, David R., 149
Office of Fair Employment Practices
  (OFEP), 101
Office of Government Ethics, 151
Office of legal counsel (Senate), 151
O'Hare, Michael V., 31
Oil interests, influence buying by, 57-58
O'Neill, Thomas P., Jr., 21, 39, 41, 149
Outside income
  of aides and staffers, 107
  regulation of, 150, 152-153, 156
  See also Honoraria
Overton, John H., 18

Pak Bo Hi, 58
Pappas, Tom, 81, 90, 103
Park, Tongsun, 21, 39, 41, 58-59, 148
Park Chung Hee, 58
Parkinson, Paula, 52, 89
Pashayan, Charles "Chip," Jr., 121
Passman, Otto E., 59, 102
Patriarca, Michael, 130-131
Patten, Edward J., 59
Patterson, James W., 7-8
Pay-ethics relationship, 149-151, 154,
  155
Pearson, Drew, 31
Pentagon Papers affair, 112-113
Percy, Charles H., 58
Personal liability of senators, 159
Peterson, Peter G., 149
Phelan, Richard J., 23
Phillips, David Graham, 152

Physical assaults by members, 36-37
Pickering, Timothy, 26
Piranha Press, 34-35
Plea bargains, 73-74
Podell, Bertram L., 72
Poland, Luke P., 7
Polk, Trusten, 17-18
Powell, Adam Clayton, Jr., 47
  added qualifications case, 11-13, 14
  indictments against, 71
  nepotism by, 99
Price, Melvin, 147, 148
Primary elections, regulation of, 10
Prior offenses issue, 16
Procurement-reform laws, 159
Proxmire, William, 56, 114-115, 132
Pryor, David, 121, 122, 124, 133, 138

Qualifications for membership in Congress, 5-6
  added qualifications issue, 11-14
Quayle, Dan, 52, 89

Railsback, Tom, 52
Randolph, Edmund, 6
Randolph, John, 20
Rangel, Charles B., 14
Ray, Elizabeth, 88-89
Rayburn, Sam, 30
Reagan, Ronald, 54, 55, 68
Reform of ethics standards. See Ethics
  reform
Registration of lobbyists, 53-54
Reid, Harry, 140
Reid, John W., 18
Remington Arms Co. Inc., 56, 57
Reprimand. See Censure/reprimand
Residence scams, 35
Resignation to avoid expulsion, 10, 18,
  19-23, 67-68
Reuss, Henry S., 57
"Revolving-door" problem, 54-55, 108
  ethics rules regarding, 150, 155, 158-
  159
Rice, Donna, 85, 94
Richmond, Fred W., 73-74, 90
Riegle, Donald W., Jr., Keating Five
  investigation, 118, 119, 121, 122, 123,
  126, 127, 129-130, 131, 134, 137, 138
Robb, Charles S., 96
Roberts, Ray, 57
Robinson, William L., 111
Rockwell International Corp., 56, 57
Rodberg, Leonard S., 112-113

Rogers, Lee, 39
Roncallo, Angelo D., 72
Rose, Charlie, 78-79
Rousseau, Lovell H., 37
Roybal, Edward R., 41-42, 59
Rudman, Warren B., 159
    Durenberger case, 129
    Keating Five investigation, 117, 120,
      122, 124, 136, 137, 139, 140-141,
      142, 143, 144
Ruff, Charles F. C., 136

Sabato, Larry J., 2
St. Cloud Times, 81
St Germain, Fernand J., 76-77
Sand, Leonard, 70
Sanford, Terry, 121, 122-123
San Jose Mercury-News, 90
Savage, Gus, 81, 91-92
Savage, Thomas John, 81
*Scandal: The Crisis of Mistrust in Ameri-
    can Politics* (Garment), 2-3, 85
Scandal rate in America, 2-3
Scherer, Roger, 35
Schine, G. David, 27, 28, 29
*Schlesinger v. Reservists Committee to
    Stop the War* (1974), 16
Schroeder, Patricia, 92
Schwartz, Morton, 115
Scott, Hugh, 57
Sebastian, William K., 17
Securities and Exchange Commission
    (SEC), 119
Sedita, Angelo, 82
Sedlmayr, Laurie, 127
Senate
    censure/reprimand cases, 26-36, 44-
      45, 117, 139-144
    chairmanships, offenders' loss of, 49
    conflict-of-interest rules, 56
    employees' rights issue, 161
    ethical issues, approach to, 47
    ethics code, establishment of, 146-147
    expulsion cases, 17-18
    office of legal counsel, 151
    personal liability of senators, 159
    voting privilege, suspensions of, 50
    See also Keating Five investigation;
      specific members and issues
Senate Ethics Committee. *See* Ethics
    committees
The Senate of the United States (Baker),
    47
Senior Executive Service, 159

Sexual misconduct, 85
    censure/reprimand for, 39-41, 43-44
    immunity protection and, 110
    influence buying and, 52
    1970s cases, 85-89
    1980s cases, 89-93
    1990s cases, 93-96
Shafran, Joe, 106
Shapiro, Richard, 99
Sickels, Dan, 85
Sickels, Teresa, 85
Sikes, Robert L. F., 41, 48, 148
Simon, Paul, 132
Simpson, Alan K., 161
Small, Pamela, 103
Smith, Denny, 121
Smith, John, 16, 19
Smith, William Kennedy, 2, 94-95
Sobsey, Chester B., 104-105
Speakers of the House, controversies con-
    cerning, 20-23
Special prosecutors, 151
Specter, Arlen, 143
Spiegel Inc., 111, 112
Staff. *See* Aides and staffers
Stallings, Richard, 77-78
Stanbery, William, 37
Stennis, John C., 45, 147
Stevens, David, 133
Stevens, Robert T., 29
Stevenson, Andrew, 37
Stewart, Rosemary, 136
Stowe, John R., 65
Strangeland, Arlan, 81
Studds, Gerry E., 39-41, 48-49, 89
Sumner, Charles, 36
Sunia, Fofo I. F., 78
Sun Myung Moon, 58
Supreme Court, U.S., 6-7
    added qualifications ruling, 14
    denial of representation rulings, 10-11
    Diggs case, 39
    disciplining of congressmen rulings, 7,
      8-9
    expulsion rulings, 9-10
    financial misconduct cases, 70, 71, 72,
      73
    Hansen case, 42
    immunity rulings, 110-115
    incompatible office rulings, 16
    lobbyist registration rulings, 53
    political work by aides and staffers,
      ruling on, 104
    primary election regulation rulings, 10

sex discrimination rulings, 102
Swaggart, Jimmy, 2
Sweeney, Mac, 106
Sweig, Martin, 21, 103
Swindall, Pat, 78
Symms, Steve, 144

Tabloid journalism, 94
Talmadge, Betty, 32
Talmadge, Herman E., 31-33, 57
Tandy Corp., 73
Tappan, Benjamin, 26
Taylor, William W., III, 123, 129, 131,
    136, 138
Teague, Olin E., 57
Teapot Dome scandal, 50
Term limitation legislation, 160
Thomas, Clarence, 2, 93, 97, 160
Thomas, J. Parnell, 71
Thompson, Frank, Jr., 48, 63, 64, 65, 66
Thompson, John G., 110
Thurmond, Strom, 58, 132, 150
Tillman, Benjamin R., 26-27, 45, 50
Time magazine, 2
Tolerance of unethical behavior, 3-4
Touya, Maria, 99
Tower, John G., 45, 57, 85
Travel expenses, reimbursement for
    aides and staffers, 108
    members, 155, 157
Trimble, Vance, 99
Truman, Harry S., 71
Tsakos, Basil A., 75
Tupper, Kari, 92-93
Twain, Mark, 1
Tydings, Millard E., 27, 28
Tye, A. Raymond, 63

Udall, Morris K., 12
Union Pacific Railroad, 7, 38, 51
Unisys Corp., 83
United States v. Brewster (1972), 112
United States v. Classic (1941), 10
United States v. Cooper (1800), 109
United States v. Harriss (1954), 53
United States v. Helstoski (1979), 114
United States v. Johnson (1966), 110-111
University of South Carolina, 75

Van Paasschen, Gwendolyn, 127
Vare, William S., 11
Voloshen, Nathan M., 103
Von Raab, William, 132-133
Voting privilege, suspensions of, 49-50

Waggonner, Joe D., Jr., 86, 110
Walco National Corp., 74
Wall, M. Danny, 131
Wallop, Malcolm, 50, 117
Wall Street Journal, 76, 83
Ward, Samuel, 51
Warren, Earl, 14
Washington Post, 58, 79, 81, 89, 90, 92, 93, 103, 122
Washington Star, 32
Washington Times, 43
Watergate scandal, 3, 147
Waxman, Margery, 136
Weaver, James, 75
Webb, James W., 37
Webster, Daniel, 51, 152

Wedtech scandal, 49, 68-70
Weicker, Lowell P., Jr., 31, 57
Weinstein, Jack B., 74
Welch, Joseph N., 29
Whalley, J. Irving, 72
Wheeler, Burton K., 19, 50
White, John, 20-21
Wild, Claude, 57
Williams, Edward Bennett, 101
Williams, Harrison A., Jr., 18, 19, 49, 50, 63, 64, 65, 67-68, 124
Williamson v. United States (1908), 109, 110
Wilson, Charles H., 39, 41-42, 48, 59
Wilson, Henry, 7, 8
Wilson, Jeremiah, 7

Wilson, Pete, 119, 121
Wise, Henry A., 37
Women, discrimination against, 99-100
Worker-protection laws, Congress' exemption from, 97, 100, 161
Wright, Betty, 23
Wright, Jim
    Diggs case, 39
    Mack case, 103
    resignation of, 3-4, 20-23, 78
Wyatt, Wendell, 73

Young, John, 86

Zihlman, Frederick N., 49
Zwicker, Brig. Gen. Ralph W., 29